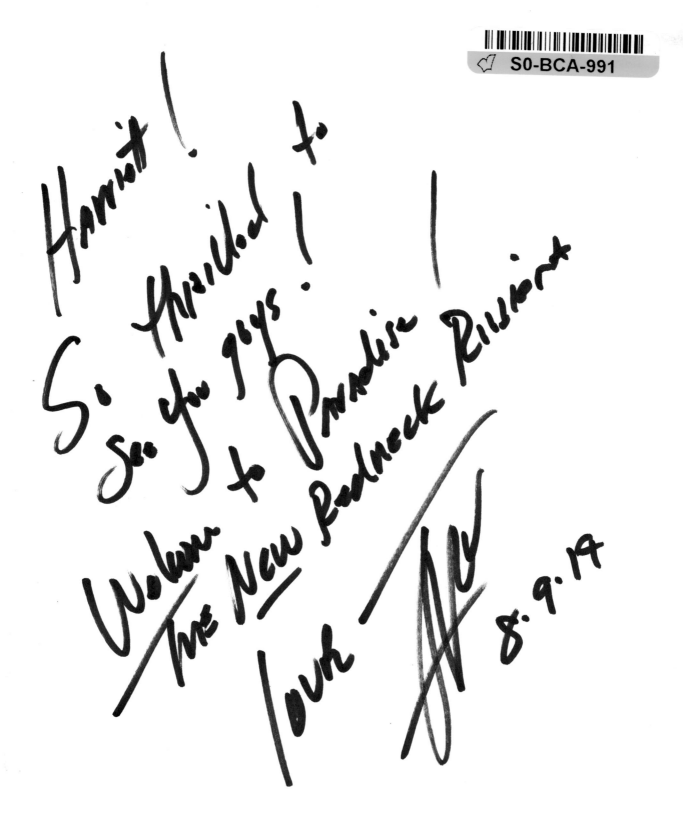

Harriet!

So thrilled!

So glad you guys!

+ Paradise Riviera!

Welcome

The New Redneck Riviera Tour

love AJ

8.9.14

Panhandle to Pan

RECIPES AND STORIES FROM
FLORIDA'S
NEW REDNECK RIVIERA

IRV MILLER

Globe
Pequot

Guilford, Connecticut

In memory of my loving dad, Norman Miller
Also to the thousands of cooks and culinarians who aspire to make a
difference wherever you plant your feet and wherever you choose to sprout roots.
To a glimpse into the future—realizing this is a special time
to be living in the Florida Panhandle.
To remembering it will not be as it is today nor has been in the past.
To the future food harvesters, thinkers, and makers of cuisine,
"the gulf is your oyster" and please never take more than can be replaced,
unless of course it's lionfish.
To these wise culinary words,
"One should have a relish for what one does;
you should also have a relish for what others have done before you."
—Robert Courtine

Globe
Pequot

An imprint of Rowman & Littlefield

Distributed by NATIONAL BOOK NETWORK

Copyright © 2015 by Irv Miller
All photography © 2015 by Bill Strength Photography unless otherwise noted on page 290.

British Library Cataloguing in Publication Information Available

Library of Congress Cataloging-in-Publication Data

Miller, Irv, 1955- author.
  Panhandle to pan : recipes and stories from Florida's new redneck riviera / Irv Miller.
    pages cm
  Includes index.
  ISBN 978-1-4930-0814-8 (paperback : alk. paper) — ISBN 978-1-4930-1948-9 (e-book)
  1. Cooking, American. 2. Cooking—Florida—Florida Panhandle. 3. Food—Florida—Florida Panhandle.
I. Title.
  TX715.M64735 2015
  641.5973—dc23

2015037278

♾™ The paper used in this publication meets the minimum requirements of American National Standard for Information Sciences—Permanence of Paper for Printed Library Materials, ANSI/NISO Z39.48-1992.

Contents

Introduction

If you're from the Redneck Riviera, you may already know me. I'm not just a flash in the pan. I like to keep my roots planted deep. I like to work with people who are risk takers, of the same mindset as me, and those who exude enthusiasm and talent for the glories of the Florida Panhandle. I'm a driven chef, a culinary visionary who has followed his efforts and has paid his dues.

When it comes to Florida Panhandle cooking, I find our unsung region's foodways are particularly southern, historically based, and unlike those anywhere else in the Sunshine State, or anywhere on the planet for that matter.

I raised my incredible daughter and make my living here. When possible I take to the coastline for relaxation and enjoyment. The beach is no stranger to me. I've lived by the water since just after high school. I hail from the East Coast and oddly enough—I can't explain it—I was summoned to the Gulf Coast. It was my destiny to live and work in Pensacola.

Perhaps being a transplant allowed me to appreciate the glories of the Florida Panhandle. Nevertheless, I wanted to capture the unique foodways of the region like no one else has ever envisioned. I believe with all my heart and soul that the timing is right for a bona fide regional cookbook seen through the eyes of a food person.

My motivation was knowing I had a story to tell and believing in my gut that I could write such a book. It wasn't easy. I knew no one was going to do my work for me. I felt alone and isolated at times as I began to create the book's contents. With a lot of encouragement from a few friends, chefs, and family, I persevered, drawing on my three continuous decades as a chef.

Those three decades are what qualify me to write this book. I'm not famous. I'm still a full-time executive chef. I've never been on *Chopped, Top Chef,* or *Iron Chef America;* I've never ever battled Bobby Flay or been nominated for a James Beard Award. I certainly have no formal experience in journalism. I don't have a recipe writer or a recipe-testing team. I am real, and I celebrate a remarkable and rewarding career as a chef that is true, foreseeable, and attainable for culinary enthusiasts both young and old. Many of my experiences are in my recipe stories and are shared in this culinary joyride.

The current interest in southern food throughout the country is undeniably hot. The foods and the people of the Deep South have long waited to be recognized for their contribution to both southern and Florida cuisine. We don't fit into a clearly defined culinary mold. Folks often don't recognize Florida cooking as particularly southern. Even more concerning is the fact that Panhandle cooking uniquely defines a region of Florida that rarely draws national interest from food experts. Our cooking is a stewpot of cultures that has influenced our region's survival and growth to date. We have a distinct, simple philosophy—use what's fresh and in season. Be it fresh shrimp, red snapper, or a mess of braising greens, there is no reason to muck a recipe up with complicated ingredients. Keep it ethnic based. Support local efforts for sustainable and responsibly farmed foods, and never forget where you come from and where you are headed!

I have tried to make this more than just a cookbook by focusing on the uniqueness of the region. I have added my own memories, thoughts, and experiences about the Florida Panhandle as it was in the past and is today. Through the course of reading my short stories and recipes, you will learn the foodways of the Florida Panhandle. You too can have a taste of my culinary journeys, discovering iconic ingredients and emblematic foods. You can meet great southern chefs and experience local lore, a bit of Florida history, the lifestyle of its people, and traditional and new-fangled farming techniques.

Along the way you will meet famous cookbook authors, seafood authorities, agriculture experts, barbecue masters, microbrewers, artisan cheesemakers, farmers, beekeepers, grits folks, shrimp farmers, and oyster folks. You'll witness farm-to-table events, get to know regional fishing legends, and rub elbows with the pioneers of Northwest Florida's new Redneck Riviera.

Florida Food and Cooking Nomenclature

The Panhandle is the last great, secret, culinary region in the state of Florida. It has a nickname that has been used over the decades by locals and tourists alike, one that might raise an eyebrow when someone hears it for the first time: the "Redneck Riviera." The term is endearing for many of us, and is synonymous with a proud type of slow and real cooking along the Gulf Coast.

Florida is known for its sunny beaches, boating, golfing, orange groves, and Disney World, an image that has been cultivated at the expense of its outstanding cuisine. The same goes for the Florida Panhandle. This region offers a lot more than just emerald green waters, white powdery beaches, new town developments, and a different time zone. The diversity of the Panhandle's restaurant scene and varieties of ethnic cooking I have witnessed over the last 30 years led me to write *Panhandle to Pan* with the intention of changing that incomplete portrayal. There's more here than meets the eye.

Just as Southern Cuisine is not a single cuisine, neither is Florida Panhandle cooking. Firmly rooted in the inland South, as well as the coastal Gulf of Mexico and its estuaries, Florida Panhandle foods comprise four distinct, yet homogeneous, cooking styles.

Old Florida

Nestled beneath fragrant magnolias and Spanish moss-draped cypress trees, one loses a sense of time when it comes to Old Florida cooking. This style harkens back to the days of close-knit, front-porch communities, a time rich in folklore, family customs, and easily accessible local ingredients, prepared simply. Old Florida cooking is casual, pure, fresh, clean, and incorporates authentic flavors that mirror cultural homegrown foods in a localized lifestyle.

Simple recipes for favorite, mainstay, dinner-table items such as baked ham, "honest" fried chicken, corn bread, hand-shucked butter beans, and strawberry shortcake are passed down by family members to ensure their future existence. In the same vein, Old Florida cooking can include a regional favorite recipe such as "Snapper Amandine" from a boat captain, given to his crew members and fish cutters.

Over 200 years ago, during the time of Spanish occupation, domestic pigs brought by De Soto graced Southern tables—including Florida and pork became a staple for the dinner and an important source of nourishment. Native American corn, grown and harvested for centuries, also found its way into everyday life. Evidence for these abundant food sources in the southern region of Florida is found in popular spin-off recipes like "Grits and Grunts" and "Hog and Hominy." Many of Florida's original and longtime restaurants borne from this time period include foods such as grouper, catfish, swamp cabbage (hearts of palm), alligator, cooters (soft-shell turtles), Hoover steak (gopher tortoise), frog legs, and armadillo.

During the "Boom and Bust" years (those years prior to the Great Depression of 1929 and the 1930s following), many regions of Florida experienced economic growth due to an increase in tourism and subsequent housing development. These were the time periods that saw the beginnings of the first somewhat modern restaurants.

One of the most recognized Florida restaurants is The Yearling, located just south of Gainesville, in Cross Creek. Famous for its Old Florida cooking, it is also known as the "Home of Florida Cracker Cooking." The term cracker is a reverent nickname given to the area's swamp-dwelling pioneers. Founder Marjorie Rawlings published Cross Creek Cookery in 1942, and in it she shares recipes based on a treasure-trove of the state's indigenous native bounty, much of which was gathered by her relatives, Florida backwoods cooks, sportsmen, and often from the kitchens of her many friends.

The former Hopkins Boarding House on Spring Street near downtown Pensacola is another example of a restaurant that featured Old Florida food. Though the restaurant didn't open until post-war 1949, the owners' intent was preserving Old Florida foods and traditions. Customers were seated next to each other on long tables and served family-style by the staff—either bowls of food were passed along or turned to the other side on a Lazy Susan. With head cook Cora Edwards in the kitchen, Hopkins became famous for Fried Chicken Day. The "pulley bone" (the wishbone attached to a chunk of breast meat) was served separately, and to get it, all you had to do was ask. There was also a surrounding porch, in the style of pre-air conditioning houses in the South, where you could sit and rock away the meal. Unfortunately, Hopkins House closed in 2004.

In keeping with family gathering traditions and casual atmospheres, many present-day Panhandle restaurateurs have re-created the simply prepared, Old Florida–style foods, and good ole Southern hospitality. You'll still find catfish cabins, crab shacks, diners, fish camps, fish houses, and beach- and harbor-side restaurants serving fried mullet, farm-raised catfish, fresh Gulf Coast fish, seafood platters, and hush puppies in the tradition of earlier times.

North Florida in particular remains spotted with Old Florida–style homes, communities, and foods. Milton (and nearby Bagdad), DeFuniak Springs, Ponce de Leon, and Florala (on the Florida-Alabama line) still maintain some serious Old Florida personae. This way of life has adapted, become modernized, and is once again a viable economical option. The challenges presented by an ever-increasing human population have borne an environmentally conscious attitude that has resulted in positive changes. Many endangered animal species have been removed from menus. Home gardens have been on the rise more than ever, featuring seasonally grown heirloom tomatoes, chili peppers, and greens. In addition, backyard chicken coops for fresh eggs have been constructed by the new wave of self-reliant locavores. The past is once again the present.

Real Florida

As Florida residents approached the late 1940s and early 1950s, foods began to revert to their cultural roots. Again, not well-defined, but succinctly recognized, the Panhandle began to spring into form with culturally inspired specialty food shops that included deep-rooted food traditions.

For me, Real Florida cooking is a celebration of all foods emblematic of Florida, both at sea and inland. For example for over a hundred years, oystermen (and women) have fished for wild oysters in Apalachicola Bays as they still do today. In East Point, live blue crabs are regularly harvested from its estuaries. There's Port St. Joe, where seasonal wild hoppers (shrimp) run and where bay scallops can still be harvested by hand in the shallow, grassy beds of St. Joseph Bay. Hook-and-line fishing still thrives throughout the waterways of the entire Florida Panhandle and off the Desoto Canyon— fingers to fathoms. Dozens of fish species including redfish, mullet, speckled trout, cobia, snapper, grouper, mahi-mahi, and tuna are still plucked from the Gulf of Mexico.

And we never have to reach too far inland to find staple agriculture such as sweet corn, tomatoes, potatoes, carrots, squash, eggplant, mushrooms, hearty greens, field peas, and sweet and hot peppers to adorn these treasures harvested from our waters.

Much of the inherent foods of the Northern Panhandle have been dominated by the down-home cooking styles of Alabama and Georgia. This proximity bred a rich exchange of cultural influences. Food traditions deep and strong came with the many immigrant populations who settled in Florida. As food and culture continued to evolve, home-style ethnic foods characterized cooking, suited for the environment during that time period. Shrimp and seafood shacks, chicken joints, breakfast and coffee houses, smoke pits, barbecue, and mom and pop ethnic foods took the lead.

Real Florida food is perhaps a continuum of Old Florida food developed and refined by predecessor cooks, travelers, and family members. Many of our festivals were created in preservation of our region's Real Florida and what we recognize now as our emblematic foods. Community events are built around food: Flora-Bama's Mullet Festival, Niceville's Boggy Bayou Mullet Festival, the Pensacola Crawfish Festival, Destin and Pensacola Seafood Festival, and the Great Southern Gumbo Cook-Off are a few current examples.

New Florida

During the 1970s, the foods of the Florida Panhandle were unmoving, still echoing the Old Florida real and simple style dominance of the slow-changing region of Florida's remote Northwest. Land and tourist development along the Gulf Coast's Redneck Riviera struggled to be recognized during the growth of Disney in Orlando and South Florida's progress. For this region, Sandestin, led by developer Peter Bos, remained the largest tourist draw for many years. It was in the mid to late 1980s when South and Central Florida began to be acknowledged as food cities, gathering national attention by creating a Florida food movement around the mega state.

Chefs from around the state sampled and developed new approaches to what would soon be coined "Florida Cuisine." As regions began emerging with new, localized, and ethnic-influenced food styles, well-known talented chefs from South Florida began receiving significant attention for inspiring the food movement. Miami chefs' heavily influenced Florida-style Chinese, Vietnamese, Jewish, and Southern cuisine all fit into the exciting Miami food mix described informally as "Floribbean." South Florida cooking began to include foods from the Caribbean with Latin-based themes—Cuban, Nicaraguan, Haitian, Dominican, Colombian, Panamanian, Bahamian, Jamaican, and Puerto Rican—combining ingredients, flavors, and cooking techniques to create rule-bending recipes and cutting-edge fusion dishes incorporating tropical fruits and vegetables that are available year-round in those areas.

Farther south, in the Conch Republic (Key West), another new regional Florida cooking was stewing. One chef's cooking was being recognized for the heavy influences of Spain's Columbus coming to the New World. The culinary visionary of Norman Van Aken—a Key West chef now considered legendary—became nationally recognized for its fusing of foods, or "fusion cooking." As The Founding Father of New World Cuisine, Chef Van Aken led the South Florida cooking scene, incorporating the fusion of ethnic and historical styles, including Latin, Caribbean, Asian, African, and American flavors. Other chefs were emerging, too, hailing from the densely populated Miami vicinity to Key West. Norman Van Aken, Mark Militello, Douglas Rodriguez, and Allen Susser came to be known as the Mango Gang.

The Florida food movement spread rapidly to the Florida Panhandle where I was chef of Bud and Alley's restaurant in Seaside, Santa Rosa Beach, Florida. In 1987 Chef Norman Van Aken, about to embark on his first cookbook tour for *Feast of Sunlight*, found his way to Seaside and served as guest chef at Bud and Alley's, promoting his cuisine. I was inspired by Chef Norman, as were many Florida chefs. The Florida food movement sparked nationwide interest in local, ethnic-based foods, and fueled the fire for chefs all over the Sunshine State to localize their menus—to seek out and rethink their region's indigenous ingredients and cooking measures and methods.

In the Florida Panhandle I became recognized for my New Florida Cooking. This was a joyful undertaking for me, since the area from the Gulf Coast's Big Bend to Pensacola supplied unending seafood treasures to showcase our neck of the woods. The Florida Panhandle's Gulf Coast seafood played a major role in our easy-to-recognize cooking. Seasonal menu highlights included soft-shell crabs, sweet calico scallops, wild clams, hand-tonged oysters, red snapper, wild shrimp, cobia, triggerfish, and grouper. We began seeking out locally farmed quail while supporting the artisan farmers and small growers throughout the Panhandle.

Modern Florida

Modern Florida cooking includes both simple and adventurous preparation methods for what may be best described as history on a plate. In all regions of the mega state, young culinary talent is eager to master this re-boiled Florida cuisine. For the first time since the 1990s, a food style that feels unique for this state is emerging, distinct, yet garnered from the loins of the Florida Food Movement. The Panhandle is the epicenter of Florida's southernmost-influenced cuisine. This trend of the modern palate includes lighter foods, healthier ingredients, and an adventurous approach using Gulf Coast horn-of-plenty produce and new artisanal products that sweep the region.

Cookbook author Robert Courtine said it best: "One should have a relish for what one does; you should also have a relish for what others have done before you." I like where Florida cuisine is headed. It has so much potential. This style of new Florida heritage cooking fuses our ethnic foods and cultures on a plate, with a nod to the Native American, Spanish, French, and English roots alongside a salute to Old Florida, Real Florida, and New Florida pioneers.

Florida Panhandle cooking in its finest form is just beginning to be considered a fashionable cuisine and respected around the state. In this neck of the woods, special attention is paid to organically grown produce, sustainable commercial fishing, livestock, and agriculture practices. A "turn back the hands of time" sort of approach to localized eating and lifestyle has made its way back to modern Florida. Both urban and rural farmers alike are inspired to sow both heirloom and newer seeds for regional staple foods.

The trend includes artisans who specialize in beekeeping and mushroom growing, and those who explore growing non-native plant species. Hydroponic and aquaponic lettuces are being grown. Florida's only successful shrimp farm resides in Gulf County in the Panhandle, and is making history for our region of the state. There's plenty of evidence of the return of the Native Floridian, the original locavore, and reverence for locally produced foods throughout the Sunshine State. It is history in the remaking. Communities have come together to ensure that localized foods are being used and how where you buy your groceries or at which restaurant you choose to eat affects our regional businesses and economy. What I think is so exciting is that it all started here in Pensacola in 1559, Florida's first settlement.

Agricultural systems are now in place so that we can grow, in our sand-based soil, delicate lettuces and non-regional vegetables—such as salsify—rather than just peppers, tomatoes, squash, and potatoes. Innovative locals construct functional gardens to replace lawns, create landscapes in their backyards, raise bees for honey, use rooftops to grow fresh herbs, raise yard birds for fresh eggs, and plant trees for nuts and fruit, including the cold-hardy satsuma. Both the posh and proletarian approach to healthier eating and greener lifestyle has come of age and is here to stay. Technology and social networking has enabled us to spread the word, easier and faster, about nutritious foods and everyday eating choices.

HISTORIC PENSACOLA - FOOD FOR THOUGHT

For thousands of years prior to the arrival of Europeans, native American Indians moved in and out of the Pensacola Bay Area, harvesting the rich marine resources of the bay and hunting the riverine forests. The arrival of Europeans resulted in an exchange of material goods, technologies and ideologies that forever changed the cultural landscape of *La Florida*. One of the best examples of this dynamic cultural evolution is reflected in the innovative and cross-cultural foodways of the modern era. It all began on the Florida Gulf Coast.

PRE-COLONIZATION PERIOD

Dave Edwards

Oysters, small shrimp, crabs, conch and scallops were gathered by native American Indians in the shallow waters and estuaries of Pensacola Bay.

Evidence of the olive, an Old World cultigen and staple of the Spanish diet, was first archaeologically documented in *La Florida* on the 1559 Emanuel Point I shipwreck in Pensacola Bay.

Native American Indians were willing to share their knowledge of edible wild plants and animals with Spanish settlers. These foods included pecan and hickory nuts; maize, various roots, tubers and wild fruits; and deer, small mammals, turtles and birds. One of many products derived from maize, grits are now a Southern staple. Coarsely ground dried corn + water or milk = Grits.

FIRST SPANISH PERIOD (1500-1763)

1559-1561
Don Tristán de Luna y Arellano and 1,500 settlers arrived at Pensacola Bay to establish a settlement and military outpost. Soon after landing, a September hurricane destroyed the fleet of ships at anchor. Several vessels were still laden with supplies, eventually dooming the colony's chances of survival.

The Spanish brought lemons, oranges and limes with them to the New World. A specific variety of citrus known as the Seville orange now grows in Historic Pensacola Village.

A variety of chiles were enjoyed by Mexico's Spanish conquerors and were subsequently introduced in *La Florida*. These peppers added flavor and color to bland, stale or fatty foods.

Pigs were initially introduced into Florida by Spanish explorer Hernando de Soto in 1539. Pork was an important and favorite meat in the Iberian diet. Cured hams, bacon and pork preserved in brine were indispenable meats for sea voyages and for overland expeditions through unfamiliar territories.

Vegetables such as mustard greens were likely brought to the Americas with enslaved Africans and cultivated in small domestic gardens.

1698-1719
After an absence of more than 130 years, the Spanish again returned to Pensacola, establishing the first permanent settlement on Pensacola Bay. The site of this outpost, *Presidio Santa María de Galve* and *Fort San Carlos de Austria*, can be visited today onboard Naval Air Station Pensacola.

1719-1722
French forces took control of the Spanish *Presidio Santa María de Galve* for three years and burned the wooden palisade fort to the ground.

Some records show that field peas first came to Florida from the West Indies in 1700. First used as food for slaves, these protein-rich peas became a primary source of nourishment for many families, both enslaved and free.

From the 1705 offshore wreck of a supply ship sent to provision the presidio, lead fishing net weights were recovered in Pensacola Bay—an indication that deep water fishing was practiced by seamen aboard these vessels.

In 1761, Pensacola resident Joseph Gutiérrez received 221 pounds of Flemish cheese, which would have cost $250 in today's currency. *Manchego*, one of the oldest and most popular types of cheese produced in Spain, may also have been imported by wealthy citizens.

Chocolate was often requested by the Spanish in Pensacola from supplies in New Spain (Mexico). It was used both as a high-status drink and for medicinal purposes.

1722-1763
By negotiated treaty with France, the Spanish regained control of Pensacola. *Presidio Isla de Santa Rosa* was first established on Pensacola Beach, and years later, *Presidio San Miguel de Panzacola* was built in the present-day downtown area. Small herds of cattle were established in the surrounding countryside.

The mirliton, a member of the squash family, was valued both as a versatile food and as an ornamental vine by French and Spanish Creoles of colonial Louisiana and Florida.

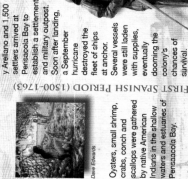

University of **West Florida**
Archaeology Institute

Two thousand years ago people harvested the rich marine resources of Pensacola Bay. Today, only the technology of the catch has changed.

Pensacola's coastal cuisine has been influenced over many years by the bounty of Gulf waters, fresh seasonal produce, healthy livestock and the culinary contributions of a multi-cultural population—you will taste family traditions and Southern hospitality in every bite!

During the 19th and early 20th centuries, the nation's largest red snapper fishing fleet was based in Pensacola. Vessels used in this industry, generally schooners, were refurbished as "Snapper Smacks" and outfitted to meet demands of the catch.

Today, the 1559 shipwrecks of the Luna Expedition provide a poignant reminder of the perils Europeans faced in settling the New World. The dynamic interactions that ensued forever changed the cultural and physical landscape of *La Florida* and what we know today as the United States of America.

TERRITORIAL PERIOD—MODERN ERA (1821-PRESENT)

In 1821, Gov. Andrew Jackson oversaw the transfer of Florida from Spain to the United States, raising the Florida territorial flag in Pensacola across the street from today's Jackson's Steakhouse, a popular downtown restaurant.

In 1861, Florida seceded from the Union. Pensacola flew the flag of the Confederacy for a little more than a year before withdrawing. Troop rations were low in vitamins and minerals, relying heavily on pickled or salted pork and beef and dried peas and beans.

SECOND SPANISH PERIOD (1781-1821)

The Tivoli House served as the center of entertainment in Pensacola, providing food, drink and amusement to a diverse clientele. A typical table at the tavern would be set with a variety of vessels, and of course, a bottle (*or two*) of wine.

The *1781 Battle of Pensacola* was one of the most significant engagements of the American Revolution. Spain, allied with the Americans, drove the British from the Gulf Coast and Mississippi River Valley, allowing Washington to focus his energies on the eastern front.

BRITISH PERIOD (1763-1781)

When the British arrived to take control of Pensacola and West Florida the fort was repaired and strengthened, and a new town plan was developed and soon implemented. An increase in trade enabled new shops to be opened, and economy improved.

Citizens were allowed to seine for oysters along the bayfront, and cattle herds continued to increase. Beef and seafood were often paired on British menus. Sherry and port wines were quite popular. Archaeologists have recovered remains of wine bottles, beef bones and oyster shells from trash pits in the British fort.

Hand colored by Dave Edwards

Images courtesy of the Archaeology Institute and UWF Historic Trust, Pensacola Historical Society Collection.

The University of West Florida Division of Anthropology and Archaeology: Documenting the physical and cultural landscapes of Pensacola's past.

A Food Tour of the Florida Panhandle

In keeping with Southern tradition we set a common table for all races, rich and poor. On the road we offer food for every socioeconomic class. Our recipes are bonded by coastline, history, iconic foods, and inherit foodways and practices. We're a proud bunch. Our culture runs deep and includes a diverse workforce—from shrimp and oyster farmers to agriculturalists and livestock farmers, fish cutters, oyster shuckers, artisans, and cooks to name a few. We stand together to make a difference with the way we think about food, where it comes from and how we cook it. I believe the Florida Panhandle is the last great regional culinary secret of the state.

These parts of Florida are sometimes called the Redneck Riviera, L.A. (Lower Alabama), Mullet Latitudes, or Middle Florida, but whatever it's called, it still translates to hurricane alley, savage sun, sandy soil, a once-vibrant oyster industry, and highly regulated recreational and commercial fishing practices. What may appear a bleak reality to many is home to others. It's all in how you view it. Generations of Florida Panhandlers have learned ways to overcome the elements, deal with sustainability rules, and ensure and preserve emblematic foods such as Apalachicola oysters and red snapper for generations to come.

Everything is subject to change, including the bounties of the land and sea provided by Mother Nature. Gulf Coast inclement weather often equates to surviving extreme heat, wind, flood and hurricane conditions, and often periods of summer drought. But humans and nature find a way to survive (and often thrive) in the midst. Filter feeders such as oysters rely on the delicate salinity balance of our bays for their survival. Our gardeners and farmers rely on the healthy soil to sow their seeds. Fisherman and divers await calm seas to go hook-and-line and spear-gun fishing. Everything is dependent on something.

People often ask what grows in the Florida Panhandle. From the outside looking in, it's not a clear food portrait, but after you spend significant time here, you begin to see the clear picture. Here, there is an appreciation for old-timey Florida coastal town foods.

Chefs and locals make a concerted effort to support old and new food culture. We buy from seafood markets that support struggling oyster folks; use sustainably harvested wild shrimp; support sustainable Gulf County farm-raised shrimp, day boat fishermen; and commercial crabbers who only know how to do one thing to put supper on the table.

The best local ingredients come from organic gardeners; pig, lamb and chicken farmers; new and aggressive agriculture practices, including hydroponics and aquaponics; and an array of artisans, farmstead cheese-makers, and urban bee keepers.

The New Redneck Riviera represents a region of the Deep South and is a real part of the diverse mega state's cooking. Chefs might agree that any degree of farm to table cooking is not easy in areas with difficult soil conditions and dramatic weather as in Northwest Florida, except I believe every location is rich in agriculture if you look for it. This has always been the case for me.

In this spirit of cooking and local sourcing, many of the best chefs in the region seek out Florida Panhandle foods and center menus on Gulf Coast Seafood and agriculture. While Central and South Florida is family, Alabama (only 20 minutes away) is next of kin to Northwest Florida, we share the bounties of agriculture, and aquaculture and artisan ingredients harvested as nearby as their own back door or as far-away Louisiana and Texas.

As chef, the task of getting the word out has taken over three decades. I believe the foods and cooking of Northwest Florida are, without a doubt, the unsung cuisine of the state. We may be the most misunderstood microregion of America's Deep South.

Chapter 1
A Gathering of Appetizers

Panhandle Phyllo Pie

Greek seamen sailed their vessels into Pensacola Bay in the mid- to late 1800s, many staking their claims as fishermen in search of opportunity. As the steady stream of immigrants increased, the newest citizens made their livings in the shrimp, oyster, and sponge-diving industry, as well as by running local grocery stores, restaurants, and other small businesses along the Panhandle. Greeks, including their predecessors, the Spanish, French, and English, all brought their beloved homeland foods to Florida, including spices and cooking techniques from Africa, South America, and the Caribbean. This cultural stew makes up our historical regional cooking; it's a blending of the Old World and the New. Their multi-sensory, savory, and sugar-laced traditional food favorites are known throughout the South and the entire country. Greek dance is a well-known, celebrated tradition, and is as integral to their culture as is family and food.

This delicious American creation—phyllo pizza—combines some of my favorite traditional Greek ingredients: tomato, spinach, greens, fennel, feta, mozzarella, and sharp Kasseri, all in one simple and fun recipe. These are the foods that make me happy and want to dance.

To make the phyllo

Preheat oven to 400°F. Place the phyllo sheets on a work surface and cover them with a towel. Place olive oil in a small dish and, with a pastry brush, spread oil evenly onto the bottom of a cookie sheet or half-size sheet pan. Layer the phyllo sheets, one at a time, onto the pans, brushing each layer with olive oil. Sprinkle 3 tablespoons of cheese between every second sheet (5 times). Repeat until all 10 sheets have been used. Brush the top layer with olive oil.

To make the spinach mixture

Place a large skillet over medium heat. Add the spinach and ⅛ cup of water. Stir until wilted completely. Transfer to a strainer and drain well. Squeeze to remove all water. Chop the spinach small, add the green onion, and place in a medium-size mixing bowl. Add the feta and goat cheese and use a fork to blend the mixture. Set aside.

To assemble

Use remaining grated cheese to sprinkle over top, leaving ½ inch of phyllo sheet edges exposed (for crust). Add the thinly sliced tomatoes side by side. Sprinkle spinach mixture on top of tomatoes and spread out evenly, leaving crust exposed. Add the sliced mozzarella and lightly season with salt and pepper. Scatter the field greens and shaved fennel over the top. Drizzle with olive oil. Bake for 25–30 minutes, or until phyllo is golden and cheeses are melted. Let rest 5 minutes before slicing with a pizza cutter.

(SERVES 4–6)

For the phyllo

10 phyllo sheets

6 tablespoons olive oil

½ cup shredded Kefalotyri, or grated Kasseri, Parmesan, or Pecorino Romano

For the spinach mixture

1 pound fresh wilted, drained, and chopped spinach

1 cup chopped green onion

½ cup crumbled feta

½ cup (4 ounces) crumbled goat cheese

For the finished dish

2 vine-ripe tomatoes, thinly sliced

6 slices fresh mozzarella

Pinch of kosher salt

Dash of fresh ground black pepper

½ pound field greens (such as chard, sorrel, mustard, dandelion, or watercress)

½ cup thin-shaved fennel bulb

2 teaspoons olive oil for drizzling

Roasted Zucchini Pan-Fritters with Corn Salsa

One of my favorite types of fritters is a pancake batter–style fritter. Batter- and dough-style fritters, savory or sweet, are perfect when cooked so they are crispy on the outside and tender and fluffy on the inside. These Johnnycake-type fritters are easy to make and simple to cook. They involve only a few more steps than making pancakes and taste particularly good when prepared in a well-seasoned cast-iron skillet. I found that the most interesting element for roasting in this recipe is the zucchini.

Zucchini is one of the most common and easy-to-grow spring and fall Florida Panhandle squashes, and is readily available year-round almost everywhere around the country. In this recipe, be sure to roast the zucchini first to enable caramelizing, which permits the natural flavors of the vegetables to take center stage. It is particularly delicious when served over roasted poblano aioli and then topped with fresh corn salsa. I like to add a drizzle of artisan honey, too.

(SERVES 6–8)

For the fritters

1½ cups small-diced zucchini

½ cup fine-diced yellow onions

2 tablespoons extra-virgin olive oil

1 tablespoon minced garlic

2 eggs

1 cup milk

1 cup all-purpose flour

1 cup corn flour

2 teaspoons baking powder

½ teaspoon kosher salt

½ teaspoon freshly ground black pepper

3 tablespoons hot sauce (Louisiana brand preferred)

Pure olive oil, extra for cooking

To make the fritters

Combine zucchini, onions, olive oil, and garlic in a medium-size bowl. Stir or toss to coat vegetables well. Pour vegetables onto a baking pan and spread out evenly. Roast for 8–10 minutes or until vegetables are tender and zucchini begins to brown on the edges.

Crack eggs into medium-size mixing bowl, and lightly beat. Add milk until blended. Place a wire mesh strainer over a separate medium-size mixing bowl. Sift the all-purpose flour, corn flour, baking powder, salt, and pepper through the strainer. Make a well in the center of dry ingredients, and pour in egg mixture. Blend until smooth using a heavy-duty wire whisk, stirring from the center out, and being careful not to overmix. Stir in the cooked zucchini. Cover and let rest in refrigerator for 30 minutes before cooking.

To make the corn salsa

Combine all ingredients in a medium-size bowl. Taste and adjust seasoning with salt and pepper.

To make the roasted poblano aioli

Preheat oven to 375°F. Place whole poblano pepper in a baking dish and bake for 15–20 minutes, then place in a ziplock bag to steam for 10 minutes. On a work surface scrape to remove skin and seeds from pepper. In food processor bowl, add egg yolks, lemon juice, garlic, and shallots and pulse to blend. Add the roasted poblano pepper and run the machine, drizzling in measured oils. Taste and adjust seasoning with salt and pepper.

To assemble

Preheat griddle or cast-iron skillet. Make a small test fritter, taste, and then make any seasoning adjustments to the batter. Ladle or spoon the fritter batter onto the well-oiled pan. Cook for 3–4 minutes on the first side, flipping when sides begin to brown and bubbles appear on the surface. Continue to cook another 2–3 minutes, until golden and center is dry to a toothpick (as a pancake).

Spoon and smear the aioli on the bottom of a platter or individual plates. Stack or shingle the fritters and then top with corn salsa. Garnish with edible flowers or micro shoots.

For the corn salsa

1½ cups shaved boiled sweet corn kernels (from 2 ears of corn)

4 tablespoons fine-diced red sweet peppers

5 tablespoons fine-diced red onion

1–2 tablespoons fine-chopped chervil or flat-leaf parsley

1 teaspoon or drizzle of artisan tupelo honey

1 teaspoon lemon juice

Pinch of salt and freshly ground black pepper

For the roasted poblano aioli

1 poblano pepper

3 egg yolks

1 teaspoon fresh squeezed lemon juice

2 teaspoons finely chopped fresh garlic cloves

2 teaspoons finely chopped shallots

¼ cup pure olive oil

¼ cup extra-virgin olive oil

Pinch of kosher salt

Freshly ground black pepper to taste

For the garnish

Edible flowers such as Johnny jump ups, nasturtiums, zucchini blossoms, squash blossoms, or micro shoots

Fried Green Tomatoes with Cucumber, Corn & Bacon Relish

Many of our country's staple dishes are Southern inspired. Green tomatoes are no exception. Perhaps the best rule of thumb when crafting winning dishes is to remember the traditional motto "vegetables that grow together, go together." Tomatoes, cucumbers, and corn certainly fit that rule. In this recipe I like to use crispy bacon to add a layer of flavor, texture, and smoky goodness. In my opinion, there's no better bacon for this dish than Benton's Smoky Mountain Country Ham's, one of the South's leading smoked bacon and cured ham producers. Owner Allan Benton uses a traditional dry-curing process that remains the same as it was in its humble beginnings in 1947.

(SERVES 4)

For the green tomatoes

3–4 medium green tomatoes

1 cup buttermilk

1–2 tablespoons hot sauce (Louisiana brand preferred)

1 cup all-purpose flour

1 cup cracker meal

1 cup cornmeal

1 teaspoon Creole spice

1 teaspoon kosher salt

For the relish

4 slices smoky bacon (Benton's bacon preferred), cooked crisp and chopped small

½ cup peeled and small-diced cucumber

½ cup fresh sweet corn kernels

3 tablespoons small-diced Vidalia onion

2 tablespoons small-diced red bell pepper

1 green onion, whites and greens, cut small

1 teaspoon finely chopped flat-leaf parsley

2 tablespoons cider vinegar

4 tablespoons extra-virgin olive oil

Pinch of kosher salt and freshly ground black pepper

To make the green tomatoes
Prepare fryer to 350°F. Slice off green tomato tops and cut into ¼-inch-thick medallions. Place buttermilk and hot sauce into a medium-size bowl. In another medium-size bowl combine flour, cracker meal, cornmeal, and Creole spice to make breading mixture. Dip each tomato slice into buttermilk mixture, let soak for 5 minutes, and then place, one at a time, into the seasoned breading mixture. Tap to shake off excess breading before deep-frying. Deep-fry the tomatoes for 2–3 minutes or until golden brown. Place fried tomatoes on paper towels to drain, then season with a pinch of salt.

To make the relish
Combine all ingredients in a small mixing bowl.

To assemble
Shingle 2–3 tomato medallions onto individual plates (or all on a platter). Scatter the cucumber and relish over the top and serve.

Eggplant Creole with Crab Meunière & Béarnaise

The tradition of Creole cooking is shared by many along the stretch of coastline from Texas to Florida, and throughout the Deep South. The epicenter for this phenomenon is New Orleans, Louisiana, and a journey to Bourbon Street will lead you to Galatoire's. This time-honored, authentic restaurant is neatly nestled into the French Quarter and is one of the only widely recognized French Creole restaurants remaining in New Orleans. That some things are just meant to stay the same is the philosophy on which the Galatoire family built their name over 100 years ago.

Friend, chef, and cookbook author Leon Galatoire and I have manned the stoves together at Jackson's Steakhouse in Pensacola, Florida, on a several occasions, preparing Mardi Gras menus for the masses. Chef Leon had prepared meals at Galatoire's for over twenty years and operated the historical institution's stoves as chef from 1991 to 1996. In the spirit of French Creole cooking, this is the most eye-appealing and interesting dish I crafted for Jackson's appetizer menu.

This particular recipe is not for the diet conscious. I have adapted this Creole-style dish to my own personalized style. *Laissez les bon temp rouler!* (Let the good times roll!)

For the eggplant

1 medium eggplant

2 cups all-purpose flour, divided

1 cup cracker meal

1 teaspoon ground cumin

½ teaspoon kosher salt, plus more for seasoning

½ teaspoon cayenne pepper

½ teaspoon sweet smoky paprika (La Chinata brand preferred)

½ teaspoon granulated garlic

½ teaspoon dried sweet basil

2 eggs

2 cups milk

For the Creole sauce

3 tablespoons olive oil

1½ cups small-diced yellow onions

1 cup small-diced celery

1½ teaspoons finely chopped garlic

1 cup small-diced green bell pepper

Kosher salt

Freshly ground black pepper

1 (16-ounce) can diced tomatoes or 2 cups peeled, seeded, and chopped tomatoes

1 (14-ounce) can tomato sauce

2 tablespoons hot sauce (Louisiana brand preferred)

1½ teaspoons Worcestershire sauce

1 teaspoon zest or microplaned orange

1 cup water or vegetable broth

To make the eggplant

Preheat deep fryer to 350°F. Peel eggplant and cut into ¼-inch-thick medallions. Cut as many perfect rounds as possible. Place 1 cup of the flour into a medium-size mixing bowl. Combine remaining flour, cracker meal, spices, and seasonings in a separate medium-size mixing bowl. In a third bowl whisk eggs and milk together.

Lightly dust the eggplant medallions with flour, then dip them, one at a time, into the milk and egg mixture to soak. Next, place them into the seasoned flour and cracker meal, coating them one at a time until completely covered. Tap off excess breading and deep-fry for 2–3 minutes or until golden brown. Remove from fryer, lightly season with a pinch more salt, and let drain on a paper towel–lined plate.

To make the Creole sauce

Heat a large skillet over medium heat and add the oil. Stir in the onions, celery, garlic, and bell peppers and sauté for 5–7 minutes over medium heat, stirring occasionally and seasoning lightly with salt and pepper as you go. Stir in the chopped tomatoes, tomato sauce, and remaining ingredients. Bring to a boil and then reduce heat to a simmer, stirring occasionally, for 30–40 minutes or until sauce begins to thicken slightly. Taste and adjust seasoning as needed. Remove bay leaf before serving.

To make the blue crab meunière

Remove any cartilage from backfin crab. Combine lemon juice and butter in a small saucepot and bring to a simmer over low heat. When butter has melted, skim surface. Add the backfin crab and parsley to warm gently, seasoning the crab with salt and pepper.

To make the béarnaise sauce

Place water in double boiler and place boiler over medium-high heat. Bring water to a boil and reduce temperature to a simmer. Place vinegar, shallots, and tarragon in top bowl of double boiler. Let reduce for 5 minutes. Add egg yolks to the tarragon mixture. Use a balloon whisk to whisk egg yolk mixture briskly over low heat until it reaches ribbon stage, 5–7 minutes. Slowly drizzle in the clarified butter while whisking. Add a few more drops of water if too thick. Remove top bowl, and turn off double boiler. Let double boiler cool for 5 minutes. Hold the prepared sauce in a warm area of the kitchen, or place back into double boiler until needed.

To assemble

Spoon Creole sauce onto plates. Place one eggplant medallion onto the sauce and top with a generous spoon of crab meunière. Top with another eggplant medallion. Divide the remaining crabmeat over the top. Spoon béarnaise sauce over the top of each stack. Garnish with parsley.

1 whole bay leaf

¾ teaspoon dried oregano leaves

½ teaspoon sweet smoky paprika (La Chinata brand preferred)

½ teaspoon granulated garlic

½ teaspoon dried sweet basil

Pinch of cayenne pepper to taste

For the blue crab meunière

1 cup backfin crab

Fresh squeezed juice of 2 lemons

2 sticks unsalted butter

1 tablespoon finely chopped parsley

Kosher salt and freshly ground black pepper

For the béarnaise sauce

2 teaspoons white vinegar

1 teaspoon peeled, fine-diced shallots

1 teaspoon dried tarragon leaf

3 eggs, separated and yolks reserved

12 ounces unsalted butter, clarified

Pinch of cayenne pepper

1 tablespoon tepid water

For garnish

1 tablespoon fresh, chopped parsley

Clarified Butter

MAKES ABOUT 1¾ CUPS

4 sticks (16 ounces) unsalted butter

Place butter in a heavy-duty saucepan over low heat. Let butter melt completely, 8–10 minutes. Let simmer gently until the foam rises to the top of the melted butter. Remove pot from heat and let sit for 10 minutes, and then skim off all the foam with a spoon.

Line a fine-mesh strainer with a few layers of cheesecloth over another metal container or heavy-duty glass bowl. Carefully pour the warm butter through the cheesecloth-lined strainer into the container and leave behind any white milk solids remaining in the bottom of the pan.

Store clarified butter in a sealed plastic container for up to 3 months. Reheat in the microwave to melt before use.

Thai-Style Jasmine Rice Cakes & Shrimp Bites

Many service men and women who have traveled the globe have either started or finished their training at Pensacola Naval Air Station. Along the way, they were turned onto the local flavors of the land in which they were stationed. Also, families from those foreign countries have immigrated to Northwest Florida for decades, especially from Southeast Asia. The longing for their homeland foods, whether adopted or inherited, is reflected in the abundance of ethnic groceries that are scattered throughout the city.

For this Thai-inspired recipe, I combine easy-to-find ingredients to create aromatic and crispy rice cakes while incorporating the gulf's bountiful local shrimp. I recommend an array of favorite sauces, such as spicy sweet red chili sauce, red chili paste, wasabi, and sweet duck sauce.

This recipe was originally submitted to Chad Kirtland, editor of *Southern Breeze,* a Gulf Coast lifestyle magazine. It was one of the centerpieces for an article in their Chef's Table section titled "Right Place, Right Time."

For the infused coconut cream

⅓ cup coconut cream (canned or boxed)

½ teaspoon Chinese five-spice powder

1½ teaspoons fish sauce

2 teaspoons thinly sliced fresh gingerroot

2 tablespoons light soy sauce

For the rice

1 tablespoon sesame oil

1 tablespoon peanut or canola oil

⅓ cup chopped onion

½ cup uncooked jasmine rice

1 cup water

To make the infused coconut cream

Place all ingredients in a small saucepan over low heat. Simmer for 15 minutes, stirring often. Remove from heat. Remove ginger with a slotted spoon and discard. Allow mixture to cool.

To make the rice

Place sesame oil and peanut (or canola) oil in a heavy saucepan over medium-high heat until hot. Add onion and cook, stirring constantly, until onion is transparent. Add rice, stirring well. Add water and bring to a boil. Reduce heat to low and simmer uncovered for 15 minutes. Cover and cook for 3 more minutes, stirring occasionally.

To make the rice cakes

Whisk egg in a large bowl and mix in cooled infused coconut milk mixture. Stir in mint, cilantro, garlic, green onion, red pepper, chile pepper, salt, and black pepper. Add cooked rice mixture, stirring until combined. Stir in flour, mixing well. (Mixture may be refrigerated at this point for a few hours before cooking if desired.) Set aside.

To assemble

Preheat grill to medium high. Thread shrimp onto skewers. Dip a hand towel into the extra oil and coat grill rack with oil. Grill shrimp on rack over medium-hot coals, covered, 3 minutes on each side or until shrimp turn pink. Remove shrimp from skewers; keep warm.

Heat vegetable oil in a large heavy skillet over medium-high heat. Fill a ⅛-cup dry measuring cup with rice mixture just until it holds its shape. Carefully remove shaped rice mixture from cup and place in hot skillet. Press gently with back of a spatula until cake is about ½ inch thick. Repeat procedure with remaining rice mixture. Cook rice cakes 2–3 minutes on each side or until lightly browned. Remove from skillet. To serve, place 2 cakes on individual serving plates. Top each serving with a grilled shrimp.

CHEF'S TIP: This recipe is delicious as a standalone rice cake and can also be easily doubled or tripled in size.

For the rice cakes

1 egg

Infused-coconut cream (recipe above)

2 tablespoons small-chopped fresh mint

2 tablespoons small-chopped fresh cilantro

1½ teaspoons finely chopped garlic cloves

3 stalks green onions (including white portion), chopped small

½ cup small-chopped red sweet pepper

1 Thai chile pepper (optional), finely diced

⅓ teaspoon kosher salt

⅓ teaspoon freshly ground black pepper

¼ cup all-purpose flour

For the finished dish

Extra oil to coat grill

16 medium Gulf Coast shrimp, peeled and deveined

2 teaspoons vegetable oil

Char-Grilled Wild Clams Casino

I first fell in love with clams casino when I learned to prepare these delicious baked clams "on the half shell" in a large seafood house in Ocean City, Maryland. After two summers of surfing the Atlantic and washing dishes (never too far from the water), I moved up the kitchen ladder and was promoted to prep cook. That season I began prepping cold appetizers to be served at dinner later that evening. One task had me shucking wild cherrystone clams one by one, filling them with traditional casino butter, topping them with Parmesan and bacon, wrapping them tightly with plastic wrap, and shelving them in the prep reach-in box. Easy enough.

Ultimately, I began to discover the wild seafood offerings from the Gulf Coast's East Bay and Cedar Key along the Florida Panhandle. I found that re-creating East Coast classics such as clams casino was a natural transition. Recently, when I was cooking outdoors for friends, I discovered that char-grilling clams on an open fire resulted in far more superior flavor than traditional broiling.

This cooking method also gives us a good reason to gather with friends, pop a cork or crack open a brew, and cook together in our slice of Gulf Coast paradise.

To shuck clams

If you're right handed, place a towel in the palm of your left hand. Firmly hold the clam in place. Use a sharp clam-shucking knife and place the blade between the tight opening to separate the clam from the muscle. Reserve the raw clam in a half shell on a tray. If this method is too difficult or the clams are too small, you can try placing them in a covered pot over medium-high heat with 1–2 cups of water and a pinch of sea salt. Bring to a boil, and when the clams begin to open, about 5 minutes, turn off heat and remove lid. Shuck the clams over a large bowl to reserve clam juice. Use a clam knife to shuck and remove top shell and loosen clam from side muscles. Place partially cooked clam back into shell. Spoon the clam juice over the clam to keep briny flavor.

To assemble

Preheat oven to 350°F. Lay bacon slices on a baking pan and cook about halfway, 6–8 minutes. Once cooked, halve each slice, and then quarter each half into 1-inch pieces, a total of 36 pieces. Place the softened butter, onions, peppers, garlic, lemon juice, parsley, salt, and pepper in a small mixing bowl. Stir to blend. In a separate small bowl, combine the Parmesan and bread crumbs. Spoon about 1 tablespoon butter mixture over each clam, then top with a sprinkle of the Parmesan mixture and top with a piece of bacon.

(SERVES 4–6)

36 middle neck or top neck clams, scrubbed

6 slices bacon

12 tablespoons unsalted butter, softened

4 tablespoons small-diced red onions

1 tablespoon small-diced red sweet pepper

1 tablespoon small-diced green bell pepper

2 tablespoons minced fresh garlic

2 tablespoons lemon juice

1 tablespoon minced fresh parsley

Pinch of sea salt and freshly ground black pepper

1 cup finely grated fresh Parmesan

½ cup panko bread crumbs

2 lemons, each cut into wedges

For outdoor cooking
Preheat an outdoor grill to medium-high heat. Grill over open fire until the bacon finishes cooking, 5–7 minutes. Serve with lemon wedges.

For indoor cooking
Preheat broiler to medium-high heat, place clams on baking pan, and place under broiler until the bacon finishes cooking, 5–7 minutes. Serve with lemon wedges.

Clams on Fire

Handling the clams one by one over an open fire can be tedious. I suggest using a standard wire cooling rack. Fill the wire rack with the prepared clams, cupped side down. Keeping the rack level at all times, grasp the far end (the end closest to the fire) using a pair of kitchen tongs and the closest end with a kitchen towel. Place filled rack over the fire, the tong end first. To char evenly and avoid hot spots, transfer the rack directly onto the grill grates. Remove rack from the grill onto a baking pan should flames get too high. Prepare a spray bottle filled with water to douse the flames if necessary.

Gulf Coast Crab Toast

Gulf Coast Blue Crab is known all over the world for its sweet flavor and tender meat. The commercial crab season extends year-round, and crab pickers from coast to coast handpick and sort wild harvested hard-shell blue crabs for all grades of crab. My favorite is backfin or jumbo lump crab. Along the Gulf Coast states, from Florida to Louisiana, commercially caught crabs are often lightly salted for boiling before the crabmeat is removed by hand for packing, shipping, or retailing.

Often, recreational crabbers and regional seafood cooks alike boil their live crabs with a mesh bag of Zatarain's Crab Boil at home and in restaurants all along the Gulf region. The robust spice bag concoction contains mustard seed, whole coriander seeds, allspice, bay leaf, and pepper—a testament to the Louisiana region.

Here in the Florida Panhandle region, I enjoy making this decadent chilled crab salad recipe to spoon onto toast rounds. It is especially delicious with Gulf Coast blue crab provided by regional pickers from Florida to Bayou La Batre in Mobile County, Alabama.

(SERVES 4–6)

For the toast

1 small French baguette for toasted rounds

Extra-virgin olive oil for brushing

For the crab

2 cups Gulf Coast backfin crab

5 tablespoons mayonnaise (Duke's brand preferred)

2 tablespoons Creole mustard (Zatarain's brand preferred)

1–2 tablespoons lemon juice

Generous dashes hot sauce (Ed's Red brand preferred)

4 tablespoons finely chopped celery, whole leaves reserved

5 tablespoons finely chopped green onions (whites and greens)

¼ teaspoon seafood seasoning (Old Bay Seasoning preferred)

½ teaspoon finely microplaned zest of lemon

Dash of freshly ground black pepper

2 tablespoons coarsely chopped parsley

To make the toast

Preheat oven to 350°F. Slice the French baguette into ¼-inch rounds. Arrange slices on a baking pan and brush lightly with olive oil. Toast until just light brown, 5–7 minutes. Turn and brush the other side lightly with olive oil, toast again until golden, and set aside.

To make the crab

Remove and discard any cartilage from the backfin crab. Set crabmeat aside. In a small mixing bowl whisk together mayonnaise, mustard, lemon juice, hot sauce, celery, green onions, seafood seasoning, and lemon zest. Gently fold in lumps of fresh crab. Season the dip with ground black pepper.

To assemble

Spoon crab dip onto toasted French bread rounds lined with reserved celery leaves. Sprinkle with chopped parsley.

Fresh Crab

Fresh crab can be particularly difficult to find if you're landlocked. It's even difficult to find a year-round supply along the Gulf Coast, where blue crab is commercially available year-round. That's why crab processors also purchase pasteurized crab meat. Pasteurization is a process where fresh crabmeat is cooked and picked, and then sealed into air-tight cans and heated to a temperature of about 185°F, then cooled quickly.

Purists are correct when they say the pasteurization process adversely affects crab meat's natural sweetness and texture. On the other hand, veteran crab men will tell you it's the closest thing to fresh and there's not a tremendous difference. I agree, and I like cooking crab dishes year-round. I know my fishmonger is pulling in the best quality pasteurized crab.

If you can't find it fresh, be attentive to domestic versus international processors. Look for processors using domestic blue crab. Metal cans always contain pasteurized meat, often from countries that sell different species of shellfish, like the red swimming crab from China.

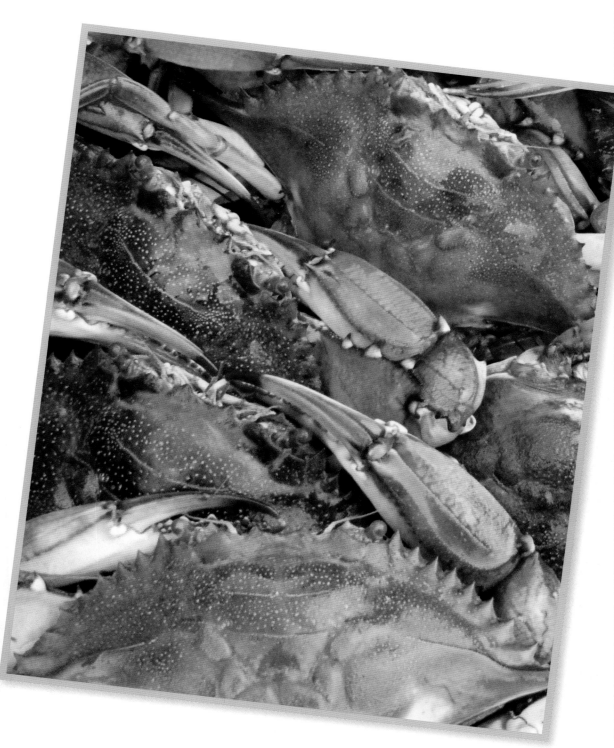

Shrimp Scampi & Grits

This southern culinary combination has many regional interpretations, from the East Coast to the Gulf Coast. There are undoubtedly as many recipes that have been created for shrimp and grits as there are cooks who created them. In the Deep South, along the North Florida Panhandle in particular, there are as many personal variations for wild shrimp as there are anywhere else in the country. While recipes for farmed shrimp have not taken center stage, this Italian-inspired preparation is perfect for wild or mild-flavored and supple-textured farm-raised shrimp. It's sure to warm the soul.

To make the grits

Place heavy cream, milk, water, grits, and salt into the top pan of a 1-quart double boiler. Bring to a boil and reduce heat to a simmer. Cover and cook for 25–30 minutes. Stir frequently with a whisk or heavy-duty wooden spoon to avoid sticking and lumps. When grits are tender, add grated cheese and stir until blended smooth. Stir in butter until completely melted and add salt and pepper.

To make the scampi sauce

Place a medium-size skillet over medium heat. Add butter and shallots and cook for 2–3 minutes. Add vermouth, garlic, parsley, and crushed red pepper flakes and, stirring occasionally, cook for 2–3 minutes more. Taste and adjust seasoning with salt and pepper. Add more garlic if you prefer.

To assemble

Preheat oven to 400°F. Spoon 4 ounces of hot grits into individual gratin dishes. Divide the shrimp and arrange on top of grits with tails in the air. Sprinkle scampi sauce on top. Top with breadcrumbs. Bake for 12 minutes. Let rest 5 minutes before serving.

CHEF'S TIP: For full-flavored grits (yellow or white), prime texture, and best nutritional results, I always recommend stone-ground grits. Liquid-to-grits ratios vary from brand to brand. C & D Mill requires a 4 to 1 ratio. Please read the label on the stone-ground grits brand you select before cooking for this recipe. Cooking time may vary depending on brand and volume cooked.

(SERVES 4–6)

For the grits

1 cup heavy cream

1 cup milk

2 cups water

1 cup stone-ground yellow grits (C & D Mill brand preferred)

¼ cup grated white cheddar cheese

⅛ cup grated Pecorino Romano

2 tablespoons unsalted butter

¼ teaspoon kosher salt

¼ teaspoon freshly ground black pepper

For the scampi sauce

This can be made in advance if desired.

6 tablespoons (3 ounces) unsalted butter

2 tablespoons finely chopped shallots

¼ cup dry vermouth

1 tablespoon minced garlic

1 teaspoon finely chopped parsley

½ teaspoon crushed red pepper flakes

Pinch of kosher salt

Dash of freshly ground black pepper

For the finished dish

40 medium shrimp, peeled and deveined

8 tablespoons panko bread crumbs

Shrimp Farms

Farming shrimp is unchartered territory for Florida. It's remarkably hands on and not a perfect science. Ed Wood and his brother-in-law Mark Godwin first began Gulf American Shrimp Farm nearly ten years ago in a remote land-locked location in Gulf County, and to this day it is the only successful shrimp farming operation in Florida. Wood and Godwin converted existing catfish ponds for farming shrimp by deep drilling an underground saltwater aquifer reaching a depth of 1,200 feet. Godwin can monitor every critical water characteristic using his cell phone by using solar-powered monitors that control diesel-powered paddle aerators for correct water oxygenation.

Every April, they stock the ponds with post-larval shrimp from the Islamorada hatchery in Key West, which are harvested in late October to allow 165 days for growth. This shrimp (*P. vannamei*) is a sixth-generation Pacific shrimp engineered specifically for farming. The operation is green-rated, which means it's been approved as a zero-discharge facility and is bio secure.

Soused Shrimp with Fresh Dill

One particular family-run seafood business that is still dedicated to Apalachicola, Florida, is Buddy Ward Seafood & Sons. Established by the late Oland "Buddy" Ward in 1957, the businesses are now operated by son Tommy Ward and his family. They later established the 13 Mile Seafood brand, and more recently 13 Mile Seafood Market on Water Street, where they dock their shrimp boats. Here they process and sell locally harvested shrimp, crab, and fish that are freshly plucked from Apalachicola Bay and the Gulf of Mexico.

Just west of Apalachicola, off Scenic Highway 30A on the Apalachicola waterway, sits the 13 Mile Seafood oyster processing plant. This is where oystermen in the vicinity bring in fresh, delicious oysters, newly plucked from the bay and surrounding estuaries. I previously worked closely there with my good friend Chef Joe Truex of Watershed restaurant in Atlanta, Georgia. Chef Joe and I ran a one-of-a-kind Gulf-to-table seafood event, hosted by 13 Mile Seafood and Outstanding in The Field organizers.

During this great gig, I was inspired by the various dishes being prepared (and sampled, of course) as all of us were being immersed in seafood. So here's my recipe for pickled, or soused, locally harvested shrimp with fresh-chopped dill to add a delicious herbal note.

For the shrimp

4 quarts water

1 onion, cut into chunks

1 celery stalk, cut into chunks

1 carrot, cut into chunks

6 garlic cloves, peeled and crushed

1 lemon, cut in half and squeezed

1 tablespoon sea salt

4 bay leaves

2 pounds raw medium Gulf Coast shrimp

For the pickling

2 medium onions, quartered

¾ cup extra-virgin olive oil

½ cup fresh lemon juice

½ cup apple cider vinegar

6 garlic cloves, peeled and sliced thin

1 teaspoon celery seed

1 teaspoon brown mustard seeds

1 teaspoon coriander seeds

½ teaspoon fenugreek seeds

½ teaspoon fennel seeds

½ teaspoon sea salt

6 bay leaves

For the garnish

3–4 large leaves of lettuce, rinsed and stems removed

2 tablespoons fresh dill pinched from the stems

1 lemon, cut into ¼-inch-thick wheels

To boil the shrimp

Place boiling ingredients into a 6-quart soup pot. Bring everything to a boil over high heat (including juiced lemon halves), reduce the heat, and simmer for 45 minutes to make a flavorful boiling broth. Add the shrimp and stir. As soon as the water returns to a simmer (in just a few minutes), remove from the heat. The shrimp will have just begun to float and the shells will have turned pink. Strain and let shrimp cool; do not rinse the shrimp. Reserve the broth, if desired. Remove shells from shrimp leaving last tail segment and tail intact. Devein the shrimp (optional) with a paring knife.

To pickle the shrimp

Combine pickling ingredients in a large bowl along with the prepared shrimp, stir well, and let marinate overnight.

To assemble

Place lettuce leaves onto a large platter or individual plates. Remove shrimp from pickling marinade with tongs and divide over lettuce. Arrange dill leaves and lemon wheels around the shrimp. Alternatively, present this in a deep, clear-glass, footed bowl, being sure to stir before serving.

Tuna Escabeche

Few American chefs exploded onto the Florida Cuisine movement in the 1980s like Chef Norman Van Aken. In addition to being Key West's famed chef, Van Aken is recognized around the globe as the "Father of New World Cuisine." He captured the attention of the nation while simultaneously cultivating the essence of South Florida—fusing Cuban soul and Latin American flavors artfully and deliciously on the plate.

I first met Chef Norman in 1987, when he demonstrated a "fusion feast" as guest chef at Bud and Alley's restaurant in Seaside, Florida, where I presided as chef at the time. In 2013, Chef Van Aken once again performed along the Florida Panhandle as guest chef at the South Walton Beaches Wine & Food Festival, where he prepared his Caesar Salad Steak "Tartare" from his first cookbook, *A Feast of Sunlight*.

Inspired by Chef Van Aken, I have adapted my recipe for seared Gulf Coast tuna from his "Snapper Escabeche Ensalada." For escabeche, historically a Spanish preparation, fish is partially cooked by heat and then finished in a flavored citrus marinade, which continues to cook it by a process called "acidulation."

To prepare the tuna

In a small, dry skillet, over medium heat, combine sesame seeds and peppercorns. Allow to heat until the white sesame seeds are toasted, 1–2 minutes. Transfer to a spice grinder and pulverize until not quite finely ground. Place in a small bowl. Cut tuna into 1 × 3-inch lengths and place in a wide, shallow dish. Rub lightly with ground spice mixture. Cover and refrigerate for at least 30 minutes or as long as 2 hours. Remove tuna from refrigerator and set aside to bring to room temperature.

To make the escabeche

Place a large nonstick or well seasoned, heavy-bottomed skillet over a medium-high flame. Add the peanut oil and heat until it begins to smoke. Immediately add tuna blocks and sear each one for 15 seconds on each side. Turn with a pair of small tongs. Transfer seared tuna to a wide, shallow dish and allow to cool. Combine marinade ingredients in a mixing bowl, add tuna, and soak well by covering and refrigerating for 2 hours, turning once after the first hour.

To make the vinaigrette

Place small saucepan over high heat, bring the orange juice to a boil and reduce to ½ cup. Transfer to a medium-size mixing bowl, add

(SERVES 4–6)

For the tuna

2 teaspoons white sesame seeds

2 teaspoons black sesame seeds

1 teaspoon black peppercorns

1 pound center cut yellowfin (ahi) tuna loin

2 tablespoons peanut or canola oil

For the marinade

3 cloves garlic, peeled and thinly sliced

½ red onion, thinly sliced

1 cup loosely packed cilantro leaves

⅓ cup light soy sauce

1 (1-inch) piece fresh ginger, peeled and grated

½ cup mirin

½ cup fresh lime juice

For the vinaigrette

¾ cup fresh squeezed orange juice

¼ cup sherry vinegar

⅓ cup extra-virgin olive oil

2 shallots, thinly sliced

Dash of freshly ground black pepper

Pinch of sea salt

For the garnish

2 Valencia or navel oranges, peeled and divided into segments

1 avocado, peeled, pitted, and sliced into thin wedges

vinegar, and whisk to blend. Add olive oil, shallots, black pepper, and salt to taste. Whisk to combine, and set aside.

To assemble

Remove seared tuna from marinade and slice into ⅛-inch pieces. Spoon a pool of vinaigrette onto each plate. Divide tuna onto plates. Arrange with the orange segments and avocado slices. Serve immediately.

Venison Chili with Smoked Gruyère & Green Onions

Centuries ago, American Indians supplied the venison that was being swapped for military subvention from Mobile, Alabama, to Pensacola, Florida. Today, whitetail deer provide the most popular large-animal hunt in Florida. Licensed hunters can hunt on privately owned properties or on seasonal public hunting grounds throughout the state. Some of the public grounds are found as close as DeFuniak Springs. Deer hunting is licensed in many areas of the Panhandle.

Hunters pride themselves on sharing their kill, filling their freezers (and occasionally mine), for the following year. In the summer months we "put up" a variety of regional fresh peas: baby butterbeans; speckled baby butterbeans; pink-eyed, cowpea, or black-eyed peas; and cream or zipper cream peas. By freezing them in ziplock bags, we can pull 'em and use 'em in the winter months. And it is during the colder months that I love adding them to venison chili.

One more special touch is to add a crafted and flavorful brewed beer from my hometown. It makes everything taste better!

Heat a heavy-duty 6-quart soup pot or Dutch oven to medium high. Add the oil. When oil begins to smoke, add the venison and cook, stirring occasionally, until well seared. Do not overcrowd the pot. Brown the venison in two batches if necessary. Add the onions, celery, peppers, and garlic and continue cooking over medium-low heat until tender. Stir in the tomato paste and cook for another 3–4 minutes. Add the tomatoes, beer, broth, water, ham hock, and spices, and bring mixture to a boil. Turn heat down to a simmer and cook for 45 minutes. Add the field peas. Simmer for another 30–45 minutes uncovered, or until chili is thick and flavorful and meat is tender and peas are cooked. Season chili lightly with salt and black pepper as you go. Remove ham hock and let cool. Remove ham hock meat from the bone, chop small, and add back to the chili. Ladle soup into soup tureen or individual bowls or cups, garnish with cheese and onions, and serve.

(SERVES 8–10)

- 4 tablespoons olive oil
- 2 pounds boneless leg or shoulder of venison, cut into ½-inch cubes
- 1 cup small-diced yellow onions
- 1 cup small-diced celery stalks
- 1 cup small-diced green bell peppers
- 2 serrano peppers, seeded and finely diced
- 1 tablespoon minced garlic
- 1 tablespoon tomato paste
- 1 (16-ounce) can chopped tomatoes
- 1 bottle beer, IPA (Pensacola Bay Brewery preferred)
- 1 cup venison or beef broth
- 1–2 cups water to cover
- 1 small smoked ham hock
- 1 teaspoon dried oregano
- 2 teaspoons chili powder
- ½ teaspoon sweet smoky paprika
- ½ teaspoon ground cumin
- ½ teaspoon ground coriander
- Pinch of cayenne pepper
- 1 cup fresh field peas (pinkeye or zipper or butter beans)
- Pinch of kosher salt and freshly ground black pepper
- 1 cup grated smoked gruyère cheese
- 2 stalks, green onions chopped

Duck Meatballs & Spicy Red Gravy

In the Deep South, cooks take as much pride in their family meatball recipes as they do in their gravies and corn bread. Duck, which is one of my favorite waterfowl, is the unique ingredient in the preparation for my Mediterranean- and Moroccan-spiced meatball recipe. Oven-roasted, slow-cooked in its own fat (confit), or in gumbo, duck provides a savory and unique flavor. Ground, as in this format, and combined with its recipe counterparts, duck makes these meatballs extraordinary.

Essential to the start of this recipe is the removal of all the duck breast meat from the carcass of a whole wild or store-bought duck. Store-bought boneless and skinless duck breast is ideal for this recipe. Also in this recipe you will find pleasure in filling your kitchen with the perfume of freshly toasted and aromatic North African spices.

To make the meatballs

Combine the ground duck, egg, chili peppers, ginger, garlic, garam masala, breadcrumbs, and salt in a large bowl until evenly mixed. Shape the meatball mixture into 12 golf ball–size rounds. In a dutch oven, add the oil and place over medium-high heat until oil surface shimmers. Carefully add meatballs, one at a time, being careful not to overcrowd the pot. Brown on all sides (about 5 minutes), then transfer to a drain pan. Adjust the heat to make sure the oil doesn't burn. Repeat until all meatballs are browned.

To make the gravy

Add the garlic, ginger, sugar, paprika, garam masala, and fennel seed to the remaining hot oil in the pan. Reduce heat to medium low and stir for 1–2 minutes. Stir the tomato sauce into the mixture and cook until the tomatoes are deep red in color, about 10 minutes. Add the water, fenugreek, and meatballs to the mixture and simmer until thoroughly reheated, another 15 minutes. Pour the cream into the mixture and cook another 2–3 minutes. Taste, and adjust seasoning with salt and pepper.

To assemble

Top the meatballs with chopped cilantro and serve.

CHEF'S TIP: If you're unable to find ground duck in the grocery store, fresh or frozen, ground turkey or pork makes a suitable substitute. If you purchase a whole duck, use the entire waterfowl by making a delicious duck stock with the carcass.

(SERVES 4–6)

For the meatballs

½ **pound duck breast meat, coarsely ground**

½ **pound pork, coarsely ground**

1 **egg, beaten**

2 **green chili peppers, seeded and minced**

1 **tablespoon minced fresh gingerroot**

2 **teaspoons minced garlic cloves**

1 **teaspoon garam masala**

⅓ **cup panko bread crumbs**

Pinch of kosher salt

1½ **cups cooking oil for shallow frying**

For the gravy

2 **teaspoons minced garlic cloves**

1 **tablespoon minced fresh gingerroot**

1 **teaspoon granulated sugar**

1 **teaspoon smoky paprika**

½ **teaspoon garam masala**

½ **teaspoon ground fennel seed**

1 **(16-ounce) can tomato sauce**

½ **cup water (optional)**

1 **tablespoon dried fenugreek leaves**

¼ **cup half-and-half or heavy whipping cream**

Kosher salt and freshly ground black pepper

For the garnish

2 **tablespoons chopped fresh cilantro**

Chapter 2
Soups and Salads

Chilled Watermelon Soup with Goat Cheese

In the dog days of summer along the Redneck Riviera, chilled soups are refreshing and fun to make. The primary and most popular picks of seasonal melons for fruit soups are cantaloupe, honeydew, and watermelon. Also prevalent are chilled vegetable soups with potatoes and vine-ripened vegetables such as tomatoes and cucumbers. However, both fruit and vegetables are compatible and complementary of one another in crossover recipes such as Watermelon Gazpacho.

This simple recipe calls for ripe, seedless watermelons that are pureed in a blender with the addition of citrus and hot peppers. For structure, body, and silky texture, add plain yogurt and a quality soft goat cheese or a salty feta cheese for great counterbalance. Also grab fresh picks from the mint and basil family to add a smart herbal note and uplift to the finish.

When preparing any chilled fruit soup, avoid making it too sweet if you're using it for an appetizer (sky's the limit if you're serving it for dessert). However you decide to create it during the hot summer months, I recommend serving your soup in an ice bowl or well-chilled soup bowl.

Place watermelon, cheese, vinegar, pepper, extra-virgin olive oil, lemon and lime juices, and basil into blender and blend on high speed until pureed. Divide into portions and place in chilled bowls. In a small mixing bowl combine cucumber, celery, and red onion with a teaspoon of extra-virgin olive oil. Sprinkle evenly with pomegranate seeds for garnish. If desired, drizzle with honey and a squeeze of lemon juice.

(SERVES 6–8)

6 cups seedless red-flesh watermelon, diced small

1 cup goat cheese

3 tablespoons pomegranate balsamic vinegar

1 serrano pepper, seeded and finely chopped

6 tablespoons, plus 1 teaspoon extra-virgin olive oil

Juice of 1 lemon, plus more for drizzling (optional)

Juice of 1 lime

10 fresh basil leaves, cut in half

½ cup cucumber, peeled, seeded, and sliced into thin half-moons

½ cup celery hearts, sliced into thin half-moons

½ small red onion, sliced into thin half-moons

3 tablespoons pomegranate seeds

Pinch of kosher salt

3 tablespoons artisan honey (optional)

Acorn Squash Soup with Honey Pecans

Honey pecans may be the star ingredients for this soup recipe, but I am a huge fan of acorn squash too. Considered a winter squash, it was first introduced to European settlers by Native Americans. The dark green color and the distinctive shape give the acorn squash its name. It is most commonly baked (best when stuffed with rice, meat, or vegetables), but also great when sautéed or steamed. Oh, did I forget about the pecans?

Raw honey and artisan honey products are crafted right here in Pensacola using regionally harvested pecans and Florida tupelo honey, which is mild, floral, and delicate, and comes only from white tupelo gum trees scattered along the Chipola and Apalachicola River basins in the Panhandle of Northwest Florida.

Unique and pure of flavor, honey pecans are not difficult to make, and using local, sustainable, hand-crafted, artisan honey from East Hill Honey Co. is a good place to start. Owner and beekeeping expert, Tommy Van Horn, harvests raw honey such as "wild flower" and "orange blossom" from his community beehives. The pecans should be purchased from a reputable farmers' market, or if you're from this neck of the woods, J.W. Renfroe Pecan Company.

Preheat oven to 350°F. Split all the squash in half, remove and discard the seeds. Place the cut sides down on baking pans. Add the carrots to the pan. Place in oven on center rack. Add 2 cups of water to the pans. Bake for 45–60 minutes or until fork tender.

The smaller squashes will become tender first. Remove them and the softened carrots and aside. After the remaining squash becomes tender, let cool slightly and remove the softened pulp with a spoon.

In a soup pot, add half the butter and sauté the onions for 5–7 minutes or until tender. Add the squash pulp, softened carrots, cider, water, and honey. Transfer to a blender and combine until smooth. Adjust consistency with water if desired.

Preheat oven to 400°F. Spread pecans out evenly on a baking pan and bake for 10–12 minutes to toast.

Reheat soup in a saucepot, stir in the remaining butter to finish, and season with salt, pepper, and nutmeg. Reheat small squash to use as soup bowls. If the openings are small, hollow them out with a spoon to increase the interior bowl size to approximately 3 inches in diameter. Ladle the soup into the cooked squash bowls. Top each soup with a dollop of sour cream and pecan halves. Drizzle with honey and fresh chives. Serve immediately.

CHEF'S TIP: Honey pecans are a specialty artisan honey product of East Hill Honey Co. and are ideal for this soup topping. To make a similar product, purchase fresh pecans, raw (local if possible) honey, and canning jars. Fill individual jars to the top with pecans. Pour in enough honey to cover. Seal in jars and boil like preserves. Store filled jars on pantry shelf until needed.

(SERVES 6–8)

1 large acorn squash

3–4 small acorn squashes

2 carrots, peeled and coarsely chopped

1 stick (4 ounces) unsalted butter, divided

1 cup small-chopped yellow onions

1 cup spiced apple cider, heated

1 cup water

2 tablespoons artisan wild flower honey, plus more for drizzling

4 honey pecans (East Hill Honey Co. preferred)

Pinch of kosher salt and freshly ground black pepper

Freshly grated nutmeg

6–8 teaspoons sour cream

1 tablespoon fresh chives, finely chopped

Ratatouille with Vegetable Broth & Pesto

Mediterranean cooking is robust in the essence of accents like garlic, fruity olive oils, saffron, tomatoes, and the aromas of rosemary and basil. Ratatouille incorporates these elements and embodies the spirit of French cooking. This summer stew, or ragout (pronounced *ragu*), usually containing eggplant, onions, tomatoes, and bell peppers was originally created in France, and has the authentic, aromatic flavor of food from the region of Provencal. But ratatouille is also popular in the spring and summer along the Florida Panhandle.

Ratatouille is a favorite of mine because it's a dish that brings more flavors from the garden into the kitchen than any other. The ingredients are available at the peak of their season and are relatively inexpensive. The best part is that it is easy to make.

I like adding zucchini and yellow squash to the customary French line-up of ingredients. Ratatouille can be created using a roasted, medley-style format or, as in this recipe, incorporated into light broth soup. Add the flavor accents of the Mediterranean with pesto or fresh herbs combined with quality Parmesan cheese, garlic, pine nuts, and extra-virgin olive oil.

(SERVES 8–10)

6 cups vegetable broth (store bought)

2 large beefsteak tomatoes

2 teaspoons herbs de Provence

For the pesto

(Makes about 2 cups)

¾ cup pine nuts

2 packed cups fresh basil leaves

1 packed cup flat-leaf parsley leaves

2 tablespoons minced garlic

1 tablespoon lemon juice

½ cup grated Romano or Parmesan cheese

½ cup extra-virgin olive oil

Pinch of kosher salt

Dash of fresh ground black pepper

To make the pesto
Preheat oven to 350°F. Spread pine nuts evenly onto a baking pan. Bake for 10 minutes. Shake the pan to turn the nuts and bake another 5 minutes. Remove, let cool completely, and set aside.

Place the basil, parsley, toasted pine nuts, garlic, lemon juice, and cheese in a food processor and pulse to chop fine. Continue to process the mixture, drizzling in the olive oil to make a smooth sauce. Taste and adjust seasoning with salt and pepper.

To make fortified vegetable broth
Place the store-bought vegetable broth into a soup pot over medium-high heat. To fortify the vegetable broth, add all the uncooked ratatouille vegetable trimmings. Once boiling, reduce heat to low and simmer for 45 minutes. Strain before using.

To prepare the tomatoes
Place a pot of water over high heat and bring to a boil. In a large mixing bowl, prepare an ice bath (equal parts ice and water). Using the tip of a paring knife, remove the shallow tomato stems from the beefsteak tomatoes. On the opposite end of the tomatoes, insert the knife tip and make a shallow X. Place the tomatoes in the boiling

water for 45 seconds, then, using a slotted spoon, transfer them to the ice bath to stop any further cooking. Peel skins from tomatoes, cut tomatoes in half, discard seeds, and then chop small.

To make the ratatouille

Place the olive oil in a deep heavy-bottomed pot over medium heat and sauté onions and garlic until translucent, about 5 minutes. Add peppers, eggplant, zucchini, and squash and stir well. Lightly season the vegetables with salt and pepper and cook over medium heat, covered, for 10–12 minutes, lifting lid frequently to stir. Remove lid and add tomatoes and broth and simmer over medium heat for 10 minutes. Add herbs and taste, adjusting seasoning with salt and pepper as needed.

To assemble

Ladle soup into individual soup bowls, using a slotted spoon to divide the vegetables evenly. Add a teaspoon of pesto in the middle of each bowl. Serve immediately.

For the ratatouille

¼ cup high-quality olive oil

1 cup small-chopped yellow onion

2 tablespoons minced garlic

1 cup small-chopped green bell peppers, seeded

1 cup small-chopped eggplant, peeled

1 cup small-chopped zucchini, skin on

1 cup small-chopped yellow squash, skin on

Kosher salt to taste

Freshly ground black pepper

French Onion "Zuppas"

At the young age of twenty-two, I was given the chance to prove myself as a kitchen manager and cook. The restaurant was a local spot called The Kitty Hawk Saloon in Ocean City, Maryland. My former boss, Greek restaurant owner Mathew Zuppas (honored by this recipe), took me under his wing and let me run the show. It was here that the "French onion connection" was made.

I like to use yellow onions as the foundation for clear vegetable soups, especially as the main ingredient in my French onion soup. Back then, Mr. Zuppas would prompt me for proper soup seasoning as I sautéed the thinly sliced onions for the French onion soup we were preparing. As I would begin to season the onions, he would say, "White pepper Irv, white pepper." He held closely that the white variety was milder yet more pungent than the black kind. "Careful Irv, season as you go!" he would warn. "If you add too much it will bite you at the end."

Equally important to the outcome of this delicious recipe was slow roasting the soup, uncovered, in a pizza oven to concentrate the flavors. This technique stands the test of time and greatly improves the recipes for which I use it. French onion soup connoisseurs everywhere (and there are many) identify with the delicate balancing act between sweet caramelized onions and a lightly salted, flavorful broth.

All Menu Items are À La Carte

Shrimp Bisque 2.25 French Onion Soup 1.95 White Gazpacho
Salmon Mousse 3.25 Pâté de Maison 2.95 Stone Crab Claws
Tossed Salad 2.75 Spinach Salad: sm. 2.25 lg. 3.25 Rice Pilaf
Cucumbers in Yogurt Sauce 1.50 Glazed Carrots 1.50 Potatoes O'Brien
Chicago Fries 1.25 Sautéed Vegetable Melange 2.25 Sautéed Mushrooms in sherry 2.

New York Strip Steak 8.25 London Broil 5.95 Broiled Scampi
Flounder Quenelles w/ Hollandaise on rice 5.95 Coquille St. Jacques 6.25 Cioppino w/ garlic bread
Baked Sea Trout w/ sorrel sauce 5.75 Quiche Lorraine 4.25 Garlic Bread .95
Banana Bread .9

Sandwiches are served w/ Chicago Fries:
Roast Beef 3.50
Baked Ham 3.50
Breast of Turkey 3.50
Chopped Sirloin 3.50

Home-made Desserts:
Cheesecake 1.95
Peaches Melba 1.75
Rum Pie 1.95

Melt the butter in a 4-quart roasting pan or Dutch oven over medium heat. Stir in the onions and season with salt and a generous fresh grind of white pepper. Reduce the heat to low. Stir until the onions are very soft and beginning to brown, 15–20 minutes. Add the sherry and increase the heat to medium-high. Keep cooking the onions until they are evenly browned and lightly caramelized, 10–15 minutes. Add the broths and bay leaves to the caramelized onions and bring the soup to a boil over medium-high heat.

Preheat oven to 350°F. Position an oven rack in the center of the oven. Place the simmering soup in its vessel carefully into the oven. Bake uncovered for 45–60 minutes, until it is reduced by one-third and browned nicely on the surface. Remove from oven, skim, and discard the bay leaves. Adjust seasoning to taste with salt, white pepper, and sugar if needed.

Place bread rounds on baking pan and bake until crisp and lightly browned, about 15 minutes. Turn and bake another 5 minutes. Set aside.

CHEF'S TIP: It's ideal if you can use correct cutter size to cut rounds to fit in the top of an onion soup crock.

To assemble
Position a rack 6 inches from the broiler and heat the broiler to high. Put six to eight broiler-proof soup bowls or crocks on a baking sheet. Fill each bowl with hot soup to a ½ inch from the top. Place and float the crouton on the soup. Sprinkle and divide the gruyère over tops, and broil until browned and bubbly, 2–5 minutes. Serve immediately.

(SERVES 6–8)

5 tablespoons unsalted butter

4 large yellow onions, thinly sliced

Pinch of kosher salt

1 teaspoon ground white pepper

½ cup dry sherry

1 quart chicken broth

1 quart beef broth

2 bay leaves

Granulated sugar to taste

8 slices white or French bread batard, cut into rounds

2–3 cups grated gruyère

Brie Soup with Oysters, Mushrooms & Homemade Brie Croutons

I discovered succulent brie soup when I moved to the Gulf Coast of Florida in 1982. After graduating from the Culinary Institute of America, I worked a short-lived poissionnier (fish cook) stint at Arthur's Restaurant along the San Antonio River Walk in Texas. I was eventually promoted to sous chef and, on a company impulse, was asked to accompany Chef Mark Cheffins (yes, that's his real last name) to Destin, Florida, to open a new, eighty-seat French restaurant.

This quaint restaurant was called "Les Saison's." It was picturesque, located right on Highway 98, the main road going through town, and overlooked Destin's breathtaking East Pass. The River Walk was wonderful, don't get me wrong, but living in the World's Luckiest Fishing Village was truly paradise.

Chef Mark was trained in German-style culinary. He was very talented, but highly temperamental. His personal habits often overshadowed his food skills (we all have flaws). However, one of his notable and delicious soup preparations for our first season's menu at Les Saison's was his velvety brie soup. I crafted my version of his soup over a decade ago, and each time I make it it's better than the last.

My recipe rendition combines three of my favorite ingredients: fresh local oysters, brie, and mushrooms.

To make the brie croutons

Preheat oven to 350°F. Place rack in the center of the oven. Place sliced bread on baking pan and bake until the bread is crisp and lightly browned, 12–15 minutes. Turn and bake for another 5 minutes. Remove from the oven and set aside to cool. When cool, place a ¼-inch-thick slice of brie on each crouton and press firmly to adhere. Place in the refrigerator until needed.

To make the soup

In a large, heavy-bottom soup pot, melt the butter over medium heat. Add onions, celery, and garlic. Turn heat to low and cook, stirring frequently with a wooden spoon, for 2–3 minutes or until vegetables are slightly tender. Add the mushrooms and cook for 2 more minutes. Add bacon and sherry and stir until the mixture turns into a smooth paste. Add the flour and continue to stir for an additional 5 minutes over low heat; do not brown. Switch over to a wire whisk and stir in the broth and milk, continuing to whisk frequently. Add the thyme and bay leaves. Bring to a boil over medium-high heat, then immediately reduce to a simmer. Taste, and season as needed with salt and pepper.

Cut brie, including its outer white flora, into 1-inch cubes and add to the soup. Continue to simmer for 30–45 minutes, then pour the soup through a mesh strainer, pushing firmly to extract all the cheese flavor from the flora. Discard the flora and strained vegetables.

Just before serving, add oysters with their liquor to the soup, stir in, and increase heat to medium to gently cook the oysters. Simmer for 5 minutes. Using a ladle, divide the soup into soup crocks and top each soup with a brie crouton. Place under the broiler for 2–3 minutes or until cheese melts and begins to turn golden on the edges. Garnish with green onions and serve immediately.

CHEF'S TIP: For a triple cream cheese such as brie, the butterfat content must be at least 75 percent. Double cream cheese only needs to have a butterfat content of 60 percent, which would also work fine for this recipe.

(SERVES 6–8)

For the croutons

1 small baguette, sliced into eight ¼-inch slices

8 slices brie cheese, to fit the baguette slices

1 stalk green onions, chopped

For the soup

2 sticks (8 ounces) unsalted butter

1 cup small chopped yellow onions

½ cup small chopped celery ribs

1 tablespoon minced garlic

1 cup sliced mushrooms (button, shiitake, or oyster)

8 slices bacon, chopped small

½ cup dry sherry

½ cup all-purpose flour

3 cups vegetable or seafood broth

3 cups milk

3 sprigs fresh thyme

2 bay leaves

Kosher salt and freshly ground white pepper

16-ounces double cream brie cheese

24 ounces of freshly shucked Gulf Coast oysters, their liquid reserved

2 green onions, chopped small

Thirty-Minute Crab Soup

The title says it all.

This recipe falls into my top five most popular and frequently made soup recipes for home or dinner parties. I fashioned it after the East Coast classic, "she-crab soup," a creamy-style crab soup originally using gravid crab and their roe. In keeping with my easy style of seafood cooking, once the ingredients are at hand and the cooking process begins, this process will produce perfect sipping crab in only thirty minutes. Time is always a luxury.

Fresh backfin crab from any coast will work for this dish. However, if you're landlocked and fresh crabmeat is not available, a top-quality domestic pasteurized crab will work just fine. To give it that extra-special touch, season your live crabs with spices and boil them for a flavorful, homemade broth. If you like, you can even break them in half and simmer right in the soup, or purchase seafood broth at any grocery store to take the least complicated route.

(SERVES 4–6)

1 cup backfin crab

1 stick (4 ounces) unsalted butter

1 cup small-diced onions

½ cup small-diced celery

½ cup dry sherry

¼ cup all-purpose flour

2 cups seafood broth or stock

2 cups milk

1 bay leaf

1 cup heavy whipping cream

½ teaspoon Old Bay Seasoning

Pinch of sea salt and freshly cracked white pepper

4 tablespoons fresh chives or green onions, chopped

Pick through the backfin crab to remove any cartilage. Place soup pot over medium-high heat and add butter. When butter melts, add the onions and celery and sauté for 2–3 minutes or until tender. Add the sherry and cook to concentrate the flavor for another 2 minutes. Add flour and stir constantly over medium-low heat for 5–8 minutes, until roux is pale white.

Add broth, milk, and bay leaf, and whisk to blend well. Increase heat and let simmer over low heat for 20 minutes, stirring frequently. Add cream and a pinch of Old Bay Seasoning, salt, and pepper to your liking, let simmer for 5 minutes, then strain. Add fresh crab directly to the simmering cream soup and stir to blend. Garnish with chopped chives or green onions.

NOTE: Florida law prohibits harvesting a female crab with eggs.

Florida Panhandle Seafood Gumbo

Before competition cooking was fashionable, I competed on a local level for philanthropy organizations along the Gulf Coast. During this heyday, I had the pleasure of winning multiple awards from the Great Southern Gumbo Cook-off, held annually in Sandestin. It was during this era that I fine-tuned my gumbo-making abilities.

A good seafood gumbo, no matter where you're from, should be full of local seafood and rich with flavor. You may use any type of seafood desired, but for this recipe, seafood gathered fresh from crab traps and shrimp casting nets is ideal. Oysters also need to be added, whether you shuck them yourself or buy them freshly shucked. Crab is no different. Fresh crabs make for a flavorful touch, but you will need handpicked jumbo lump crab to add to this gumbo.

This gumbo is rich and dark, with a spicy kick provided by andouille sausage and hot sauce. There is no other dish that is more of a true testament to the emblematic foods of the Gulf Coast than gumbo.

(SERVES 12–14)

For the seafood stock

3 tablespoons olive oil

Shells from 1 pound medium Gulf Coast shrimp, deveined and reserved

2 onions, coarsely chopped

2 stalks celery, coarsely chopped

2 carrots, coarsely chopped

4 cloves garlic

5 quarts water

1 bunch parsley stems

2 bay leaves

For the gumbo

½ cup peanut oil

1 cup all-purpose flour

2 cups yellow onions, diced small

6 large Florida blue crabs, cut in half

To make the seafood stock

Place a large pot over medium-high heat. Add the oil and shells; stir for 5 minutes or until shells turn pink. Add onions, celery, carrots, garlic, water, parsley stems, and bay leaves. Increase heat to high and bring to a boil. Immediately reduce heat and simmer stock until it is reduced by one-third, 1½–2 hours. Strain through a fine sieve.

To make the gumbo

Make a roux by heating the oil in a heavy-bottom skillet or dutch oven over medium-high heat. Whisk the flour into the hot oil; it will begin to sizzle. Reduce heat to medium and continue whisking until the roux takes on a deep brown color, about 20 minutes. Add the onions, stirring them in with a wooden spoon or heavy-duty whisk; be careful not to let it splash onto your hands or arms. Reduce heat to medium low and continue whisking until roux changes from the deep brown color to a rich, dark brown, 10–12 additional minutes. Remove from heat to cool slightly, about 5 minutes.

Add the crab and sausage and cook, stirring for a few minutes before adding the celery, peppers, garlic, crushed tomatoes, and okra. Increase the heat to medium high and cook, stirring, for about 3 minutes. Add the fresh thyme, seafood stock, and bay leaves. Bring to a boil, stirring frequently. Reduce heat to medium low and simmer for 1 hour.

Add the shrimp, oysters, and crabmeat to the pot and cook for 15 minutes. Add the green onions and season with salt, pepper, Worcestershire, Creole spices, and hot sauce. Skim surface to remove fat. Serve in bowls over white rice.

2 cups andouille sausage, sliced ½-inch thick

1 cup small-diced celery

1 cup small-diced green pepper

2 tablespoons minced garlic cloves

1 (16-ounce) can tomatoes, crushed

2 cups sliced okra

1 teaspoon fresh thyme leaves

3 quarts shellfish stock (see recipe above)

2 bay leaves

1 pound medium Gulf Coast shrimp

1½ cups freshly shucked oysters and oyster liquor

1 cup Gulf Coast backfin crab

1 cup small-cut green onions

Pinch of kosher salt

Dash of freshly ground black pepper

3–5 tablespoons Worcestershire or to taste

2 tablespoons Creole spice blend

6–8 tablespoons hot sauce (Louisiana brand preferred) or to taste

2 cups cooked basic white rice

Sweet Corn and Snap Bean Salad

Like so many facets of Panhandle cooking, the famed combination of Florida sweet corn and snap beans is frequently celebrated. Whether in a salad, salsa, or a succotash side, these two are a winning combination. Sweet corn varieties grow throughout the country at the peak of the summer months. In Florida super sweet corn varieties reign supreme for nine months, and snap beans for seven months of the year, enabling availability year-round. Fresh corn and snap beans are not exotic ingredients, nor is a simple red wine vinaigrette. The key in this salad is that the corn and beans be gathered at their peak.

(SERVES 4–6)

4–5 ears sweet corn

Kosher salt

1 pound fresh snap or green beans, trimmed

½ cup small-chopped red onion

1 teaspoon minced garlic

⅛ cup red wine vinegar

¼ cup extra-virgin olive oil

½ cup fresh basil leaves

Freshly ground black pepper

Fill a pot large enough to hold all the corn with water. Bring to a rolling boil over medium-high heat. Shuck and remove silk from the corn and place cobs in boiling water. Reduce to a simmer and cook for 5 minutes. Remove with tongs, reserving the water, and transfer cobs to a towel-lined plate to drain and cool completely before handling.

Cut the ends off the ears so cobs are flat. Stand cobs upright and use a sharp knife to remove the kernels. Leave as many clusters as possible—there is no need to break them up. Place kernels in a large bowl and set aside.

Prepare an ice bath (equal parts ice and water) in a large bowl. Return corn water to a boil and add a generous amount of salt. Add the beans and cook until just tender, about 4 minutes. Remove them to the ice bath to stop the cooking process. Chill beans completely and then drain them well on a towel-lined plate. Cut beans in half using a sharp bias cut, and place in the bowl with the corn kernels and chopped red onion.

In a small mixing bowl, add the garlic and vinegar, and then slowly whisk in the oil to make vinaigrette. Drizzle over the corn and bean mixture. Roll basil leaves like tobacco, use a sharp knife to cut them into thin threads, then sprinkle them over the salad. Add salt and pepper to taste and toss gently. Serve immediately.

Wilted Greens & Shiitake Mushrooms with Creole Mustard and Bacon Dressing

Agritourism is a style of vacation that takes place on a farm. Agritourists have an opportunity to live and work on the farm caring for animals and crops, and to become involved in an assortment of agricultural activities. This industry not only provides an economic boost for farmers, but also for their local community.

Coldwater Gardens in Milton, Florida, is one such farm benefiting from this agricultural trend currently sweeping across the state. Owners Natalia and Tom Ritter operate forest management tours, bird watching, beekeeping, mushroom growing, and host a number of other rural functions. Their outdoor gardens are landscaped using modern permaculture methods and flourish with certified Naturally Grown varieties of hearty kale, tomatoes, mushrooms, fennel, and other delicate greens.

In one of their gardens, the Ritters utilize pebble-rooted plant beds and a nutrient feeding supply to sustain a variety of lettuces, protecting them from extreme outdoor environmental conditions. Natalia explains, "Worms eat our kitchen scraps and clippings from the garden and reproduce. Their castings promote healthy soil and amend the sandy loam found in this region. The worms themselves are a food source for the fish that power our aquaponics system, providing renewable nutrients directly to the plants."

To grow shiitake mushrooms, forest logs are cut into three-foot lengths, drilled, and seeded with live mushroom spores, and sealed with wax. The logs are then soaked in large tubs of water overnight. As they bear mushrooms through the wax-sealed holes, the logs are stacked and rotated for harvesting. In approximately six weeks, if conditions are ideal, abundant mushrooms are handpicked and brought to my kitchen door by the Ritters themselves. How's that for service?

(SERVES 6–8)

For the wilted salad

1 pound triple washed spinach, Russian kale, or chard

8 large shiitake mushrooms (or 16 medium)

4 tablespoons extra-virgin olive oil, divided

2 shallots, minced

Dash of freshly ground nutmeg

Dash of freshly ground black pepper

Pinch of kosher salt

For the Creole mustard and bacon dressing

12 slices bacon

4 tablespoon small-diced yellow onion

5 tablespoons cider vinegar

2 tablespoons dark brown sugar, packed

1–2 tablespoons Creole mustard

Dash of freshly ground black pepper

4 tablespoons olive oil

To make the wilted salad

Remove any thick stems from your greens. Remove mushroom stems and reserve for broth or compost. Slice the mushrooms ⅛-inch thick and divide into two batches. Place a sauté pan over medium heat. Add 2 tablespoons oil and half the sliced mushrooms, and sauté for 2–3 minutes. Add 1 minced shallot and half the greens. Turn leaves in warm oil until they wilt, 1–2 minutes. More hearty greens may need 2–3 minutes longer. Repeat with remaining oil, mushrooms, and greens until wilted.

To make the Creole mustard and bacon dressing

In a saucepot, render the bacon over low heat until crispy. Remove from pan with a slotted spoon, drain onto paper towel, and chop. Reserve the bacon fat in pan. Add onion, vinegar, sugar, mustard, and ground pepper to the bacon fat and whisk in olive oil. Keep in warm area. Whisk well before spooning over greens.

To assemble

Transfer wilted greens and mushrooms onto individual plates or a platter. Whisk together warm dressing before spooning over greens. Add crisp crumbled bacon and serve immediately.

Field Greens with Bacon & Blue Cheese and Buttermilk Dressing

Urban produce grower Robert Randel is an incredibly passionate organic micro-gardener who lives in Gulf Breeze, Florida. He owns and cultivates a humble 6,000-square-foot, residential garden that yields 400–600 pounds of produce each year. "This is still small scale," Randel says. "But the white sand is now a living soil and a thriving bio-active culture."

"The overall concept is to convert barren lands to bearing lands. The goal is to build a biologically active, living earth that feeds the plants a wide spectrum of micro-elements, so the food produced is a high-nutrient, high-energy input as a process of life," he explained. He has no problem painting a perfectly clear picture to explain his process. "The methods may be called organic, but the concept is to create as lush a natural relationship of earth process as possible. Man with nature, rather than man against nature." Intense, to say the least.

This simple and delicious recipe complements any variety of field greens, foraged or store-bought. Use the best vine-ripe tomatoes you can get your hands on, artisan blue cheese, and excellent smoky bacon for a one-of-a-kind salad.

(SERVES 6–8)

1 pound shiitake mushroom caps, sliced ⅛-inch thick

Extra-virgin olive oil for drizzling, plus 2–3 tablespoons for dressing

Pinch of kosher salt

Dash of freshly ground black pepper

8 ounces crumbled artisan blue cheese

¼ cup buttermilk

1 tablespoon lemon juice

1 tablespoon finely chopped fresh chives

½ pound Osaka mustard greens

½ pound baby arugula

½ pound baby red leaf, green leaf, or romaine lettuce

1 cup halved Florida heirloom cherry tomatoes

1 Florida (Fuerte) avocado or 2 California (Hass) avocados peeled, seeded, and sliced thin

8 slices bacon, cooked crispy and crumbled

Preheat oven to 350 F. Place mushroom slices in a small bowl, drizzle with olive oil, and gently toss to coat evenly. Lightly season the mushrooms with salt and pepper and place them on a baking tray. Bake for 10–12 minutes, remove from oven, and set aside.

Place crumbled cheese into a medium-size mixing bowl. Add half the buttermilk and stir together with a fork, mashing a little to break up the cheese. Add olive oil and remaining buttermilk to the dressing. Keep chunky or blend smooth according to your preference, I like mine chunky. Add lemon juice and season with salt, pepper, and chives. Set aside.

On a large platter, or on individual plates, arrange the field greens. Combine the tomatoes with the dressing and toss well, seasoning with more pepper if desired. Arrange dressed tomatoes on the center of the fresh greens. Arrange roasted mushrooms and avocado slices on salad. Top with crumbled crisp bacon and serve.

Spicy Blue Crab Salad with Avocado & Mango

Before Emeril's *Florida* and *How to Do Florida*, *Flavors of the Coast* was a first-of-its-kind destination and food cooking show. I participated in the show from 2002 to 2004. The series (fifty-one episodes in all) captured the heart and soul of food from the Florida and Alabama Gulf Coast. Never reaching syndication, the show was produced by WSRE Public Television in Pensacola, and in its original format took viewers on culinary road trips.

Season one and season two excursions were accompanied by field travel hosts Melia Allen and Heather Gilchrest respectively. I stayed in the studio kitchen preparing mouth-watering feasts. Eventually, funding for the program began to dwindle, so for the following two seasons I single-handedly held down the position of host, bringing in local cooking talent. Those were interesting years.

One of my favorite recipes from *Flavors of the Coast* was featured in an episode called "Crabbing with Maria's Seafood." Using only the freshest ingredients, I combined naturally ripened exotic mango with creamy ripe avocado and contrasted that by using fresh backfin crab dressed with cayenne pepper-spiced mayonnaise and made the quintessential crab salad.

Pick through the backfin crab to remove any cartilage. Avoid breaking up the lumps. Place into medium-size mixing bowl. In a separate small mixing bowl combine mayonnaise and cayenne pepper. Whisk well to blend. Pour mayonnaise mixture over lumps of crab and toss gently to coat evenly.

Place the avocado on a cutting board and, using a sharp knife, cut lengthwise into the skin and cut around and remove the seed. Use a spoon to remove the meat from the skin or just peel back the skin to remove. Dice the avocado meat small, and set aside.

Hold the mango flat on a cutting board and, using a sharp knife, cut lengthwise into the skin and cut over the top of the oblong large seed. Lay flat on cut side and repeat to other side. Use a sharp paring knife to make deep square crosscuts down through the mango meat to the skin. Spoon out the diced meat and set aside.

Place 6 3-inch ring molds on a pie pan. Spoon and divide the crab mixture evenly to partially fill the ring molds, about 1 inch high. Use the back of a spoon or dowel to press down firmly on the crab mixture. Next add about a 1-inch layer of diced avocado on top of the crab mixture. Firmly pack the molds again. Repeat with diced avocado for top layer. Wrap top of exposed molded avocado and, keeping them on the pie plate, place them in the refrigerator. Let chill for 1 hour before removing the ring molds.

To serve, place a filled ring mold in the center of each plate. Push firmly on the top layer and carefully remove the ring molds. Top each stack with micro greens and surround the salad with scattered berries. Serve immediately.

(SERVES 4–6)

2 cups fresh Gulf Coast backfin crab

¼ cup mayonnaise (Duke's brand preferred)

⅛ teaspoon cayenne pepper

2 ripe Mexican or Champagne mangoes

1 ripe Florida (Fuerte) avocado

1 ounce micro greens, bull's blood or amaranth shoots

6 fresh strawberries or blackberries

CHEF'S TIP: If you do not have 3-inch ring molds, 10-ounce soup cans, with both ends removed, can be used.

Joe's Tomatoes Filled with Crab Salad

Pensacola local Joe Cunningham is recognized far and wide by his unmistakable lofty stature, larger than life personality, and boisterous laugh. But what's he's best known for are his delicious tomatoes. Endeared with the title "Tomato Joe," he and his equally amazing wife, "Tomato Pam," take to the road each year to find the freshest ripe tomatoes just off the vine for loyal customers like me. "They must be moved out fast for perfect, ripe, succulent tomatoes and handled with care," says Joe. "We can provide the tastiest tomatoes year-round by hand selecting and tasting every supplier's garden-fresh batch. No hot house tomatoes, period!"

At the beginning of each year, Joe and Pam head as far south as Homestead, Florida, and eventually wind up through central Florida on their tomato-collecting trips. Their next destination is back north to the short-lived tomato season (May to June) in the Florida Panhandle. After returning home, Joe and Pam pack up their gear and travel as far north as Sand Mountain, Georgia, to escape the Panhandle's dog day summer months. Then they return to the much warmer climate of South Florida to begin the cycle all over again.

The simple vinegar-seasoned crab salad called "West Indies salad" originated in the 1950s at Bayley's Steakhouse south of Mobile, Alabama, just fifty miles from Pensacola. For my version, I have adapted a comparable crab salad and put it inside a hollowed vine-ripe tomato—an idea I got from a presentation done by Jacque Pepin. In addition, I add a Mediterranean touch by including scooped and chopped tomato, toasted pine nuts, capers, niçoise olives, fresh chives, and extra-virgin olive oil. Then I add a fresh basil sprig to the center of the inverted tomato to top it off.

(SERVES 6–8)

6 small vine-ripe tomatoes, rinsed

2 tablespoons finely diced red onions

4 tablespoons finely diced poblano peppers

3 tablespoons lemon juice

¼ cup tarragon vinegar

⅛ cup pure olive oil

3–5 dashes hot sauce (Tabasco brand preferred)

2 cups backfin crab, shells removed

Select medium and unblemished vine-ripe tomatoes. Slice tops off, just under the stem. Using a tablespoon, remove all the pulp and seeds in one swoop. Reserve tops and pulp for dicing.

In a mixing bowl combine the onion, peppers, lemon, vinegar, oil, and hot sauce; lightly blend with a whisk. Gently fold in the crabmeat, marinate, and chill for 1 hour.

Preheat the oven to 350°F. Place pine nuts on a baking pan and toast for 8–10 minutes or until lightly golden. Set aside to cool.

Use a tablespoon to fill each tomato with chilled crab salad. Invert an individual salad plate on top of tomato opening. Using both hands, carefully turn both the tomato and plate at the same time. Repeat for each stuffed tomato. Do not lift the tomato once it's been turned over.

In a mixing bowl combine the diced tomato tops and pulp, capers, olives, toasted pine nuts, and chives. Stir in olive oil and black pepper. Spoon this mixture around each salad-filled tomato. Using a toothpick, poke a small hole in the center of each inverted tomato bottom. Place a sprig of basil with a ¼-inch short thick stem pushed in the hole. Place in refrigerator or serve right away.

1 tablespoon pine nuts

1 teaspoon capers, drained

2 teaspoons pitted and sliced kalamata olives

4 tablespoons fresh chives, cut into ¼-inch lengths

6–8 tablespoons extra-virgin olive oil

Dash of freshly ground black pepper

8 fresh sweet basil sprigs with stems

Tarragon Shrimp Salad with Avocado & Tomato

In my opinion, there is no easy-to-make shrimp preparation more enjoyable than shrimp salad. All it takes is the combination of tender Gulf shrimp, fresh tarragon mayonnaise, and some of the flavor nuances from the coastal Deep South. My secret for the perfect pair of ingredients for this dish is to find just-ripened avocados and tomatoes. This dish will not work if the avocados are not ripe enough, or if they are too soft.

Still, one of my most recognized and touted salads, my Tarragon Shrimp Salad remains on the Jackson's Steakhouse lunch menu today. I might be blamed for causing a riot if I tried to remove this one. (In the past, I've experienced many vocal displeasure–style riots from guests due to the pulling of popular menu items.)

While shrimp salad is simple to prepare in general, assembling for this particular presentation will take some time and requires a lot of love. Believe me, it will be worth the effort. The avocado and shrimp portion can be molded a few hours in advance and then wrapped, chilled, and held until unveiling time. Just before serving, I like to dress the tomatoes with a little fresh herb vinaigrette. As you place each salad in front of your guests, prepare to claim your "oohs" and "ahs."

(SERVES 4–6)

3 tablespoons fine-chopped red onion

3 tablespoons fine-chopped celery

1 teaspoon minced garlic

2 tablespoons lemon juice

¼ cup lightly packed fresh tarragon leaves, removed from stem and chopped fine

½ cup mayonnaise (Duke's brand preferred)

1 pound medium Gulf Coast shrimp

1 tablespoon Old Bay Seasoning

4–6 ripe Haas avocados

3 corn tortillas cut into shards

In a small mixing bowl, combine onion, celery, garlic, and lemon juice with the fine-chopped fresh tarragon and mayonnaise. Whisk to blend well.

In another mixing bowl combine shrimp and Old Bay Seasoning and toss to coat evenly. Place the shrimp on a steaming rack in a skillet with 1 cup of water. Cover and place over medium-high heat and steam for 3–5 minutes or until shrimp have turned white in the center. Let cool, and then peel and devein the shrimp. Do not rinse off seasoning from the cooked shrimp. Slice each shrimp in half lengthwise.

Place the sliced shrimp in a separate mixing bowl and add 4–6 tablespoons of the mayonnaise mixture. Blend, being careful not to break up the shrimp. Chill mixture for 1 hour before filling the avocados.

Remove skins and pits from avocados, and slice in half lengthwise. Place half of an avocado on the bottom of a 3-inch ring mold, smooth side down. Place ¼ of the shrimp salad mixture on top of the molded avocado half, and then place the other half of avocado as a top and push down to form over top of the shrimp salad. Cover with plastic wrap and place filled mold in refrigerator for 30 minutes.

Preheat fryer to 350°F. Fry tortilla shards in hot oil for 1–2 minutes, and then drain on paper towel. Season with salt and pepper, then set aside for final garnish and presentation.

To assemble the salad, place each filled ring mold in the center of a round plate. Shingle the thinly sliced tomatoes tightly around the ring mold to form a circle. Gently push down on top of avocado and slide ring mold up to remove. Garnish the top of avocados by spearing with (pointy end first) 4–5 crispy tortilla shards per avocado. Serve immediately.

CHEF'S TIP: If you don't have 3-inch ring molds, you can use 10-ounce tin cans with ends removed.

Pinch of kosher salt

Dash of fresh ground black pepper

12 plum or small vine-ripe tomatoes, sliced ⅛ inch thick

Seared Toro and Seaweed Salad

Toro is the prized lower-belly cut of the enormous bluefin tuna (as big as 990 pounds). Authentic bluefin toro is well-marbled and light pink to pink in color. There is only a small portion of this rich and tender tuna belly available per fish, and if fresh and prepared correctly, it melts in your mouth like butter. It is indeed a rare treat.

The not-quite-as-enormous (as big as 400 pounds) yellowfin (ahi) tuna, on the other hand, is a more common and affordable option for the Gulf Coast region. "Honestly, our restaurants and customers are only looking for high-grade tuna loin for searing and slicing and for steaks," explains Charlie Knodt of Maria's Seafood in Pensacola. "We usually can't sell tuna belly. The fish cutters take it home, and some customers will call ahead to reserve if they like."

Graded and primarily used for its loin cut, yellowfin tuna belly is smaller and has a lower fat content than bluefin. Yellowfin toro, if you will, can be found on the seafood retail counter at Joe Patti's Seafood along with other more exotic parts of the fish like throats, cheeks, and backbones. Though it's not the melt-in-your-mouth toro variety, yellowfin tuna belly remains underutilized. Here is a terrific way to prepare a magnificent yellowfin tuna toro.

In a medium-size mixing bowl, whisk together soy sauce, mirin, ginger, sesame oil, and garlic. Cut tuna belly into 2 pieces and slice into 1-inch lengths. Place it in the bowl and marinate for 20 minutes.

In a small bowl, whisk together the rice vinegar, sugar, ginger, soy sauce, and sesame oil. Spoon half the dressing over the seaweed and toss well, taste and adjust seasoning if necessary.

Place a non-stick skillet over medium-high heat. Sear each length of marinated toro, flat side down, for 1 minute per side. Remove from heat and let sit in hot pan for 3–4 minutes to carry over cooking. Remove from pan and use a sharp slicing knife to slice on a bias into 1-ounce rectangles until all has been used.

Divide the dressed seaweed salad into the center of individual plates. Arrange tender slices of toro around the salad. Top with carrot, cucumber, and avocado slices, drizzle with the remaining dressing, and top with toasted sesame seeds and scallions. Serve immediately.

(SERVES 4–6)

1 cup light soy sauce

¼ cup mirin

1 tablespoon chopped ginger

1 teaspoon toasted sesame oil

3 garlic cloves sliced thin

1–2 pounds yellowfin tuna belly, skin removed

2 tablespoons seasoned rice wine vinegar

1 teaspoon granulated sugar

2 teaspoons grated ginger

2 teaspoons soy sauce

6 ounces frozen wakame seaweed salad

1 small carrot, peeled and sliced paper thin

1 small cucumber, peeled and thinly sliced

1 firm, ripe avocado, sliced

1 teaspoon white sesame seeds, toasted

1 teaspoon black sesame seeds, toasted

4 green onions, slivered

Thai-Style Spicy Beef and Hydroponic Lettuces

Northwest Florida and nearby Alabama are notorious for their sandy loam and piney woods. Due to these geographical conditions, traditional earth farmers have vested interest in alternative and creative farming methods such as hydroponics. The Craine family owns and operates Craine Creek Farm, off Highway 59 in Loxley, Alabama. They have tremendous success with indoor hydroponic practices. In fact, a wet wall in the summer and heating techniques in the winter allow for consistent lettuce crops year-round.

Some of my favorite indoor-grown lettuces include red and green oak leaf, red pak choy, tatsoi, spicy mustard, and endive. Hydroponic lettuces such as these are ready two days after harvesting. This additional hang-time allows for lettuce head hardening for healthier handling.

My good friends Barbara Williams and Sandy Veilleux are the owners of Flora-bama Farms in Pensacola. They arrange for frequent pick up of harvested, ready-for-use lettuces from Craine Creek Farm, and deliver them to restaurant chefs throughout the region.

(SERVES 4–6)

For the beef marinade

6 tablespoons olive oil

1 teaspoon sesame seed oil

4 tablespoons seasoned rice wine vinegar

1 tablespoon fresh grated ginger

1 tablespoon Thai fish sauce

1 tablespoon red chili paste (Sambal Oelek brand preferred)

6 garlic cloves, sliced thin

2 pounds flat-iron or flank steak

For the salad dressing

⅛ cup olive oil

2 tablespoons lemon juice

¼ cup loosely packed small-chopped cilantro leaves

½ teaspoon sesame oil

2 tablespoons light soy sauce

1–2 tablespoons chopped lemon grass

To make the beef marinade

Place marinade ingredients in a mixing bowl, whisk together, and then pour over steak. Let steak marinate for 2 hours in the refrigerator, turning once after the first hour.

To make the salad dressing

Place dressing ingredients in a mixing bowl and whisk together, making sure sugar is dissolved. Set aside.

To assemble

Preheat a fryer to 350°F. Cut wontons into strips and deep fry for 1–2 minutes until golden brown, place onto paper towel to drain, and season with salt and pepper.

Preheat the grill to medium high. Brush bok choy heads with olive oil, place over medium-high heat to char all over and wilt, 5–7 minutes. Transfer to cutting board, discard stem, and cut leaves into medium-size pieces.

Prepare grill grate surface for steaks by dipping a used kitchen towel into oil and rubbing it over grill grates. Cook steaks medium to medium-rare, 5–7 minutes on each side. Remove from heat, place on cutting board, and let rest for 5 minutes before slicing. To slice, hold knife at a 45-degree angle and cut the steak crosswise into very thin slices.

1 minced Thai chile or hot pepper (add seeds for additional heat)

1 tablespoon light brown sugar

1 teaspoon Thai fish sauce

Dash of freshly ground black pepper

For the finished plate

6 wonton wrappers

Salt and pepper to taste

Extra olive oil for grilling

2 heads baby bok choy (optional)

1 head leafy red or green oak lettuce, all leaves

1 head spicy mustard, all leaves

1 head red pak choy, all leaves

2 tomatoes, cut into thin wedges

1 cucumber, thinly sliced

1 small red onion, thinly sliced

1 bunch fresh spearmint, chopped small

For the garnish

1 ounce radish micro shoots

Transfer the meat with its juices into a large mixing bowl and toss with the cut bok choy, oak leaf lettuce, spicy mustards, red pak choy, tomatoes, cucumber, onion, and chopped mint. Drizzle with dressing and toss gently. Divide salad on individual plates or a platter. Garnish with wonton crisps and radish micro shoots.

Turducken Gumbo

Turducken was made famous by Louisiana celebrity chef Paul Prudhomme, proprietor of K-Paul's Louisiana Kitchen in New Orleans. He introduced the idea to popular culture during the early 1980s. Turducken is a portmanteau, or combination of two (or more) words and their definitions to make one new word, something Prudhomme likes to do; the name K-Paul is a portmanteau of Chef Paul and his previous wife Kay. In this case, the combination of the recipe's main players (turkey, duck, and chicken) are combined to make turducken.

Prudhomme's distinctive preparation requires the handiwork of a skilled charcutier, or butcher, to insert a deboned, sausage-stuffed chicken into the cavity of a deboned, corn bread–stuffed duck, which is then jammed into a deboned, oyster-mash-stuffed turkey.

I decided to take it one step further. The idea of using turkey, duck, and chicken to make gumbo came about when I toyed around with the thought of starting my own food product line. To my knowledge, pairing turducken with gumbo had never been done before. Everyone liked my idea! I thought this would be a fun and delicious spin on Cajun cuisine classic, and it became one of my signature dishes among a circle of friends around the Christmas holiday season. I never pursued my product line, but this one-of-a-kind, roasted, three-bird gumbo is loved by my friends, and that's all that matters.

To cook the turkey, duck, and chicken

Rub the skin of the turkey with oil, salt, and pepper and place on roasting pan and roast for 12 minutes per pound.

Remove gizzards and neck from inside the duck. Place on roasting pan and rub the skin with oil, salt, and pepper. Roast for 1½ hours.

Remove gizzards and neck from inside the chicken. Place on roasting pan and rub the skin with oil, salt, and pepper. Roast for 1–1½ hours.

To check for doneness, insert a cooking thermometer into the thickest portion of the meat, either the breast or thigh. Each bird should have an internal temperature of 165°F when done and the juices should run clear (not pink) when skin is pierced. Remove from oven and let sit for 30 minutes to rest.

Remove breast and thigh meat from bones, and then pull the meat into spoon-size pieces. Remove small meat morsels by hand. Reserve each carcass and the turkey rib bones for stock.

(SERVES 12–14)

For the turkey, duck, and chicken

1 small (2- to 3-pound) rib-on turkey breast

1 small (4- to 5-pound) duck

1 small (about 2½-pound) chicken

2 tablespoons pure olive oil

Salt and pepper to taste

For the turducken stock

1 onion, coarsely chopped

1 carrot, coarsely chopped

1 stalk celery, coarsely chopped

10 garlic cloves

Roasted chicken carcass (from roasting)

Roasted duck carcass (from roasting)

Rib bones from roasted turkey breast

1 bay leaf

1 sprig fresh thyme

20 black peppercorns

For the gumbo

½ cup duck fat (reserved from roasted duck)

½ cup peanut oil

1 cup all-purpose flour

2 cups yellow onions, diced small

2 cups andouille sausage, sliced ½-inch thick

1 cup small-chopped celery

1 cup small-chopped green pepper

2 tablespoons minced garlic

1 teaspoon fresh thyme leaves

3½ quarts turducken stock (recipe below)

2 bay leaves

2 cups sliced okra

Pinch of kosher salt

Dash of freshly ground black pepper

2 tablespoons Creole spice blend (your favorite brand)

3–5 tablespoons Worcestershire sauce

6–8 tablespoons hot sauce (Louisiana brand preferred)

2 cups cooked basic white rice

To make the Turducken stock

Place a 10-quart stock pot over medium-high heat. Add the onion, carrot, celery, and garlic. Break up and add the roasted chicken carcass, duck carcass, and turkey breast rib bones, the bay leaf, thyme, peppercorns, and 6 quarts of water. Increase heat to high and bring to a boil. Immediately reduce heat to a simmer and cook for 1½–2 hours or until stock is reduced by one-third. Strain through china cap (metal strainer with medium-size holes), and then again through a fine sieve.

To make the gumbo

Make a roux by heating the reserved duck fat and oil in a heavy-bottom skillet or dutch oven over medium-high heat. Carefully whisk the flour into the hot oil. It will begin to sizzle. Reduce the heat to medium and continue whisking until the roux takes on a deep brown color, about 20 minutes. Add the onions, stirring them in with a wooden spoon or heavy-duty whisk; be careful not to let it splash on your hands or arms. Reduce heat to medium-low and continue whisking until roux becomes rich dark brown, 10–12 minutes. Remove from heat to cool slightly, about 5 minutes.

Add the sausage and cook, stirring, for a few minutes before adding the celery, bell peppers, and garlic. Increase the heat to medium–high and cook, stirring, for about 3 more minutes. Add the fresh thyme, turducken stock, and bay leaves. Bring the gumbo to a boil, stirring frequently. Reduce heat to medium-low and simmer for 1 hour.

Add the okra to the pot along with roasted chunks of turkey, duck, and chicken. Season with salt, pepper, Creole spice blend, Worcestershire, and hot sauce. Simmer for another 45 minutes. Skim surface to remove fat. Serve in bowls over cooked white rice.

Browning Flour

Lightly browning flour (in the oven) is a time-saving method used to significantly speed up roux cooking time. Browning flour creates a unique nutty aroma that will fill the kitchen. It's a fine line between a chocolate roux and a burnt roux, so be attentive and careful not burn the roux; if you do, you will have to start over again.

To lightly brown flour, preheat oven to 375°F. In casting off the shackles of traditionalism, I suggest browning flour before beginning the roux. Browning in advance will significantly speed up the roux cook time, and the time needed to whisk the roux to a rich dark brown or chocolate brown will be reduced by approximately one-third.

Pour the flour onto a sheet tray and spread it out, containing the flour dust when handling. Bake for 25 minutes or until the flour begins to turn light brown. Use the back of a fork to stir the flour after 10 minutes. Then repeat after another 10 minutes. Use the browned flour as you would regular flour.

Chapter 3
Oysters

Raw Oysters with Ed's Red

Anywhere you go along the Gulf Coast, raw oysters are widely known as "oysters on the half shell." Along the Apalachicola River basin they're also called "topless oysters" or "nude oysters." This classic shuck-and-suck-style oyster is also famous at Indian Pass Raw Bar located at the intersection of C-30 and C-30B (Indian Pass) in Port St. Joe.

These days the best tasting oysters from the Gulf Coast are enjoyed by locals and tourists alike at this landmark raw bar. Don't look for a fancy menu—the short menu is posted on the wall. Oysters are shucked and served raw, baked with toppings, or steamed, but never fried since there is no fryer.

The Indian Pass Raw Bar building was a former general store, Oyster Company, and once housed a seafood company managed by my friend and local Port St. Joe legend Ed Creamer. Ed is a life-long Port St. Joe resident and knows his way around the St. Joseph and Apalachicola Bay better than anyone. To keep busy during his retirement, he developed Ed's Red, a hot sauce first offered on the counter at Indian Pass Raw Bar to adorn oysters. It's the only hot sauce they serve. Ed's hot sauce has intense fruit and his bottled recipes offer several degrees of spiciness. Ed's Red is truly "An Oyster's Best Friend."

This raw oyster preparation is as simple and "stripped down" as it gets. All that is required are fresh oysters, oyster shucking skills, plenty of ice, and Ed's Red hot sauce.

(MAKES 36 OYSTERS, 4–6 SERVINGS)

36 wild oysters, such as Apalachicola, shucked

3 pounds crushed ice, divided equally into bowls or oyster serving trays

Ed's Red Hot Sauce

Saltine crackers

Dill and Mustard Seed Mignonette, Spicy Tamari, or Ceviche Sauce (recipes follow)

Place the shucked oysters, freed of the muscles that tether them to the shells, into a half-shell, and place them over crushed ice on a large serving tray or individual serving bowls. Serve with Ed's Red Hot Sauce and one of the following sauces.

Raw Oyster Sauces

Spicy Tamari Sauce

Shortly after I graduated from the Culinary Institute of America (CIA) in 1982, I resettled in Destin, Florida. Known as "The World's Luckiest Fishing Village," Destin is recognized for its excellent fishing (and also claims to have the biggest fishing vessel fleet in the state). Between the three years spent at the CIA and before the permanent Florida move, I had a brief restaurant stint in San Antonio, Texas. My boss would take frequent fishing trips to the Destin area, refreshing vacation getaways from his corporate empire, Universal Restaurants, centered in Dallas, Texas.

At that time, there wasn't much land development in Destin, and a good restaurant was difficult to come by. Company proprietor Phil Vacarro decided it was time to open a second location for his famed Les Saison's Restaurant in Dallas, this time in Destin. After my promotion from poissonnier (fish cook) to sous chef (assistant chef), I was asked to join the operation. I eagerly packed my bags for the journey to the Gulf Coast's Florida Panhandle.

I quickly settled into the laid-back culture of the Redneck Riviera. I established new friends and relationships in the quaint coastal fishing village. I also picked up a few life lessons and cooking tips from its inhabitants. This recipe was inspired by one of my Vietnamese prep chefs at the restaurant. It's easy to make and a great dressing for oysters. It brings back good memories, too.

Combine the sesame seeds in a small, dry sauté pan, and place over medium heat for 2–3 minutes, shaking the pan continuously until the white sesame seeds have turned light brown. Whisk together all remaining ingredients, and chill for 1 hour. Whisk again before serving. Use as directed over raw oysters.

CHEF'S TIP: If you can't find fresh lemongrass, frozen cut lemongrass may be substituted and is often available in the freezer section of Asian markets.

(SERVES 4–6, ENOUGH FOR 3 DOZEN OYSTERS)

1 teaspoon black sesame seeds

1 teaspoon white sesame seeds

3 tablespoons fresh lemon juice

3 tablespoons finely chopped cilantro

2 tablespoons extra-virgin olive oil

¼ teaspoon sesame oil

¼ cup tamari or low-sodium soy sauce

1 tablespoon chopped lemongrass (frozen may be substituted)

1 teaspoon minced serrano chiles

1½ tablespoons Vietnamese fish sauce

Dash of freshly ground black pepper

Ceviche Sauce

South Florida cooking blends culinary flavors from many cultures. The two most notable are Caribbean and South American. This is due to both the steady flow of imported ingredients into the area and tropical produce that is either grown locally (the climate is similar) or imported, as well as to the large number of ethnic groups that make up a sizable percentage of the population there.

While flavors from the Caribbean and South America are by far more easily obtained in South Florida, many of them make their way north to the Florida Panhandle and are not too hard to find if you're an avid shopper. Of course, a drive from anywhere around these parts to South Florida is only half a day's drive.

I'm glad they are reasonably available, because two of the fresh and exotic ingredients in this ceviche sauce just happen to be Caribbean and South American. Ceviche is one of my favorite seafood dishes. I find it the perfect vehicle for seafood that is just plucked from the Gulf of Mexico, especially in the heat of summer. Basically, it is classic "heatless cooking." Technically, it is cooking by acidulation, when a citrus marinade cooks raw seafood.

(SERVES 4–6, ENOUGH FOR 3 DOZEN OYSTERS)

2 pink or sweet grapefruits, segmented

2 navel or Seville oranges, segmented

6 tablespoons lime juice, zest of 1 lime reserved to add to mixture

1 slightly firm mango, finely chopped

1 minced shallot

1 minced jalapeño pepper, seeds discarded

½ red bell pepper, finely chopped

3 tablespoons finely chopped cilantro

1 tablespoon extra-virgin olive oil

1 teaspoon pomegranate seeds (optional)

Pinch of sea salt and freshly ground black pepper to taste

Combine grapefruit, oranges, lime juice and zest, mango, shallot, peppers, cilantro, olive oil, and pomegranate seeds in a small mixing bowl. Stir with a spoon to blend and break up citrus sections to make ceviche sauce. Chill for 1 hour in the refrigerator. Spoon ceviche sauce over the raw oysters and serve. Taste, and adjust seasoning with salt and pepper.

Dill and Mustard Seed Mignonette

I have always been captivated by the ever-yielding and colorful array of sea-food from Florida's bountiful Gulf Coast. And I have always been open to creating new dishes using local ingredients. During the time that the Florida food movement swept through the Florida Panhandle, an unfamiliar sauce called mignonette began topping oysters on the half shell in fine dining restaurants in metropolitan cities throughout the South.

Mignonette sauce is usually made with minced shallots, cracked pepper, and vinegar, and is traditionally served with raw oysters. Different mignonette sauces use different types of vinegar, but all contain pepper. I did some adapting of my own, making what is a very French and boutique-style sauce into something more pickled, herbal, and southern.

Place the mustard seeds and water in a small pan over medium-high heat, bring to a boil, reduce heat, and let simmer for 5–7 minutes. Strain and rinse seeds under cool water. Repeat the entire cooking and rinsing process 3 times.

In a small bowl, combine rinsed seeds with wine, vinegars, shallots, peppers, freshly ground pepper, dill, and salt. Chill for 1 hour. Stir well. Spoon over raw oysters and serve.

(MAKES 4–6 SERVINGS, ENOUGH FOR 3 DOZEN OYSTERS)

2 tablespoons white or yellow whole mustard seeds

¼ cup water

¼ cup chardonnay or other white wine

¾ cup champagne vinegar

¼ cup cider vinegar

¼ cup minced shallots

1 tablespoon seeded and minced serrano peppers

2 tablespoons minced red sweet peppers

1½ tablespoons freshly ground black peppercorns

2 tablespoons of small-chopped fresh dill

Pinch of sea salt

Raw Oyster Fact

Raw oysters require very little adornment. If you'd like, add a squeeze of fresh lemon juice, some hot sauce, or some homemade cocktail sauce alongside a dab of prepared horseradish. If you're feeling adventurous, prepare and serve an array of each of these sauces, to be spooned over each oyster before slurping it down.

Cannonball Oysters with Sweet and Spicy Chili Sauce

In Pensacola's historic downtown district rests Plaza Ferdinand, a landmark park where General Andrew Jackson oversaw the transfer of Florida from Spain to the United States in 1821, eight years before he became the seventh President of the United States (1829–1837). He's the namesake for the original Jackson's Restaurant right across the street, a one-of-a-kind eatery that I founded along with my business partners Barry Phillips and Walter Steigleman in 1999. The award-winning restaurant is now Jackson's Steakhouse and is owned by Collier Merrill and his brothers Will and Burney.

Jackson's is only a cannonball's fire away from several enormous, black replica cannons positioned throughout the park. One evening at the restaurant, I was visiting with my good friend and marksman "Cannon Ball Curtis" and created this simple oyster recipe for him.

Select Apalachicola oysters are ideal for this panko-breaded, crispy-fried preparation adorned with an easy-to-replicate, Vietnamese-style, sweet and spicy chili sauce.

To make the oysters

Create a milk wash by combining eggs and milk in a small mixing bowl and whisking until blended. Place the flour in a shallow mixing bowl, add the salt and pepper, and blend well. Place the panko in a third mixing bowl. Roll the oysters in the seasoned flour. a few at a time, until they are completely dusted and evenly coated. Transfer them to the milk wash, coat well, immediately place them in the bowl of panko crumbs, and coat well.

In a deep skillet, heat the frying oil to 350°F. Deep-fry the breaded oysters for 1–2 minutes (depending on their size) until golden brown. Drain well and transfer fried oysters to paper towels to drain further.

To make the sauce

Combine all ingredients in a small mixing bowl and blend with a whisk. Let the sauce sit for 30 minutes to allow the flavors to fully combine.

To assemble

Toss oysters with as much of the Sweet and Spicy Chili Sauce as you like. Serve with toothpicks.

(SERVES 4–6)

For the oysters

4 eggs

1 pint milk

3 cups flour

2 teaspoons kosher salt

1 teaspoon freshly ground black pepper

5 cups panko bread crumbs

24 Gulf Coast oysters, freshly shucked and drained

Oil, for frying (vegetable or peanut)

For the sweet and spicy chile sauce

⅛ cup seasoned rice wine vinegar

½ cup corn syrup

3 tablespoons fish sauce

3 tablespoons sugar

3 tablespoons lemon juice

1 tablespoon grated fresh ginger

1 teaspoon minced garlic

1 tablespoon red chili paste (Sambal Oelek brand preferred)

1 teaspoon red chile flakes

Char-Grilled Oysters with Aged Country Ham

In 2012 I represented Florida at the Great American Seafood Cook-Off, a nationally recognized seafood competition held annually in New Orleans. Sixteen chefs from around the country prepare their best dishes using the domestic seafood indigenous to their states. The event is one of the most exciting and highly respected culinary events in the country.

In 2012 chefs prepared their regional fresh catches. Louisiana's Keith Frenzt prepared black drum and gulf shrimp; Oregon's Gregory Gourdet prepared Chinook salmon and butter clams; Alabama's Chris Hastings prepared an array of gulf shellfish, crustaceans, and fish for bouillabaisse; and I, of course, prepared red snapper and gulf shrimp.

The Great American Seafood Cook-Off was an opportunity to tout our regions' seafood, meet creative chefs, and dine at some of the city's proudest restaurant seafood supporters. The night before the cook-off, we all visited Drago's Seafood Restaurant, home of the Original Charbroiled Oyster—buttery Louisiana oysters hot off the flaming charbroiler!

Here is my version of this delicious recipe, Florida Panhandle-style.

Apalachiola, Florida

Apalachicola remains one of the more remote Old Florida cities along the Gulf of Mexico. It is in the heart of Florida's "Forgotten Coast"; a regional name used to designate the relatively undeveloped, quiet section of the Panhandle's "Big Bend" coastline stretching from Mexico Beach to Apalachee Bay. A trip to this area is as good as it gets for getting away from it all.

The "Forgotten Coast" is known for its pristine bays, sugar white beaches, coastal marshlands and estuaries that are rich with sea life. Apalachicola Bay, in particular, is widely recognized for its wild oysters; however, these days the shrimping industry is equally important. Seasonally harvested "brownies" (brown shrimp) and "hoppers" (pink shrimp with a black dot on their shell) are the catch in these parts. An active blue crab industry also exists in Apalachicola Bay. Blue crab, both hard-shell and soft-shell, or "peelers", are typically harvested from the estuaries inshore.

Today, the once-vibrant oyster industry manages to show some signs of life in Apalachicola Bay on any given day. There are a good number of Oystermen and women who still tong for wild oysters and are able to harvest 3 or 4 bags a day. Bay closures and new oyster handling and harvesting procedures are managed by government agencies to prevent proper handling of product, over harvesting and provide time for juvenile oyster growth. Natural oyster reefs aren't spawning as plentiful as in the past. For Apalachicola, the dormant oyster industry manages to stay focused on replanting oyster beds as best they can while local and state agencies provide constant water testing. If and when Apalachicola ever bounces back, there might again be a bounty of oysters hitting the market again someday in the near future.

Lingering effects from the Deepwater Horizon incident, current litigation concerning Georgia water drainage and the interference of local politics will eventually work themselves out over time (fingers crossed). In the meantime, industry leaders around Alabama's Mobile Bay are still producing wild oysters and Grand Bay are already having some success with alternative measures such as sustainable off-bottom aquaculture and sustainable oyster farming practices. "Our greatest challenge over the next 20 years is dealing with coastal salinity change in each of our important estuaries that we grow oysters," said Chris Nelson, vice president of Alabama's Bon Secour Fisheries and a Gulf Seafood Institute board member.

It is ironic that at a time when shellfish consumption is at an all time high, and good oysters are in vogue, the natural harvest is on the decline. Crab harvests are starting to gain momentum after several years of record low harvest. Shrimp harvests are also starting to follow the low harvest trend. From Florida to Texas, the gulf coast is suffering from high prices and the lowest oyster production on record.

Combine butter, garlic, chives, sherry, jalapeños, paprika, red pepper flakes, and salt in a saucepot. Whisk together over low heat until sauce reaches a smooth, yogurt-like consistency, then remove from the burner.

Mix Parmesan and panko in a small bowl. Set aside.

Preheat gas grill or prepare and light a charcoal grill to medium-high heat. Place the loosened oysters in their half-shells on a wire baking rack (see note below). Sprinkle each oyster with a light dusting of the Parmesan and panko mixture to give the sauce some texture to adhere to. Apply a generous teaspoon of butter onto each oyster, and then divide the remaining Parmesan mixture among the 36 oysters.

Cut each ham slice in half, then quarter each half into 1-inch pieces for a total of 40 pieces. Place one piece of ham on each oyster, then transfer oysters, one by one, onto the hottest spot on the grill. Let the oysters cook for 3–5 minutes, placing a bit of additional sauce over the oysters as they flame and brown a bit on the edges. Let them continue to cook in their own juices for a few minutes, just until the edges curl and the butter bubbles. Remove from grill. Squeeze lemon wedges over the oysters just before serving.

CHEF'S TIP: Although the amount of butter may seem excessive in this recipe, much of it will end up in the flames due to the shallow-cupped shape of the oyster. The butter provides a quick cook and intense char flavor when cooked by the open-fire grilling process.

(MAKES 36 OYSTERS, SERVES 4–6)

4 sticks (1 pound) unsalted butter at room temperature, cut into 1-inch pieces (see note)

6 cloves garlic, minced

¼ cup finely chopped chives

¼ cup dry sherry

1 tablespoon minced jalapeño peppers (ribs and seeds removed)

1 teaspoon sweet smoky paprika

1 teaspoon crushed red pepper flakes

Pinch of sea salt

1 cup finely grated Parmesan

½ cup panko bread crumbs

36 Gulf Coast oysters, cleaned and shucked, bottom shells reserved

5 slices cured ham (serrano or prosciutto)

2 lemons cut into wedges

Oyster Fry with Corn Relish, Blue Cheese & Bacon

Our regional oyster preparations are prized along the Gulf Coast from Louisiana to Florida, and one of the most popular ways to prepare oysters is to deep-fry them. It's easy and delicious—especially when you buy them fresh, already shucked, and packed in their own liquor.

Readily available, freshly shucked oysters packed in their own liquor arrive from the oyster plant to the seafood market packed in gallon buckets, and then are broken down in-house into 12-ounce (or smaller) containers for retail sales. They can be found on retail seafood counters and labeled as fresh shucked oysters. These pre-shucked oysters are ideal for frying and baking.

To ensure quality, before they're shucked, the oysters are first rinsed and then selected by size and shell condition as they are sorted for wholesale and retail packaging. Common practice when selecting oysters used for pre-shucking is to choose the larger, pillow-shaped oysters—those too large for slurping—along with the frequently found imperfect cluster oysters.

I'm fascinated when I see skilled oyster shuckers filling gallon containers as they hand-shuck oysters, one by one, at lightning speed. Shucking and slurping fresh oysters is a local tradition and, to many, a favorite way to eat them. I must admit though, just cracking open a container lid and eating pre-shucked oysters straight out of the bucket makes for time better spent at the table.

This recipe may look intensive because it's in three parts, but don't let that dissuade you from preparing this tasty, fried-oyster combination; it's really quite simple.

(SERVES 4)

For the relish

6 strips bacon

4 ears fresh sweet corn, husk and silk removed

2 tablespoons unsalted butter

2 tablespoons finely chopped red onion

3 tablespoons finely chopped red bell pepper

2 jalapeño peppers, charred on the grill, seeded, and finely chopped

2 tablespoons finely chopped parsley

To make the relish
Preheat charcoal or gas grill to medium. Panfry the bacon until crispy, drain onto paper towels, reserving the bacon fat, and chop bacon into bits. Set aside.

Dip a paper towel in the reserved bacon fat, and rub it all over the ears of corn. Place the oiled corn on the grill and turn every few minutes until the ears are charred all over, 5–7 minutes. Remove from grill and let cool. Cut off the thick end of the cobs so the corn stands upright on your cutting board. Hold the top firmly and slice straight down the sides with a sharp knife to remove kernels. You should end up with about 2 cups of shaved kernels. Set these aside.

Melt the butter in a medium skillet over medium heat. Add onions, peppers, jalapeño, and parsley and sauté for 2 minutes. Add charred corn kernels and stir in honey and lemon juice. Taste and adjust seasoning with salt and pepper.

To make the blue cheese cream

Place a medium-size skillet over medium heat. Pour in the cream, bring to a boil, then reduce heat to low and simmer, whisking frequently, until cream is reduced by a third, 8–10 minutes. When cream thickens, 1 cup of blue cheese to the saucepan and whisk to combine. Taste, and adjust seasoning with salt and pepper.

To make the oysters

Preheat a deep-fryer or heat frying oil in a deep skillet to 350°F. Combine egg, buttermilk, and hot sauce in a small mixing bowl. Combine flour and Cajun spice in another small mixing bowl. Place panko in a third bowl. Dust oysters, a few at a time, with seasoned flour, tapping to remove any excess flour. Dunk the dusted oysters into the buttermilk mixture a few at a time, coating each oyster completely. Then place the wet oysters into the bread crumbs and coat them evenly. Place directly into hot oil and fry the breaded oysters for 3 minutes or until golden brown.

To assemble

Pour a pool of blue cheese cream onto each plate. Arrange fried oysters on top of the cream, and then spoon relish over the oysters. Crumble additional blue cheese on top and sprinkle with the reserved crisp bacon bits.

1 tablespoon artisan honey (optional)

1 tablespoon lemon juice

Pinch of kosher salt

Dash of fresh ground black pepper

For the blue cheese cream

½ pint heavy whipping cream

1 cup blue cheese, plus ¼ cup additional for sprinkling at the end

Pinch of kosher salt and ground black pepper

For the oysters

Vegetable or peanut oil, for frying

1 egg

2 cups buttermilk

¼ cup hot sauce

1 cup all-purpose flour

1 tablespoon Cajun spice

3 cups panko bread crumbs

24 Gulf Coast oysters

Oysters in Ginger Broth with Thai Chiles

During the mid-1980s, many Vietnamese, Philippine, and Taiwanese people found a new home along the coastlines of Florida, Alabama, Mississippi, and Louisiana. Many brought fishing skills from their native land and used fish-cutting, oyster harvesting, and shrimping as ways to support their families. Of course, many also brought exotic recipes and fundamental flavors and ingredients from the Far East.

Early on I was inspired by this Asian cultural infusion and discovered that one of my favorite ways to prepare oysters was in a quick-and-easy stew with Asian flavors. It doesn't really matter which section of the coast your oysters are gathered from for this stew, any one will do. The soup broth for this dish is light and rather delicate. It is only ever so slightly thickened with flour, and not too rich.

(MAKES 36 OYSTERS, SERVES 4–6)

6 tablespoons unsalted butter

2 bunches scallions, whites cut on a thin bias (greens reserved for garnish)

3 tablespoons all-purpose flour

3 cups coconut milk

3 cups vegetable broth

2 tablespoons fish sauce

1–2 tablespoons soy sauce

¼ cup mirin

36 oysters, shucked with their liquor reserved

1 tablespoon grated fresh gingerroot

1 small garlic clove, minced

2 tablespoons coarsely chopped cilantro

1 tablespoon thinly sliced Thai chile peppers

1 tablespoon lime juice

Pinch of sea salt and freshly ground black pepper

1 small French baguette

Melt the butter in a soup pot over medium heat. When the butter is bubbling, add the scallion whites and stir to coat. Cook slowly for 5 minutes, stirring frequently. Sprinkle the flour over and cook for 2 minutes longer, stirring well to blend. Stir in the coconut milk, broth, fish sauce, soy sauce, mirin, and oyster liquor and bring to a boil. Reduce to a simmer and then add ginger, garlic, cilantro, and chiles. Bring to a boil, remove from heat, and add lime juice. Taste and adjust seasoning with salt and pepper as desired. Ladle into soup into bowls and garnish each bowl with scallion greens. Serve with torn French bread.

CHEF'S TIP: Fellow oyster lovers and cooks will attest to the fact that as soon as the edges of the oysters begin to curl in a soup, gumbo, or stew, they are ready to serve. This stew can be ready to go in 10–15 minutes from when the cooking process begins. Pick a reliable seafood market in your region to buy either fresh or pre-shucked oysters in their liquor.

Endangered "Miracle Spot"

In 2012, the historically pristine Apalachicola Bay, a.k.a. the oyster "Miracle Spot", experienced its lowest oyster production in twenty years. Drought-like conditions across the Southeast had reduced its freshwater flow from Georgia, especially due to the increased freshwater demands of the highly populated city of Atlanta. The water quality issues for the "Miracle Spot" had begun to deepen. Culling for oysters these days is dire, but oysterfolks continue to remain hopeful.

Also contributing to the decline in oyster numbers is the effects due to juvenile oyster harvesting. The fear created by a potential contamination of the oyster beds from the 2010 BP oil spill, nearby hurricanes, and the Florida rock snail parasite have caused frequent premature harvesting. In recent years, the dwindling oyster populations have garnered the attention of health environmentalists and the federal government. There are renewed commitments in establishing and adapting sustainable water-use regulations and new oyster measures to ensure a healthy, sustainable oyster habitat for Apalachicola oysters. Some bay closures are set in place; however the real concern is that by letting oysterfolks continue to work the bars, they are doing more damage to the bay, pushing the day of true recovery further and further back. Other serious conversation continues to escalate on closing the bay for an extended amount of time to let it rebuild: Ensuring the preservation an iconic symbol of Real Florida.

"Apalachicola is the last place in the United States where wild oysters are still harvested by tongs from small boats."

—*The Oyster Guide* by Rowan Jacobsen

Baked Oysters with Hot Peppered Collards

Along the Gulf of Mexico oysters are baked with a variety of regional favorite ingredients and are served for any occasion, any time of the year. Salinity of a great oyster is often predicated by wind direction and freshwater flow into the salty Apalachicola Bay. The perfect nude oyster should be a fine balance of freshwater and saltwater. I developed this recipe to complement both degrees of salinity.

This recipe is one of my most talked about and requested oyster recipes. There are a few extra steps in the recipe, but they are well worth the effort. I created this recipe with many of the Florida Panhandle's soulful southern ingredients—assembled and cooked my way—complementing each perfectly baked oyster in its shell.

This extraordinary recipe graced a notable farm-to-table dinner for 13 Mile Seafood Outstanding in the Field event in 2015, when I was the featured guest chef.

(SERVES 4–6)

For the ham hock broth

1 gallon water

2 smoked ham hocks

2 yellow onions cut into quarters

1 celery rib, cut into 2-inch lengths

2 carrots, peeled and coarsely chopped

2 tablespoons kosher salt

3 bay leaves

½ teaspoon whole black peppercorns

For the corn bread

5 tablespoons olive oil (or bacon fat), divided

1 cup unbleached all-purpose flour

1 cup yellow cornmeal

1 tablespoon baking powder

1 teaspoon salt

2 cups buttermilk

3 eggs, well beaten

To make the ham hock broth

Combine all ingredients in an 8-quart stockpot. Bring to a boil and simmer for 3 hours. Remove ham hocks from the broth, let them cool, and remove meat, discarding skin and bones. Use meat and broth as directed below. Strain and reserve the liquid.

To make the cornbread

Preheat oven to 375°F. Sift flour, cornmeal, baking powder, and salt together into a large mixing bowl and set aside. Mix buttermilk with 2 tablespoons of olive oil and the eggs. Add to the dry ingredients and stir briefly to combine.

Heat 2 tablespoons of olive oil (or bacon fat) in a skillet. Remove pan from heat and set aside until cornbread batter is ready. Heat a 10-inch round cast-iron skillet over a low flame and pour in the remaining 1 tablespoon of olive oil. Swirl the skillet around so the oil completely coats bottom and sides of pan. (If a cast-iron skillet is not available, oil an 8 × 8 × 2-inch or 1 × 7 × 2-inch glass baking dish well with the olive oil.)

Pour in the corn bread batter. Bake for 40–60 minutes or until a toothpick inserted into middle comes out clean and top is golden brown. Remove and let cool completely, then crumble into fine crumbs and place in a mixing bowl. (This can be made one day in advance and stored in a sealed container until needed.)

To make the andouille cream

In food processor, combine chopped sausage, garlic, and shallots and pulse until ground. Place a thick-bottom saucepot over medium-high heat and add processed mixture. Stir mixture over medium-high heat for 2 minutes, then add brandy and let simmer an additional 2 minutes to concentrate flavors and burn off the alcohol. Add the cream and stir mixture to blend well. Let simmer over medium heat for 15–20 minutes or until slightly thickened and velvety. Whisk the sauce frequently as mixture simmers. Add salt and pepper to taste just before serving.

For the andouille cream

1 andouille sausage link, coarsely chopped

2 teaspoons minced garlic

2 teaspoons minced shallots

⅛ cup brandy or sherry

2 cups heavy cream

Pinch of kosher salt

Dash of freshly ground black pepper

For the finished dish

24 Gulf Coast oysters

1 bunch fresh collard greens

Pinch of sugar (optional)

Hot sauce to taste

2 cloves garlic, finely chopped

1 shallot, finely chopped

2 tablespoons good brandy or sherry

1 pint heavy whipping cream

Salt and freshly ground black pepper to taste

To prepare the finished dish

Preheat oven to 350°F. Shuck oysters, straining oyster liquor into a container, and add the shucked oysters to the strained liquid. Discard the top half of each oyster shell, but reserve bottom half, and place cupped side facing up on a baking pan.

Bring the ham hock broth back to a boil and then reduce to a simmer. Place the fresh collard greens on a flat work surface, use a utility knife to remove ribs from leaves, then cut the collards into 1-inch cubes. Plunge the cut greens into the broth and cook for 30–40 minutes. If greens are slightly bitter, add a pinch of sugar. Add hot sauce. Strain into colander, reserving the liquid. Spread the cooked collards on a baking pan to cool slightly. Chop them small enough to fit easily in an oyster shell.

Finely chop the cooked ham hock meat. Place a saucepot over medium-high heat. Add the ham hock meat, garlic, and shallot. Stir mixture over heat for 2 minutes then add brandy. Let simmer, stirring frequently to concentrate flavors and burn off the alcohol. Add the andouille cream, a few tablespoons of reserved oyster liquor, and a few tablespoons of the collard greens pot liquid. Stir to blend well. Stirring frequently, let simmer over medium heat until slightly thickened, 15–20 minutes. Taste, and adjust seasoning with salt, pepper, and additional hot sauce to your liking.

Fill each oyster shell with a full teaspoon of chopped collards. Place an oyster over each greens-filled shell, and cover each oyster with crumbled corn bread. Place the oyster pan in the oven and bake for 8 minutes. Remove and then sauce each individual oyster with 1–2 tablespoons of the ham hock–cream reduction, then place pan back in oven and bake another 4 minutes. Remove and serve immediately.

The Oyster: Jewel of the Gulf Coast

The ancient native bivalve mollusk—the oyster—is the jewel of the Gulf of Mexico. Found in its finger estuaries, the oyster is as much a prized jewel to our waters as the naturally formed pearl is to the Persian oyster. In this sense, one cannot appreciate the glories of our prized harvests from the Gulf without acknowledging its Mediterranean counterpart near the "mouth" of the Adriatic Sea. The earliest known oyster cultivation there began roughly 2,000 years ago. Here's to you, Adriatic oyster!

Today, five oyster species enter the U.S. marketplace. Of these, it is the *Crassostrea virginica* that is most common. It can be found living in waters from the upper East Coast into the Gulf of Mexico. In the Gulf, oysters are primarily established along the upper coast: Apalachicola's East Bay (and adjoining bays) westward to Santa Rosa County's East Bay; Bon Secour Bay in Alabama; the public fisheries of Louisiana; and Galveston, Texas. Each one of these region's jewels (as oysters are affectionately called) is a piece of Gulf Coast pride to its natives, with each staking its regional claim to oyster variety preference and recipe excellence. A way of life to some, an indulgence to others.

It's the taste of the freshly shucked oyster along with its liquor slurped straight out of its shell that dictates the unique flavor nuances of the oyster in its purest form. The oyster delicacy begins with a partiality to size, shape, and degree of clarity. Salinity levels and texture contribute to the flavor, which derives from the watery habitat of each oyster bed's regional "merroir". It's a balancing act of salinity where freshwater feeds from rivers interacting with the salty Gulf's tidal action and protective barrier islands. These variable elements make for the size, flavor, health, and general survival of the oyster. Chefs and oyster connoisseurs from the region know that all Gulf Coast oysters (although all are the same species) do not look and taste the same.

Naming particular oysters is easy because they are identified by their regional estuary location. Just as Louisiana oysters are only native to Louisiana estuaries, the Apalachicola oyster variety is specific only to Apalachicola, in the Florida Panhandle. Throughout Apalachicola Bay, for instance, the oyster beds themselves are named by their oyster watermen. The watermen and area oyster companies lease the beds individually from the state. This relationship helps to keep oyster beds planted, and continually keep existing beds replanted and restored.

For the livelihood and survival of these wild filter-feeders, the Apalachicola River finger-arteries draining from South Georgia through the Florida highlands are key to providing nourishment and a low-saline freshwater flow into the bay. Along with good weather conditions, this determines optimum blending with saltwater and creating ideal salinity levels by mixing with the saltier waters of the Gulf of Mexico. Wind coming from the east brings more freshwater into the bay from the river. Wind from the west brings more salt-water from the Gulf. Oystermen read the wind to know when and where to get their catch.

Even with current small harvest issues, Apalachicola Bay oysters (on more than one occasion) have been recognized as some of the finest in the world. They are medium size, sharply-ridged, shallow-cupped, elongated, and yield a plump, opaque, creamy-gray oyster resting in clear liquor. They are ideal for shucking and make for ideal eating; often served with a squeeze of lemon, some prepared horseradish, hot sauce and crispy saltine crackers.

Louisiana oysters are slightly larger, round-shaped, deeply cupped and thicker, yielding a patty-shaped, very tasty oyster. The smaller ones are ideal for shucking and eating raw (also recommended to be served with the usual suspects: lemon; horseradish; hot sauce; and crispy saltines). The larger oysters are superb for grilling on the half shell over open flames while being doused with ladles of garlic butter and fresh herbs. The other important prep-aration for the bigger ones is being baked in the traditional New Orleans-style Rockefeller or Bienville.

Every now and then (fortunately not too often) Gulf Coast residents must combine their resources in times of crisis. For Louisiana, two milestone moments occurred in 2005 in the aftermath of Hurricane Katrina and in the equally terrifying aftermath of the BP oil spill in the spring of 2010. It was not uncommon for Louisiana to call upon Apalachicola for oysters when their populations were severely damaged. Nor was it uncommon for Apalachicola to call upon Louisiana and Alabama to meet demand when they suffered from low harvests.

Many of the factors related to production and availability include extreme weather conditions, low harvests, and the timing of a particular state's open season. It's no surprise to me that when it comes to oysters, we "Gulf Coast-ers" will always pull our resources together by supplying fresh oysters from each other's oyster-producing estuaries, in order to provide a seamless supply of oysters for the region and the country.

Oyster Harvesting

The Apalachicola Bay oyster has been called the best-tasting oyster in the world. Due to temperate water conditions along the Florida Gulf Coast, as compared to other U.S. oyster estuaries, Apalachicola oysters are usually ready for harvesting in 18 to 22 months. They are medium-size, sharply ridged, shallow-cupped, elongated, and yield a plump, opaque, creamy-gray oyster resting in a clear liquor — equally balanced with the brackish water's low saline content and delicate meat flavor.

Ninety percent of oysters harvested in Florida come from the Apalachicola Bay system. In recent years, the dwindling oyster harvests have received the attention of both health environmentalists and the federal government. The Apalachicola river system is threatened by a lack of fresh water coming downstream from federally controlled dams on the Chattahoochee and Flint rivers in Georgia. The two rivers merge at the Florida state line where the Jim Woodruff Dam rises in Chattahoochee to provide the Apalachicola freshwater flow. With too much salt water, oyster predators flourish. The oysters suffer.

The promising news is: There are strong commitments to establish and adapt sustainable water-use regulations and new oystering measures to ensure a healthy, sustainable oyster habitat for Apalachicola oysters, an iconic symbol of Real Florida. Following the recent success of oyster aquaculture (oyster farming) with Point Aux Pin Oysters Co. and Murder Point Oyster Co. in Alabama, Apalachicola was recently approved by the state to begin limited leasing of small sections of the Apalachicola Bay for new oyster farming practices.

Chapter 4
Red Snapper Riviera

Red Snapper with Pecan Meunière

Red Snapper is the fish that built Northwest Florida. I am so passionate about it that I had originally titled my book *Red Snapper Riviera, a re-created Redneck Riviera.* My desire was to pay tribute to the champion fish that has shaped our history for over a century, and acknowledge our well-known pristine coast. Ultimately, I decided to change the title to *Panhandle to Pan;* but the significance of snapper to my seafood cooking has not been lost, as I have dedicated an entire chapter to it.

Snapper, or any flakey and firm white fish, is best served when it has just been plucked from the water and prepared simply. Recently, this classic French meunière preparation has taken on various adaptations throughout the Gulf Coast. The best-known alteration to the original was done by famed Louisiana chef Paul Prudhomme. He created his own Louisiana-style version by adding spices, garlic, Worcestershire, and Tabasco Sauce.

But, for the more classic French preparation, I simply heat the butter until foaming and then add some parsley and lemon juice. I then pour the sauce over the snapper, which has already been topped with perfectly toasted pecan halves. This is sort of a sister-sauce to the more well-known "butter pecan sauce."

Preheat the oven to 350°F. Place pecans on a baking pan and bake 8–10 minutes or until nicely toasted.

In a medium-size mixing bowl, combine flour, salt, and pepper. Set aside.

Pat the fish dry with paper towels and season with salt and pepper on both sides. Place the fillets in the seasoned flour to coat both sides evenly.

Place a large ovenproof sauté pan over medium-high heat. When it is very hot, add the oil and swirl to coat the pan. Pat the dusted fillets to remove the excess flour, then lay the cut sides of red snapper fillets in the pan so the pieces are not touching. Sear until the fish is deep golden brown on the bottom and moves easily in the pan. Turn the pieces over and immediately place the pan in the oven to finish cooking, 7–8 more minutes.

Remove fish when done and pat dry with a paper towel. Place the fish on individual plates. Divide and arrange the toasted pecans over top the red snapper fillets. Wipe out the sauté pan with a paper towel. Place pan back on medium heat. When hot, add the butter and let bubble and foam. Add lemon juice, chopped parsley, and a pinch each of salt and pepper, swirl to combine, then spoon sauce directly over each piece of fish and serve immediately.

(SERVES 4)

½ cup pecan halves

1 cup all-purpose flour

1 teaspoon kosher salt, plus more for seasoning

1 teaspoon freshly ground black pepper, plus more for seasoning

4 (6- to 8-ounce) skinless red snapper fillets

4 tablespoons olive or vegetable oil

3 tablespoons unsalted butter

2 tablespoons lemon juice

2 tablespoons minced fresh parsley

Whole Roasted Snapper

Commercial snapper fishing first began in Pensacola in 1871. Crews of experienced New England fisherman wished to avoid the treacherous winter storm months of the North Atlantic, so they made their way south to the Gulf of Mexico to fish the more temperate waters. Many of the men were seasoned sailors who brought their schooners to the area. Since these ships were built in the Northeast, they were equipped with holds called "well-smacks." These storage chambers were designed for cold-water catch, which were packed in ice cut from frozen lakes—a glimpse into the future for holding red snapper in the Gulf of Mexico's sub-tropical climate.

The trick to preparing whole fish is to begin with the right one. The best from the waters along the Florida Panhandle include red snapper, grouper, sheepshead, triple tail, and pompano, in the 2–3 pound range. Roasting is the ideal way to ensure tender, just-cooked meat at the bone with crispy skin on the surface.

Historic Pensacola

(SERVES 4)

1 (2- to 3-pound) head-on red snapper, scaled, gutted, and gills removed

3–4 tablespoons extra-virgin olive oil

Pinch of kosher salt

Dash of freshly ground black pepper

1 teaspoon minced garlic

2 sprigs fresh thyme

1 small red onion, thick sliced

6 ½-inch-thick lemon wheels

6 ¾-inch-thick slices Roma tomatoes

½ cup good-quality white wine

2–3 tablespoons Green Sauce (see recipe in chapter 5)

Preheat the oven to 350°F. Score the fish by making several shallow 3-inch cuts on each side, in the thickest part of the fillet. Place the oil, salt, pepper, and garlic in a mixing bowl and combine. Pour half into the baking dish along with thyme sprigs. Add the onions and lemon wheels. Place the fish onto the mixture. Rub in remaining oil mixture and arrange tomatoes around the fish. Drizzle with the wine. Roast for 30–40 minutes. Transfer onto a platter and arrange lemons, onions and tomatoes; pour over pan juices. Drizzle with green sauce and serve immediately.

Steamed Whole Snapper with Citrus and Herb Dipping Sauce

Pensacola was the home for early America's largest red snapper fleet from the 1880s to the 1930s. Besides being Northwest Florida's largest coastal port, ideal for the burgeoning snapper industry, Pensacola harbored two of the coastal region's largest snapper schooners. The city's port led the way in the processing and shipping of red snapper and, at one time in history, provided the majority of the world's supply. Most of the country's major cities had the fish shipped to them by railroad, either packed in tins or stored fresh in refrigerated cars.

Eventually red snapper would be discovered in other areas of the Gulf of Mexico. The gradual dwindling supply of snapper in Panhandle waters enabled the industry to become more widespread. Also contributing to the downturn in the area's snapper industry were the inability to forecast catastrophic weather, fishing restrictions resulting from strikes, and the frequent economic discontent of the fishermen. Nothing that good lasts forever. Now other states and their governing bodies would set their own specific rules and regulations.

Historic Pensa

During that golden era, red snapper was touted for its health benefits and heavily marketed as brain food. One of the simplest and most nutrient-packed preparations for any fish is to steam it whole. Here is my recipe for simple steamed red snapper with dipping sauce.

To make snapper

Rinse the fish under tap water and pat dry with paper towels. Score the fish by making several shallow 3-inch cuts on each side in the thickest part of the fillet. Place the oil, salt, pepper, and garlic in a mixing bowl and combine. Rub the fish inside and out with the mixture. Place the fish on a 9-inch pie pan, bending the fish slightly if it is too long.

Pour 1–3 cups of water into a wok or braising pot and elevate the pie pan with three small saucers. Bring the water to a boil over high heat, cover, and steam for about 25 minutes or until the white meat flakes from the bone.

To make citrus and herb dipping sauce

While the fish is steaming, stir together the dipping sauce ingredients in a small bowl. Set aside.

To serve

When the fish is ready, carefully remove the pan from the steamer and pour off any accumulated liquid. Transfer the fish to a platter, spoon some of the dipping sauce mixture over the fish, and serve the rest in bowls for dipping. Garnish with fresh dill sprigs and sliced lemon. Serve immediately.

(SERVES 4)

For the snapper

1 (3-pound) red snapper, scaled, gutted, gilled, and head on

3 tablespoons extra-virgin olive oil

Pinch of kosher salt

Freshly ground black pepper

1 teaspoon minced garlic

For the citrus and herb dipping sauce

⅓ cup fresh orange juice

2 tablespoons lime juice

4 tablespoons aged balsamic vinegar

4 tablespoons water

2 teaspoons wildflower honey

1 teaspoon grated peeled ginger

1 teaspoon minced garlic

½ teaspoon minced and seeded serrano chile

1 teaspoon chopped fresh chives

1 teaspoon chopped fresh dill

Dash of hot sauce (Tabasco brand or sriracha preferred)

For garnish

Sprigs of fresh dill

2 lemons for slicing

Red Snapper with Roasted-Peanut Slaw and Soy-Ginger Sauce

Silas Stern, co-owner of the historic Pensacola Warren Fish Company, is noted for saying, "For a long time, the fishing in Florida was done by farmers and settlers for home consumption, while the growth of the larger towns and fishing industries arose simply to supply the immediate neighborhoods." During the mid-nineteenth century this was true. That was until Pensacola pilot boats began to notice the vividly colored red snapper in abundance as they merely fished to pass the time. It soon became obvious to the locals that there was the potential to create a seafood industry based on red snapper as the food source.

As fishing expanded in Pensacola by the late nineteenth century, so did the cultural base of the polyglot crews, including Frenchman, Spaniards, Italians, Greeks, and others. It wasn't long before the increase in activity and interest made Pensacola the epicenter for the snapper industry. The Pensacola Fish Company opened in 1872, becoming the first company to handle and ship red snapper. During the 1880s to 1930s, Pensacola, Florida, and its port were recognized around the country as the "Snapper Capital of the World."

Those European fishing crews from long ago brought with them influences on how local seafood was to be cooked that are still prevalent throughout the Gulf Coast region today. The same can be said about the Asian cooking influences brought to these parts shortly thereafter. This red snapper recipe is prepared with fresh-dressed peanut slaw along with soy and ginger.

Historic Pensacola

To make the roasted-peanut slaw

Place a dry sauté pan over medium heat and add the sesame seeds. Shake pan and let seeds toast for 1 minute. Set aside to reserve. Place green onions, cilantro, olive oil, sesame oil, vinegar, and pickled ginger in a mixing bowl and blend well. Add Napa cabbage, bok choy, and red pepper. Use two forks to toss the cabbage in the oil and vinegar mixture to coat evenly. Add the toasted sesame seeds and peanuts. Taste, and adjust seasoning with salt and pepper.

To make the soy-ginger sauce

Place the cornstarch in a small mixing bowl; add sugar, soy sauce, sherry, ginger, shallots, garlic, cilantro, sesame oil, and olive oil. Whisk to combine and then pour into a small saucepan. Place over medium-high heat and bring to a boil, whisking occasionally. Turn off and whisk before using.

(SERVES 4)

For the roasted peanut slaw

½ **teaspoon white sesame seeds**

½ **teaspoon toasted black sesame seeds**

4 **tablespoons chopped green onions**

3 **tablespoons fresh cilantro leaves**

3 **tablespoons pure olive oil**

¼ **teaspoon sesame oil**

2 **tablespoons seasoned rice wine vinegar**

3 **tablespoons fine-sliced pickled ginger**

1 cup firmly packed, thin-sliced Napa cabbage leaves

1 cup firmly packed, thin-sliced bok choy

½ cup loosely packed, thin strips of red pepper

¼ cup coarsely chopped roasted peanuts

Pinch of kosher salt and freshly ground black pepper

For the soy-ginger sauce

1 teaspoon cornstarch

1 teaspoon brown sugar

⅔ cup light soy sauce

2 tablespoons dry sherry

1 tablespoon fresh grated ginger

2 tablespoons finely chopped shallots

1 teaspoon minced garlic

1 tablespoon finely chopped cilantro

¼ teaspoon sesame oil

¼ cup olive oil

For the red snapper

4 (6- to 8-ounce) fresh skinless red snapper fillets

4 tablespoons olive oil or vegetable oil, plus more for grilling

Pinch of kosher salt and freshly ground black pepper

For the garnish

1 teaspoon sriracha

To make the red snapper

Preheat grill to medium-high heat. Rub fish fillets with oil, salt, and pepper. Rub the grill grates with a kitchen towel dipped in oil. Gently place fish fillets onto grill over open fire for 3–4 minutes on each side.

To assemble

Place a tall pile of slaw onto each plate. Place grilled snapper fillet on top and spoon soy-ginger sauce over and around the fish. Dab sriracha onto plate and serve right away.

Red Snapper Throats with Ket-nam

From Pensacola to Destin, fishermen and locals alike know the value of locally caught snapper. It is the Gulf Coast's most cherished recreational and commercial catch. There is a far-reaching demand across North America for commercially caught red snapper, which is often shipped to Canada, New York, and Chicago, bringing in big money for suppliers.

Snapper throats on the other hand are a Florida Panhandle sensation! Local seafood markets and dockside fish cutters recognize the underlying demand for these tasty gems. "Throats, both snapper and grouper, are in such high demand with the locals that I need to keep a sign-up sheet," says Ray Borden, manager of Maria's Seafood in Pensacola. "A sort of snapper throat waiting list for alerting regulars when the throats are fresh and plentiful."

If you look for them, it is possible to find these jewels iced down on the fish market counter at both Maria's Seafood and Joe Patti's Seafood in Pensacola. However, if you do spot them among the other fish offerings, rest assured, they are just off the boat and will be succulent when prepared properly. Frying is my favorite way to prepare snapper throats. The meat is exceptionally moist and flavorful and separates easily from the bone once it's cooked.

This recipe includes my ket-nam dipping sauce, the perfect accompaniment with herbal notes of cilantro and just the right amount of kick.

Historic Pensacola

To make the ket-nam sauce

Place mayonnaise, chili sauce, Creole mustard, lemon juice, garlic, cilantro, and hot sauce in a mixing bowl and whisk together. Let sit in refrigerator 1 hour before using.

To make the snapper

Have your seafood market remove the snapper throats from the whole snapper. A 3- to 4-pound snapper is ideal for meaty throat. Each snapper has one throat that can be served whole or cut down and skillfully partially deboned or deboned completely (whereby a fish cutter leaves only the throat meat with fins attached).

Preheat the fryer to 350°F. Place flour, cornmeal, cracker meal, and seasoning in a mixing bowl and blend with a whisk. Place buttermilk and hot sauce in another mixing bowl and blend with a whisk. Place prepared throats into the seasoned buttermilk for a few minutes and then dredge in the flour mixture, shaking off excess. Deep-fry for 3–5 minutes or until golden brown.

Squeeze lemon over the crispy fried throats and garnish with fresh parsley if desired. Serve a dollop of ket-nam on the plate or as a dipping sauce and serve immediately.

(SERVES 4)

For the ket-nam sauce

1 cup mayonnaise

½ cup chili sauce

¼ cup Creole mustard

1 tablespoon lemon juice

1 tablespoon minced garlic

3–4 tablespoons chopped cilantro leaves

For the snapper throats

2 tablespoons hot sauce (Ed's Red XX brand preferred)

4 (6- to 8-ounce) snapper throats, fins intact

½ cup rice flour or all-purpose flour

½ cup yellow cornmeal

½ cup cracker meal

2 teaspoons seafood seasoning (Old Bay Seasoning preferred)

3 cups buttermilk

¼ cup hot sauce (Louisiana brand preferred)

Peanut oil or vegetable oil for frying

Lemon (optional)

Fresh parsley sprigs

Red Snapper with Heirloom Tomatoes & Sweet Corn Sauce

Harbor Docks Seafood Market, owned by Charles Morgan, is one of Destin's longtime by-the-book seafood suppliers. In addition to owning its own boats, Harbor Docks contracts with over 100 commercial fishing vessels who supply a host of locally owned independent restaurants looking for Gulf-caught fish. For every fish reeled in, Harbor Docks Seafood Market complies with all regulations and cooperates with several agencies that monitor the sustainability of domestic fisheries.

Just a rod cast away, their Harbor Docks Restaurant prides itself for being the quintessential catch-to-kitchen experience, and is one of my favorite Destin spots.

There are eleven or so varieties of snapper often gracing the fillet station at the seafood market. Charles Morgan will tell it like it is when it comes to fresh line-caught Gulf snapper, grouper, triggerfish, tuna, amberjack, and cobia. "If you're coming to our area and want to find fresh seafood, go to independently owned restaurants where people give a damn!" Enough said.

Also, if you're in our area during the summer time, there's nothing quite like Florida sweet corn and tomatoes. Here is one of my simple recipes for a regional preparation of red snapper with those two summer sensations.

Historic Pensacola

To make the corn sauce

Shuck, rinse, and cut the ends of the ears flat. Stand upright and use a sharp knife to remove the kernels and scrape the milk from the cob. Reserve the shaved corn. Save corncobs for stock or discard. Place a medium sauté pan over medium-high heat. Add butter, shallots, corn, and peppers and sauté the mixture for 3 minutes. Add cream and bring to a boil. Lower heat and simmer for 10–12 minutes or until thickened, whisking occasionally. Adjust seasoning with salt and pepper to your liking. Set aside until assembling.

To prepare the red snapper

Preheat grill to medium-high heat. Snapper must be very fresh for easy handling on a grill. Rub the fish fillets with oil, salt, and pepper. Rub the grill grates with a kitchen towel dipped in oil. Gently place fish fillets onto grill over open fire for about 3–4 minutes on each side.

Core and slice the tomatoes into ¼-inch-thick slices. Shingle slices onto individual plates. Place grilled snapper over tomatoes with part of the tomatoes slices remaining exposed, alternating by colors for presentation purposes. Spoon corn sauce and sprinkle with fresh chives.

(SERVES 4)

For the corn sauce

3 ears of corn

8 tablespoons (1 stick) unsalted butter

2 tablespoons finely chopped shallots

3 tablespoons finely chopped sweet red peppers

1½ cups heavy cream

Granulated sugar to taste

Pinch of kosher salt

Dash of freshly ground black pepper

For the red snapper

4 (6- to 8-ounce) skinless red snapper fillets

3 tablespoons olive oil

Pinch of kosher salt

Dash of freshly ground black pepper

Extra oil for the grill grates

1 pound assorted heirloom tomatoes

1 tablespoon finely chopped fresh chives

Butter-Basted Red Snapper with Pecan, Orange, and Shaved Fennel

Destin, Florida, is located approximately fifty miles east of Pensacola and was mostly uninhabited until the late 1840s when Captain Leonard Destin began to make it his home. The coastline, with its sugar-white sand and aqua-blue, emerald waters was almost a completely undeveloped territory along the Florida Panhandle. For decades Destin was inhabited by a few families who fished commercially to feed the families in their community. The eleven-mile-long, unspoiled strip of paradise ultimately adopted the founding name, Destin.

The East Pass, the waterway connecting the Choctawhatchee Bay to the Destin Harbor and the Gulf of Mexico, was built in 1926. This passage, reportedly dug by the founding families (including the Destins) using only shovels, was key for the development of the commercial fishing industry, giving way to easier access in and out of the Gulf of Mexico. Years later, the main artery for road travel, Highway 98, was paved and more modern industries like recreational charter boat fishing and tourism made their mark. By this time, the red snapper fishing legacy had already shifted to Destin from Pensacola, where the industry had begun years before.

This delicious salad is made with easy-to-grow fennel (easier than digging the East Pass), Florida oranges, and pecans. These ingredients are some of the staple foods that have been growing in some form since the days of Captain Leonard Destin. They are a perfect accompaniment for the butter-basted and delicate, white, flaky meat of red snapper, especially when using this unique, crispy cooking technique.

(SERVES 4)

For the salad

3 oranges (Florida naval or Valencia preferred)

¼ cup pecan halves

2 small or 1 large fennel bulb, core removed and shaved

¼ cup thinly sliced red onion

1 cup loosely packed mizuna greens, watercress, or arugula

For the dressing

½ teaspoon minced garlic

Pinch of grated zest and 2 tablespoons lemon juice

2 tablespoons white balsamic vinegar

To make the salad
Segment the oranges and reserve in their juice. Place the pecans on a baking pan and bake for 8–10 minutes or until nicely toasted. Set aside. In a large bowl add the fennel, onions, mizuna, orange segments, and pecans.

To make the dressing
Place garlic, lemon juice and zest, balsamic vinegar, parsley, and coriander in a mixing bowl. Whisk in the olive oil and season with salt and pepper.

To make the red snapper
Preheat oven to 350°F. Pat the fish dry with paper towels and season with salt and pepper on both sides. Pour the oil in a sauté or cast-iron pan over medium-high heat. When the pan is hot but not smoking, place fish in pan skin side down, gently pressing on it so it does not curl up. From this point turn down the heat to medium and do not touch the fish. The skin will become crisp and free itself from

the pan. Cook for 4 minutes on the skin side, then turn the fish over. Add butter and cook, tilting pan and spooning butter over fish, until butter is brown, and fillet meat has turned white throughout, about 2 minutes.

To assemble

Divide salad onto individual plates. Place red snapper fillet on top of salad and drizzle with butter sauce before serving. Spoon additional dressing around the plates.

2 tablespoons coarsely chopped parsley

¼ teaspoon ground coriander

⅛ cup extra-virgin olive oil

Pinch of kosher salt

Dash of freshly ground black pepper

For the red snapper

4 (6- to 8-ounce) skin-on scaled red snapper fillets

Pinch of kosher salt and freshly ground black pepper

4 tablespoons olive oil or vegetable oil

2 tablespoons butter

Red Snapper with Tarragon Crust & Provençal Sauce

David Krebs first began fishing in 1969 at the age of eleven. His fishing partner was the legendary Dewey Destin, descendant of Captain Leonard Destin, who settled in this region of the Florida Panhandle between 1845 and 1850. In the 1970s Krebs hauled seafood with his father from the Gulf Coast up into the Northeast and Canadian markets. He then worked with his father at Tripp's Seafood in Destin until opening Ariel Seafood on Mountain Drive in Destin in 1991.

Today he owns five commercial fishing boats and remains quite vocal on the issues of sustainable commercial red snapper fishing throughout the Gulf of Mexico. The "one giant leap for fisher-mankind" was taken with his signing onto the Gulf Wild tagging system. This collection of initiatives from the Gulf of Mexico Reef Fish Shareholders Alliance helped make snapper traceable, confirming their authenticity and point of origin. This system currently provides assurance to retailers, restaurants, and consumers around the country who want to be assured that the snapper they purchased is the real deal. It is no wonder that David Krebs is widely recognized as the "Red Snapper Guy."

Here is one of my favorite recipes from the early days at Les Saison's in Destin in honor of the man who continues to lobby for proper laws and regulations for red snapper fishing.

(SERVES 4)

15 slices of white bread

¼ cup coarsely chopped fresh tarragon leaves

1 teaspoon kosher salt

1 teaspoon freshly ground black pepper

2 cups buttermilk

4 (6- to 8-ounce) skinless red snapper fillets

1 tablespoon olive oil

1½ cups diced tomatoes

3 cloves finely chopped garlic

1 sprig fresh thyme, leaves removed, or ½ teaspoon dried leaf thyme

2 bay leaves

Pinch of sugar

1 tablespoon finely chopped parsley

Cut and remove crust from the white bread. Discard the crust and place bread in a food processor. Use pulse button to make fine bread crumb, add chopped tarragon, salt, and pepper. Place into a shallow dish.

Pour buttermilk into a small mixing bowl. Place each cut fillet in the buttermilk, and then place directly into the tarragon crumb. Only coat the removed skin side. Press the fresh tarragon bread crumbs firmly when breading.

Heat olive oil in a saucepan until almost smoking. Add diced tomatoes, garlic, thyme, bay leaves, and a pinch of sugar. Cover and simmer sauce over medium-low heat for 30 minutes. Remove and discard bay leaves. Stir in parsley.

Place a large ovenproof sauté pan over medium-high heat; when it is very hot, add the oil and swirl to coat the pan. Pat off any excess bread crumbs and then place the coated side of the fillets in the pan so the pieces are not touching. Cook until the fish is light brown on the bottom and moves easily in the pan. Turn the pieces over and immediately place the pan in the oven to finish cooking, 7–8 more minutes or until the bread crumbs have turned golden brown. Spoon sauce onto individual plates, place crusted snapper atop of sauce, and serve right away.

Red Snapper with Zucchini–Chorizo Caponata

I first fell in love with Mediterranean country cooking when American chefs made it popular in the mid-1980s. This style of cooking eventually swept through the Florida Panhandle. It inspired me to prepare our local produce and indigenous seafood following the tradition of regional dish styles published from the works of notable Mediterranean cooking experts Richard Onley, Elizabeth David, Paula Wolfert, and American cooking guru James Beard.

During this culinary renaissance, I discovered caponata, a Sicilian eggplant recipe originally passed down from the seventeenth century. It's an easy recipe that blends ripe vegetables and robust flavors. I like to make this wonderful Italian accompaniment using peppers, tomatoes, onions, and celery, combined with sweetened vinegar and capers. This blending of ingredients produces a sweet and sour sauce perfect for fresh local seafood. Over the years, I have applied these sun-drenched cooking ingredients to snapper, grouper, swordfish, and mahi-mahi.

In this non-traditional preparation for caponata, I swap out zucchini (or squash) for eggplant. I also add diced spicy pork chorizo (a nod to our Spanish roots) for depth of flavor and texture. (However, the pork can simply be left out for vegetarian eaters.) This is a perfect accompaniment to freshly sautéed or broiled red snapper. Your creation can be made a day in advance, put into the fridge, and then reheated when your fresh catch is ready to be served.

(SERVES 4)

For the caponata

2 tablespoons extra-virgin olive oil

½ cup small-diced chorizo sausage

½ cup lightly peeled and small-diced zucchini

To make the caponata

Place a large sauté pan over medium heat. When hot, add the olive oil and the chorizo. Lightly brown in the oil for 3–5 minutes, stir, and add zucchini, red peppers, onions, and raisins. Sauté for 2–3 minutes or until vegetables begin to soften. Add vinegar, salt, pepper, and sugar and simmer another 3 minutes. Add diced tomatoes and oregano. Simmer over medium-low heat until the flavors blend and the mixture thickens, stirring often, 10–12 minutes. Stir in capers just before serving.

To make the red snapper

In a medium-sized mixing bowl, combine flour, salt, and pepper. Pat the fish fillets dry with paper towels and season with salt and pepper on both sides. Place the fillets in the seasoned flour to coat both sides. Place a large ovenproof sauté pan over medium-high heat. When it is very hot, add the oil, and swirl to coat the pan. Pat the dusted fillets to remove the excess flour. Lay the cut sides of red snapper in the pan so the pieces are not touching and sauté until the fish is deep golden brown on the bottom and moves easily in the pan. Turn the pieces over and immediately place the pan in the oven to finish cooking, 7–8 more minutes.

Remove fish when done and pat dry with a paper towel. Place the fish on individual plates. Reheat the caponata, and spoon evenly over fillets. Sprinkle with chopped parsley and serve immediately.

¼ cup small-diced sweet red pepper

¼ cup small-diced yellow onion

3 tablespoons golden raisins

⅛ cup red wine vinegar

Pinch of kosher salt and freshly cracked black pepper

Pinch of sugar (optional)

1 cup peeled and small chopped tomatoes

½ teaspoon dried oregano leaves

1–2 teaspoons drained capers

For the red snapper

1 cup all-purpose flour

1 teaspoon kosher salt

1 teaspoon freshly ground black pepper

4 (6- to 8-ounce) skinless red snapper fillets

¼ cup olive oil or vegetable oil

For garnish

½ teaspoon chopped flat-leaf parsley

Chapter 5

Seafood from Fingers to Fathom

Lionfish Sashimi

The magnificent and voracious prehistoric-like lionfish is not just edible, but has been a delicacy throughout the Caribbean for decades and now along the Gulf Coast. Eighteen spines (thirteen dorsal spines, two pelvic spines, and three anal spines) of the lionfish are venomous and can deliver a painful sting, but are not deadly. Beneath their red-striped lion camoflage lies pearly-white, delicate, grouper-like meat. When cooked the fillets are a similar texture to Florida hogfish.

The species is non-native and has unfortunately become the largest serious threat facing our Gulf fisheries, feeding on the native invertebrates and juvenile populations of snapper, grouper, and triggerfish. Lionfish are found in massive numbers along the reef structures off the coast of Pensacola, and in smaller numbers west into Alabama, Mississippi, and Louisiana.

You can sometimes cast into them with a baited hook, but, for the most part, catching lionfish remains a spear-fishing-only proposition. Acquiring fresh lionfish requires divers to spear and gather them under near-perfect weather conditions. To ensure the future of our native species, sustainable removal efforts are needed to significantly reduce lionfish densities along the Florida Panhandle.

Should you get your hands on some sizable lionfish, make sure they are absolutely fresh. I recommend, at minimum, a whole lionfish weight of 1–1½ pounds to yield nice size fillets. Remember the fin rays can stick you, so fillet them with care.

So after reading all of that, you may be thinking, Why bother? Well, lionfish meat is excellent fried, spice-rubbed, and pan-seared whether used in ceviche, sushi, or, more specifically, my favorite—as sashimi. Here is my recipe for lionfish sashimi with a variety of Asian sauces. Sesame seaweed salad is an ideal accompaniment.

To make the sweet sriracha sauce

Place sriracha sauce and sugar in a small saucepan over low heat. Stir frequently until sugar dissolves, 8–10 minutes. Set aside

To make the red curry aioli

In a food processor, combine the egg yolk, red curry paste, and mustard and pulse to process. With the machine running, slowly drizzle in oil until all has been used. Aioli mixture should be thick and creamy. Add lime juice, taste, and adjust seasoning with salt and pepper to your liking.

To make the soy ginger syrup

In a medium saucepan, combine the soy sauce, orange juice, brown sugar, pickled ginger juice, and sesame oil. Bring to a boil slowly over medium heat, turn down the heat, and reduce the mixture by two-thirds or until it becomes syrupy, about 30 minutes. Let cool before using or make in advance and store in a covered container. It will keep for a long time.

To prepare the sashimi

If using whole fish, place the whole lionfish flat on a cutting surface. Avoid all the spines, hold the fish by the pectoral fin, and carefully slip the fillet knife behind the head to make the first downward cut. Turn the knife blade downward and run the knife flat along the fish's backbone, cutting all the way to the tail. Leaving the tail attached, flip the cut fillet over to lay it flat on the work surface. Make a notch down to the tail skin, slide the blade flat, and carefully jiggle the blade as you cut to separate the meat from the skin. Once the skin is removed, cut any small rib bones from the fillet. Rinse under cold water and pat dry with a paper towel.

To assemble

Place the fillets on a clean work surface and, with a sharp knife, cut as many slices (approximately ⅛-inch thick) as possible on a bias approximately. Arrange slices on a chilled platter or individual chilled plates. Drizzle or spoon on sauces, add a pinch of pickled ginger, and serve immediately.

(SERVES 4)

For the sweet sriracha sauce

¼ cup sriracha sauce

¾ cup granulated sugar

For the red curry aioli

1 egg yolk

½ teaspoon red curry paste

1 tablespoon Dijon mustard

¾ cup olive oil

1 tablespoon fresh lime juice

Pinch of kosher salt

Dash of freshly ground black pepper

For the soy ginger syrup

1 cup low sodium soy sauce

⅛ cup fresh orange juice

½ cup light brown sugar

2 tablespoons pickled ginger juice

¼ teaspoon sesame oil

For the sashimi

2 whole (1½- to 1¾-pound) lionfish or 4 (6- to 7-ounce) lionfish fillets, skinless

2 tablespoons sweet sriracha

2 tablespoons red curry aioli

2 tablespoons soy ginger syrup

Pinch of pickled ginger

Peel 'n' Eat Hoppers

North Florida "hoppers," produced by the high salinity waters of St. Joseph Bay, may just be the best peel 'n' eat shrimp in the world. These succulent shrimp migrate off the grass flats of the bay from the middle of March to early May. These firm shrimp are in the middle of the flavor spectrum and range from pink to golden brown in their pretty cooked colors.

Unlike most shrimp that have one distinct color, hoppers are chameleons of the sea, matching their color to the seabed below. In St. Joseph Bay they exhibit an almost translucent green hue, off the shores of Cape San Blas they have a golden brown color, and around the Florida Keys they flash a cooked pink look, hence the name "Key West Pinks." One common trait they all share, though, is the circular spot on their side.

Hoppers are incredibly delicious pink shrimp that have a crisp texture and bite, with a light, sweet ocean flavor. They are great for boiling; the fresher the shrimp, the better. So if you are fortunate enough to gaze out over St. Joseph Bay on a spring evening and see the sunset procession of shrimp boats heading out for the night, rest assured the hopper run is under way.

(SERVES 4–6)

1 onion, cut into chunks

1 celery stalk, cut into chunks

1 carrot, cut into chunks

6 peeled garlic cloves, crushed

1 lemon, cut in half and squeezed

1 tablespoon sea salt

4 bay leaves

4 quarts water

2 pounds raw medium-size Gulf Coast shrimp

Place onion, celery, carrot, garlic, juiced lemon halves, sea salt, bay leaves, and water into a 6-quart soup pot. Bring to a boil over high heat, reduce the heat, and simmer for 45 minutes to make a flavorful boiling broth. Add the shrimp and stir. As soon as the water returns to a simmer (just a few minutes), remove from the heat. The shrimp will have just begun to float and the shells will have turned pink. Strain, reserving the broth if desired, and let shrimp cool. Do not rinse the shrimp. Remove shells from the shrimp, leaving last tail segment and tail intact. Devein the shrimp with a paring knife if desired.

Barbecued Shrimp

Wood's Fisheries is located along the Port St. Joe canal where shrimpers bring in their catch. Owner Ed Woods and his family have been in business for 150 years. The fishery also buys boatloads of wild-caught shrimp, which it processes, cold stores, markets, and sells. Offerings include seasonal East Bay harvested wild white shrimp, wild brown shrimp or "brownies," sweet pink North Florida hoppers, royal reds, Gulf of Mexico rock shrimp, and US farm-raised shrimp. Ed supplies Gulf wild shrimp to coastal seafood markets Gulf wide and around the United States, and is the largest shrimp processor from Biloxi, Mississippi, to Jacksonville, Florida. Wood's Fisheries also processes both wild and Gulf County farm-raised shrimp.

One of my favorite shrimp preparations is barbecued shrimp, with wild shrimp with the shell and head still on. The New Orleans Gulf shrimp dish is enjoyed throughout the southeastern region of the country including the Florida Panhandle.

Here is my recipe for a silky, Worcestershire-spiked butter and garlicky shrimp dish. It's is a bit messy, so keep a wet napkin handy to wipe your hands. I serve it with white rice and French bread for sopping.

2 tablespoons olive oil

1½ pounds medium whole Florida shrimp, heads and shells intact

2 tablespoons minced garlic

½ cup heavy cream

½ teaspoon chopped fresh rosemary

⅓ cup Worcestershire

4 teaspoons freshly cracked black pepper

1 tablespoon Creole spices (your favorite brand)

2 bay leaves

1–2 tablespoons lemon juice

¼ cup water

2 sticks (8 ounces) unsalted butter, chilled and cut into chunks

Pinch of kosher salt

Dash of hot sauce (Ed's Red brand preferred)

4 tablespoons chopped green onion (whites and greens)

1 loaf French bread (such as Leidenheimer brand)

2 cups cooked white rice (follow instructions on label)

Place a large heavy-duty skillet over medium-high heat. Add oil, shell-on shrimp, and garlic and stir for 5 minutes. Remove shrimp with a slotted spoon and place on a holding dish. Add cream to the hot pan and reduce the heat to medium for 3–5 minutes to let sauce thicken.

Add the rosemary, Worcestershire, black pepper, Creole spices, bay leaves, lemon juice, and water. Whisk together and bring to a boil. Once the liquid is boiling, immediately reduce heat to moderate and begin to add the chunks of butter. Whisk until smooth and slightly thickened, using all the butter. Once sauce is made, return shrimp to the pan to warm in the sauce, 5–7 minutes over medium-low heat. Taste and adjust seasoning with salt, pepper, and hot sauce to your liking.

Remove shrimp from sauce (peel them at this point if you choose, but do not rinse them) and arrange in individual bowls. Pour sauce over the shrimp, top with green onions, and serve with crusty French bread and hot white rice.

Bay Scallops with Mushroom Cream Sauce & Bacon

In the not-too-distant past I could pick up my phone and place an order for Gulf of Mexico sweet calico scallops (*Argopecten gibbusa*) by the gallon from the Florida Big Bend region. Not anymore. Commercial calico scalloping in Florida became restricted when the state permanently restricted harvesting within three miles of the coast in order to preserve this priceless mollusk. With the restriction in place, commercial scalloping came to a halt and became a bycatch of shrimping.

There are only a few places left in Florida where bay scallops (*Argopecten irradians*), a relative to the Calico scallop, can be harvested—St. Joseph Bay along Port St. Joe on the Panhandle is the place. Seasonal recreation–only bay scalloping begins around late June and lasts through mid-to-late September. With a Florida saltwater fishing license, you can harvest bay scallops by hand with a dipping net or aboard a landing boat. (Look for good scalloping grounds along 30A near Indian Pass.) And of course follow the limits set in place to preserve these succulent bay scallops for future generations.

St. Joe Bay, in particular, is where the water is shallow, pure, and inviting. With little to no freshwater inflow, this is the perfect place for bay scallops to retreat from the interference caused by human civilization. There's nowhere more remote than just east of Mexico Beach to Florida's Big Bend.

If you can't get these sweet Calico scallops, don't worry—quality bay scallops from any coast will work for this recipe. This caramelized scallop preparation makes for an impressive first or main course for a small coastal dinner party.

Add bacon slices to a medium-size skillet over medium heat. Cook until crispy, 8–10 minutes. Let bacon drain and cool slightly, then chop small. Set aside on a paper towel–lined plate.

Preheat a grill to medium high. Brush bread slices lightly with olive oil, and then season with salt and pepper. Place on grill grates and make crosshatch marks on one side, 2–3 minutes. Set aside.

Place a large nonstick sauté pan over medium heat and add oil and butter. Pat the scallops dry with a paper towel and lightly season with salt and pepper. Add half the scallops to the hot pan, spreading them out with a ¼-inch space between them. Sauté for 2 minutes, shake pan, and cook 1–2 minutes longer.

Remove from pan with a slotted spoon and set aside on a dish. Wipe the pan dry with a paper towel and repeat for second half of scallops, leaving pan juices in the pan after cooking the second batch.

(SERVES 4)

8 strips smoked bacon

4 (1½-inch-thick) slices French bread cut on a bias

Olive oil for brushing

Pinch of kosher salt

Dash of freshly ground black pepper

2 tablespoons olive oil

1 tablespoon unsalted butter

3 cups bay scallops

¼ cup small chopped leeks, rinsed well

1 teaspoon minced garlic

2 cups sliced chanterelles or your favorite mushroom

½ cup dry sherry

2 cups heavy whipping cream

1 tablespoon finely chopped fresh chives

1 tablespoon finely chopped red bell pepper

Add leeks, garlic, mushrooms and sherry to the juices. Cook until the mushrooms are tender, about 3 minutes. Add cream and bring to a boil. Reduce heat and let simmer until thickened, 5–7 minutes. Taste, and adjust seasoning with salt and pepper.

Place one slice of grilled French bread in the center of each plate. Reheat scallops by dropping them back into the sauce for 2 minutes, just before serving. Spoon mushroom mixture and pan sauce over the French bread moments before serving. Divide scallops over top and around the mushroom mixture. Sprinkle chopped bacon, fresh chives, and diced peppers over top. Serve right away.

Soft-Shell Crab with Andouille & Sweet Corn Pan Sauce

Blue crabs are caught off the shoreline, local bridges, and in the brackish waters from the Florida Panhandle to Louisiana. Commercial crabbing is permitted year-round in Florida; crabs are caught in baited traps and sold throughout the country. Recreational crabbing is also allowed year-round with a limit of one gallon per person. People often use string baited with chicken necks to lure the crabs in for hand netting.

Soft shell crabs are molting crabs. A crab molts (sheds its old shell) twenty to twenty-five times during its lifetime. To peel away its hard shell, a crab swells its body with water to help crack and peel it (giving it the name "peeler"). Then the crab backs out of its old shell, and the soft, new shell begins to harden immediately.

During the sorting process, live, ready-to-molt crabs are identified by cracked carapaces. The crabs are plucked from among the hard-shell crabs and placed into a molting pond for live harvesting in twenty-four hours, and then sorted in their soft shell for sizing and shipping. If you get the chance to eat one of delicious crustaceans, they are best when found alive and must be cleaned first before eating.

Here is my recipe for a Deep South–inspired soft-shell crab preparation. These steps are done to remove the parts that are inedible or are bitter and will impart unwanted flavors.

To make the corn
Preheat the grill to medium high. Lightly rub corn with oil on the cob, place on grill grates, and char all over, rolling occasionally for 5–7 minutes.

Let cool for 5 minutes. Cut the ends of the ears flat. Stand upright and use a sharp knife to remove the kernels and scrape the milk from the cob. Shave corn off husks and reserve.

To make the pan sauce
Place a medium sauté pan over medium heat. Add butter and sausage and sauté for 2–3 minutes. Add corn kernels, shallots, red peppers, parsley, lemon, and wine and sauté another 5 minutes. Add cream and reduce heat to low. Stir and swirl in chilled butter to make a smooth sauce. Keep pan moving until all the butter has been used. Taste and season the pan sauce with salt and pepper to your liking.

To make the soft-shell crab
Add oil to a cast-iron skillet and preheat to 350°F. Prepare the soft shell crab by lifting the protective shell and removing the gills or fingerlike lungs. Use kitchen shears to cut away the eyes and mouth. Pierce the legs and claws with the tip of a sharp knife to prevent

(SERVES 4)

For the corn

2 tablespoons olive oil

2 ears of corn

For the pan sauce

1 tablespoon unsalted butter, plus 4 tablespoons chilled

½ cup small-diced andouille sausage

1 tablespoon finely minced shallots

2 tablespoons finely chopped red bell peppers

2 tablespoons finely chopped flat-leaf parsley

1 teaspoon fresh lemon juice

1–2 ounces chardonnay or white wine

2 tablespoons heavy whipping cream

Pinch of kosher salt

Dash of freshly ground black pepper

For the soft shell crab

3 cups vegetable oil for cast-iron-skillet frying

4 jumbo soft-shell crabs

2 eggs

1 cup milk

1 cup water

1 cup all-purpose flour

½ cup cornmeal

1 teaspoon granulated garlic

1 teaspoon granulated onion

Dash of cayenne

Pinch of kosher salt

Dash of freshly cracked black pepper

For garnish

Fresh parsley leaves, chopped

them from bursting in the hot oil when frying. Finally, you must pull away and remove the bottom tail flap, known as the apron.

Place the eggs in a medium mixing bowl and beat with a fork. Add the milk and water and beat to blend. In a separate bowl add the flour, cornmeal, granulated garlic, granulated onion, cayenne, salt, and pepper and use a fork to blend. Place the soft shell crab into milk wash to coat evenly, then into the flour mixture to coat evenly all over again. Tap off any excess flour before frying. Fry the soft shell crab about 4 minutes or until golden brown, and then drain onto a paper towel–lined dish.

Place crabs on individual plates, spoon over all the andouille and corn pan sauce and sprinkle with chopped parsley leaves.

CHEF'S TIP: A good quality, frozen soft-shell crab is acceptable from a reliable seafood market. Talk directly to the seafood market manager. I recommend not buying frozen soft-shell crabs from just anyone. They may not have been so fresh when they were put up, or could easily be imported crabs mistaken for domestic once they are removed from the box. Check for a freeze date, and make sure they are not older than six months before purchasing.

Chef Irv's Premium Crab Cakes with Tarragon Aioli & Cucumber and Corn Relish

Crabs are the sweetest shellfish in the sea. I have rarely tasted a crab dish I didn't love. Crab cakes are no exception, as they are a specialty from coast to coast. Chefs pride themselves on their own unique, signature preparations. I spent significant time in Ocean City, Maryland, where crab cakes are practically a religion, so I understand the purist approach to great crab cakes and the beauty in their simplicity. The chief ingredients for a Marylander are backfin blue crab, mayonnaise, dry mustard, Old Bay Seasoning, and bread crumbs. My crab cakes are engineered to my liking and are not authentic, Maryland-style crab cakes—they're better!

In the final stage of binding the crab mixture, I make sure to use just enough and not too many bread crumbs. I like to use seasoned, dry, Italian-style bread crumbs. After making the crab mixture, use your fingers to gently blend in the bread crumbs making sure not to break up the lumps of crab. To finish, the mixture must sit for a minimum of 1 hour in order to fully absorb the wet mix before you shape the crab mixture into patties.

I was once labeled the Crab Cake King by Robert Tolf, *Florida Trend* magazine's top food critic. In this multi-award winning crab cake recipe, the mayonnaise is replaced by eggs and cream, giving it a richer texture and leaving plenty of moisture to be gently absorbed into the dry bread crumbs. The crab cake toppings change with every season (or menu) and are countless, fun, and interesting. My customers keep coming back year after year to see what new accompaniment I've created.

For the aioli

¼ cup coarsely chopped fresh tarragon leaves

3 egg yolks

2 teaspoons fresh lemon juice

1 teaspoon finely chopped garlic

1 teaspoon finely chopped shallots

½ cup pure olive oil

¼ cup extra-virgin olive oil

1 dash hot sauce (Ed's Red brand preferred)

Pinch of kosher salt

Dash of freshly ground black pepper

For the relish

½ cup peeled and small-diced Kirby cucumber

½ cup shaved sweet corn (1 ear fresh sweet corn)

3 tablespoons small-chopped Vidalia onion

2 tablespoons small-chopped red bell pepper

1 teaspoon finely chopped parsley

2 tablespoons cider rice vinegar

4 tablespoons extra-virgin olive oil

Pinch of kosher salt and freshly ground black pepper

For the crab cakes

2 cups (1 pound) fresh or pasteurized backfin crab

4 tablespoons (2 ounces) unsalted butter, divided

4 tablespoons finely chopped red sweet pepper

To make the aioli
Place the chopped tarragon into the food processor along with egg yolks, lemon, garlic, and shallots and process for 30 seconds. Drizzle in measured oils one at a time in a slow and steady stream until creamy thick. Add hot sauce to your liking. Taste, and adjust seasoning with salt and pepper.

To make the relish
Combine all ingredients in a small mixing bowl.

To make the crab cakes
Preheat oven to 350°F. Remove any cartilage from the backfin crab, being careful not to break up lumps of crab. Heat sauté pan over medium heat and add 2 tablespoons butter. When butter begins to bubble, add the peppers and onions and sauté until tender, about 2 minutes. Place picked backfin crab in a medium-size mixing bowl, then add sautéed onions and peppers on top of the crab.

In a separate bowl, whisk egg, cream, and hot sauce to blend, then add Old Bay Seasoning, Coleman's dry mustard, pepper, and parsley. Use a whisk to blend well. Pour this mixture over the backfin crab, using your fingertips to blend the wet mixture lightly and evenly without breaking up the lumps of crab.

Scatter the bread crumbs over the mixture, again using your fingertips to blend and make a delicate crab mixture. Cover with plastic wrap and let mixture sit for 1 hour in the refrigerator before shaping into 8 1-inch-thick patties.

Heat oil in a large skillet or non-stick pan over medium heat. Place the chilled crab cakes carefully into the hot oil, being careful not to overcrowd. Add remaining butter and cook until the crab cakes are golden brown, about 3 minutes per side. Using an offset spatula, remove the cakes from the skillet and transfer to a baking pan to bake for 7–8 minutes. Drain on paper towel–lined dish. Place onto individual plates, dab with the aioli, spoon over the relish, top with crispy bacon, and serve.

CHEF'S TIP: Chef Irv's Premium Crab Cakes are available at Maria's Seafood in Pensacola or by email: Irv@ChefIrvMiller.com.

4 tablespoons finely chopped red onion

1 egg

¼ cup heavy whipping cream

1 tablespoon hot sauce (Ed's Red brand preferred)

1 tablespoon Old Bay Seasoning

2 tablespoons Coleman's dry mustard

Dash of freshly ground black pepper

1 tablespoon fine-chopped parsley

¾ cup seasoned Italian bread crumbs

3 tablespoons olive oil

6 slices bacon cooked crispy and chopped small (reserve for topping)

Pompano with Tasso Spice & Herb Butter

Florida pompanos, also known as jacks, are thought of by many along the Florida Panhandle as fish royalty. I can't say enough about this delicious and local fish; there just isn't any other that boasts the tantalizing and exotic flavor of pompano. In Florida waters, their season starts in October and runs through May. I use them when I can get my hands on them, which is not always so easy. So, if you spot them iced down at the seafood market retail counter, get as many as you can.

Gulf Coast commercial fishermen often buzz the flats with wide-open motors in order to locate pompanos before setting their nets. Pompano fishermen, in particular, are a wise, experienced, and dedicated lot. Their preferred technique of hauling in these silver, toothless, mackerel look-alikes is line fishing on foot. The thing to do is to spot schools of them in the emerald green waters, running and hugging the surf zone, shorelines, and sand bars, from fishing piers and bridges, and cast lines to catch them.

Being a flat fish, they can be prepared in numerous ways. One of my favorite ways is whole, either broiled or baked, in parchment paper. This is known as Pompano en Papillote, originally

created by Jules Alciatore at Antoine's Restaurant in New Orleans. But I believe that the following time-honored recipe, Pompano with Tasso Spice & Herb Butter, is the most beautiful and simple preparation for fresh pompano fillets, combining open-fire grilling and baking for both crispy skin and delicious moist meat.

To make the tasso spice
Place the spices in small mixing bowl and blend with a whisk or fork and set aside.

To make the herb butter
Place butter into a medium-size mixing bowl and add rest of ingredients. Use a heavy wooden spoon to blend mixture well. Cut a 10-inch-square sheet of baking paper, place butter on closest end, and roll into cylinders, twisting the ends snug in opposite directions. Refrigerate until firm, about 1 hour.

To make the pompano
Preheat oven to 350°F and grill to medium-high. Rub fish fillets with oil and about ½ teaspoon of tasso spice for each fillet. Rub the grill grates with a kitchen towel dipped in oil. Gently place seasoned fish fillets onto grill, skin side down, over open fire for 3–4 minutes, using a fish spatula to rotate once. Remove and place onto baking pan, skin side down, and bake for another 4 minutes or until pompano is white and tender.

Unwrap and discard baking paper around the herb butter, then cut 4 thick herb butter medallions. Place 1 slice over the cut side of each pompano fillet and allow it to partially melt before serving. Pompano skin will be crispy and delicious. Place onto platter or individual plates and serve immediately.

(SERVES 4)

For the tasso spice

1 teaspoon granulated garlic

1 teaspoon granulated onion

½ teaspoon sweet smoky paprika (La Chinata brand preferred)

½ teaspoon cayenne

1 teaspoon fresh ground black pepper

1 teaspoon kosher salt

For the herb butter

4 ounces (1 stick) unsalted butter, room temperature

2 teaspoons finely chopped fresh chives

2 teaspoons finely chopped parsley

2 teaspoons finely chopped fresh dill

1 teaspoon fresh thyme leaves removed from the stem

1 teaspoon lemon juice

1 teaspoon minced garlic

Pinch of kosher salt

Dash of freshly ground black pepper

For the pompano

4 (6- to 8-ounce) skin-on pompano fillets

3 tablespoons olive oil

2 teaspoons tasso spice (above recipe)

Extra oil for the grill grates

Fried Mullet with Dill Tartar Sauce & Hush Puppies

The mullet is one of Old Florida's most symbolic and adored fish species. Generally it is skinned, fried, and served with hush puppies, grits, and fresh lemon. Sound familiar? Occasionally, mullets are tossed, as when people gather to compete on the beach at the Flora-Bama Lounge & Package in Perdido Key, Florida. Each April, individuals throw a mullet (some as far as 150 feet) from a ten-foot circle across the state line into Alabama. This is the World Famous Annual Interstate Mullet Toss, a great excuse to throw a weekend-long party. Sounds like adoration to me.

Silver and black mullet are caught year-round along the shores, bays, and estuaries of the Gulf Coast in Alabama and throughout Florida and just off the coastline of the Panhandle. Native to our Gulf Coast waters are silver (or white) mullets, which are harvested mostly in the spring, and striped (or black) mullets, which are harvested in the fall. Mullets travel in schools and have a habit of jumping, which makes it easy for fishermen to spot them.

In the Pensacola area, we stick with a more familiar and simple Florida Panhandle recipe for fried mullet fillets, accompanied by my delicious dill tartar sauce. This can easily be served for lunch or dinner. It is essential to have the freshest mullet available.

(SERVES 4)

For the dill tartar sauce

1 cup mayonnaise (Duke's brand preferred)

¼ cup drained and fine-chopped bread and butter pickles

3 tablespoons fine-chopped yellow onion

1 tablespoon coarsely chopped fresh dill

1 tablespoon lemon juice

For the hush puppies

Oil for frying

2 cups yellow or white cornmeal

2 tablespoons all-purpose flour

1 teaspoon granulated sugar

2 teaspoons double-acting baking powder

To make the hush puppies

Preheat the oil to 365°F. In a large bowl, whisk together cornmeal, flour, sugar, baking powder and baking soda, salt, black pepper, and cayenne. Make a 3-inch well in the center of the dry ingredients.

In a second bowl, add onions, red peppers, jalapeño, egg, and buttermilk. Whisk together and add to center of dry ingredients. Whisk from the sides of the bowl to make a smooth batter. Batter should be stiff and easily fall from the scoop.

Use a 1-ounce scoop to portion batter and carefully release each hush puppy into the hot oil, one at a time. Fry for 3½ minutes or until hush puppies turn a deep golden brown and float. Place on paper towels to drain.

To make the mullet

Preheat the frying oil to 350°F. Place eggs, mustard, hot sauce, and water into a medium-size mixing bowl. Place flour, salt, and pepper in a shallow dish and blend with a fork or whisk. Place cornmeal and cracker meal in a separate shallow dish and blend with a fork or whisk.

1 teaspoon baking soda

¼ teaspoon kosher salt

Dash of freshly ground black pepper

Pinch of cayenne pepper

½ cup finely minced yellow onion

¼ cup finely diced red sweet pepper

1 teaspoon finely diced jalapeño, seeds removed

1 large egg

1 cup buttermilk

For the mullet

Oil for frying

3 eggs, lightly beaten

3 tablespoons Creole mustard

2 tablespoons hot sauce (Louisiana brand preferred)

2 tablespoons water

1 cup all-purpose flour

½ teaspoon kosher salt

Freshly ground black pepper

¾ cup cornmeal

¼ cup cracker meal

4 (6-ounce) skinless mullet fillets

1–2 lemons, cut into wedges

Dust each fillet with seasoned flour, then dip into egg mixture, then coat with the cornmeal mixture. Panfry or deep-fry for 3–4 minutes, or until golden brown. Drain on paper towels.

Arrange hush puppies and mullet on a platter or onto individual plates. Serve with tartar sauce and garnish with lemon wedges.

To make the dill tartar sauce
Place measured ingredients into a mixing bowl and combine. This sauce can be made up to a week in advance and chilled in the refrigerator.

Sheepshead with Green Sauce & Succotash

My formula for fresh seafood is simple: Maintain direct dialogue with your local seafood suppliers, who in turn support your fishermen, seek out the freshest Gulf Coast seafood, and buy from local sustainable fisheries. My good friend Ray Boyer, manager of Maria's Seafood in Pensacola, does just that. He works directly with local commercial fishermen and fisheries to be sure he has premium seafood. Whether it's fresh Apalachicola Bay oysters, Port St. Joe shrimp, Alligator Point wild clams, Destin deep-water yellowfin tuna, or Pensacola sheepshead, they are all bountiful treasures across the Florida Panhandle.

One of my favorite fish is sheepshead or bait stealer. Sheepshead, which is a rather curious name for a fish, can be found iced down on the retail counter during spawning season, between February and April. Another name for it is convict fish because of its jailhouse stripes. Ray Boyer claims, "Whoever coined the bizarre name for the species was damn smart." Boyer explains, "They are so delicious, the name has most likely saved the species, preventing them from being fished out. Another theory for the unusual given name is most likely from its sheep-like incisors."

Sheepshead are seasonal, fun, and easy to catch. They are plentiful just off water structures, jetties, and bridge pilings. The flaky white meat is delicate and sweet. Along the Florida Panhandle sheepshead is often branded as poor man's snapper; the monkfish of the not-so-deep.

Here's my recipe for pan-sautéed sheepshead with seasonal succotash and a green fresh-herb sauce to adorn.

(SERVES 4)

For the green sauce

1 teaspoon minced garlic

Juice and zest of 1 lemon

2 lightly packed cups flat parsley leaves

2 lightly packed cups fresh basil leaves

½ cup pure olive oil

¼ cup extra-virgin olive oil

Pinch of kosher salt

Dash of freshly ground black pepper

To make the green sauce

In a food processor add garlic, lemon juice and zest, parsley, and basil. With processor running, slowly add both olive oils in a slow steady stream. Taste, and adjust seasoning with salt and pepper.

To make the succotash

In a medium skillet, add butter and place over medium heat. Add the tasso and stir for 3 minutes. Add onions, celery, garlic, and peppers and cook, stirring frequently, for another 5 minutes or until onions become translucent. Add diced tomatoes, field peas, corn, and broth. Simmer for 40 minutes or until peas are tender. Taste, and adjust seasoning with salt and pepper.

To make the sheepshead

In a medium-size mixing bowl, combine flour, salt, and pepper. Set aside.

Preheat oven to 350°F. Pat the fish dry with paper towels and season with salt and pepper on both sides. Place the fillets in the seasoned flour to coat both sides. Place a large ovenproof sauté pan over medium-high heat. When it is very hot, add the oil and swirl to coat the pan. Pat the dusted fillets to remove the excess flour. Lay the fillets, cut side down, in the pan so the pieces are not touching. Sear until the fish is deep golden brown on the bottom and moves easily in the pan. Turn the pieces over and immediately place the pan in the oven to finish cooking, 7–8 more minutes. Remove pan from oven. Add butter to the pan and tilt the pan to baste with the bubbling butter.

Spoon herb sauce onto individual plates. Place cooked fillet onto sauce and spoon succotash directly over top of each fillet. Serve immediately.

For the succotash

2 tablespoons unsalted butter

1 cup small-chopped tasso or country ham

½ cup small chopped Vidalia onions

⅓ cup finely chopped celery

½ teaspoon minced garlic

⅓ cup small-chopped green bell peppers

⅓ cup small-chopped red sweet pepper

1 cup seeded and diced Creole or vine-ripe tomatoes

1 cup field peas (such as fresh pink-eyed or white acres)

2 cups (2–3 ears) shaved sweet white or yellow corn

1 cup vegetable or chicken broth

Pinch of kosher salt

Dash freshly ground black pepper

For the sheepshead

1 cup all-purpose flour

2 teaspoons kosher salt

1 teaspoon freshly ground black pepper

4 (6- to 8-ounce) skinless sheepshead fillets

Pinch of kosher salt and freshly ground black pepper

4 tablespoons olive oil or vegetable oil

2 tablespoons (¼ stick) unsalted butter for basting

Panhandle Redfish with Worcestershire-Spiked Butter Sauce

Redfish was made famous in the South and throughout the country during the mid-1980s by renowned Louisiana chef Paul Prudhomme. His recipe for blackened redfish quickly became a sensation in this region. Soon all of America discovered how to blacken fish in a cast-iron skillet. Chefs and foodies everywhere sought out redfish for their menus and soon enough consumption became so extreme that it was nearly fished-out.

Florida Panhandle native Jeff Dutrow, educational coordinator at the Apalachicola National Estuarine Research and Reserve, avid redfish fisherman, and longtime friend of mine explains, "Redfish are designed to hunt their favorite things, crabs and shrimp; two ingredients that may explain why they taste so good. Also called red drum and channel bass, redfish juveniles grow up in the shelter of tidal marsh creeks and rivers and move offshore after maturity. They are one of the most abundant and sought-after game fish across the entire Gulf Coast and represent a true success story of cooperative management after years of decline in population from over fishing. If the Gulf Coast chose an icon to wave on its flag, our spot-tailed redfish would fly well as a proud representative for the entire region."

For a magnificent taste with little hassle and no blackening, try this pan-sautéed redfish with creamy Worcestershire-spiked butter sauce.

(SERVES 4)

For the Worcesteshire-spiked butter sauce

1 lemon, juiced

¾ cup chardonnay

2 coarsely chopped shallots

1 bay leaf, broken

6 whole black peppercorns

¼ cup heavy whipping cream

3 tablespoons Worcestershire sauce

4 ounces (1 stick) unsalted butter, chilled and cut into eight pieces

Dash of hot sauce (Tabasco brand preferred)

Pinch of kosher salt

Dash of freshly ground black pepper

To make the Worcestershire-spiked butter sauce

Bring lemon, wine, shallots, bay leaf, and peppercorns to a boil in a small, heavy, nonreactive saucepan over medium-high heat. Cook until the mixture is reduced by half, then add whipping cream and return to a boil. Reduce heat and simmer until thickened, 3–5 minutes. Remove saucepan from heat, add Worcestershire sauce, and whisk in a few pieces of chilled butter, one at a time. Whisk constantly until the sauce is creamy thick. Return saucepan to burner and, over very low heat, add remaining pieces of butter, one at a time, whisking constantly. Add hot sauce and seasonings to your liking. Strain through a fine-mesh strainer and keep in a warm area.

To make the red fish

In a small mixing bowl combine egg, milk, and water and beat with a fork and set aside.

Sift the flour, parsley, paprika, garlic, thyme, oregano, cayenne, salt, and pepper through a hand sifter into another mixing bowl and also set aside.

Preheat oven to 300°F.

Pat the fish fillets dry with paper towels and place in the milk mixture, then into the seasoned flour to coat both sides. Place a large ovenproof skillet over medium-high heat. When it is very hot, add the oil and swirl to coat the pan. Lay the fillets, cut side down, in the pan so the pieces are not touching. Sear until the fish is a deep, golden brown on the bottom and moves easily in the pan. Turn the pieces over and immediately place the pan in the oven to finish cooking, 3–5 more minutes.

Remove fish when meat has turned white and flakes. Pat dry with a paper towel. Place the fillets onto individual plates and spoon the sauce and directly over each fish. Serve immediately.

For the red fish

1 egg

½ cup milk

½ cup water

1½ cups rice flour

3 tablespoons finely chopped flat-leaf parsley

3 tablespoons smoky sweet paprika (La Chinata brand preferred)

2 tablespoons granulated garlic

1 teaspoon dried thyme leaves

1 teaspoon dried oregano

1 teaspoon cayenne

1 teaspoon kosher salt

1 teaspoon freshly ground black pepper

4 (6- to 8-ounce) skinless red fish fillets

2 tablespoons olive oil or vegetable oil

Trout Amandine

Many restaurants ago, in a kitchen far, far away, I wondered when I was going to learn how to cook on the hot line of a kitchen like the other seasoned cooks. At age twenty-two, after having worked in seafood houses for a few years and watching kitchen crews hustle in preparation of their daily line setup, I knew that sooner or later my time would come. Then one night, the occasion arrived, just not in the way I expected it.

When a scheduled line cook was a no-show for his shift (a frequent industry happening), all eyes turned to me. Literally. I was next in line. Kate, the restaurant manager, smiled at me and said, "Looks like you're going to learn how to sauté tonight!"

My first task was to cook the mountain trout, one of the restaurant's biggest sellers. I cleared my throat, took a deep breath, and stepped up to the stove. With no experience, I began to learn how to cook whole trout to order for the restaurant. For that reason, trout will always have a special significance for me.

Speckled trout, my favorite, is found throughout the Panhandle waters, and is the prized variety of trout around these parts. Limited amounts of local silver sea trout (or white trout) are sometimes discovered at the end of a fishing line just off the 3-mile bridge in Pensacola and in brackish waters throughout the local waterways. Bone-in and head-on is one of my favorite ways to cook any trout. Here's one of the tastiest recipes with the easiest preparation that is referred by the local inhabitants from the eastern seaboard to the Gulf Coast.

Preheat oven to 350°F. Wash the cleaned trout well under cold running water. Pat fish dry inside the cavity and outside thoroughly with paper towels. Season each trout with salt and pepper inside the cavity.

In a shallow dish, combine the flour, cornmeal, cayenne, and a pinch each of salt and pepper. Blend with a fork. Dredge trout through cornmeal and flour mixture, coating the exterior of each fish thoroughly and evenly.

Place the oil in a heavy-duty skillet over medium heat. Add the trout and skillet-fry until crisp and golden brown on both sides, 5–7 minutes per side. For whole trout, place in oven for an additional 7–10 minutes. Drain on paper towel–lined plate.

Place butter in a small skillet over medium heat and let bubble. Do not burn. Add almonds and toss well, making sure they are covered in butter and lightly browned, about 2 minutes. Stir in lemon juice, parsley, and Worcestershire sauce.

Place trout onto a platter or individual plates skin-side up. Spoon almonds and sauce over fish and serve.

(SERVES 4)

4 (12- to 14-ounce) speckled trout, cleaned but left with head intact or 8 (6- to 8-ounce) skin-on fillets

Kosher salt

Freshly ground black Pepper

1 cup all-purpose flour

1½ cups yellow cornmeal

½ teaspoon cayenne

1–2 cups vegetable oil

8 tablespoons (1 stick) unsalted butter

1 cup sliced almonds

3 tablespoons lemon juice

2 tablespoons finely chopped parsley

1 teaspoon Worcestershire sauce

Triggerfish Gratin

Being employed as a chef from Seaside to Pensacola enabled me to discover native Florida Panhandle fish species from local "fish heads" (fish cutters and delivery guys reeking of fish in their tall, white, rubber boots), who regularly fished red snapper and grouper for a living. Checking in daily seafood orders at the restaurants' back doors often led to conversation, and I soon learned about triggerfish (gray triggerfish). In the early days, triggerfish was referred to as "trash fish," and was a bycatch of snapper fishing. Triggerfish was often left behind dockside for boatmates

who knew how to artfully cut through the sandpaper-like skin with their razor-sharp fillet knives.

Triggerfish are identified by their piranha-like front teeth and a deadly trigger fin system used to dissuade its predators. Most restaurants would never buy triggerfish due to its difficulty with handling. Because they were considered "trash fish," the fish were previously difficult to give away as whole fish, let alone sold or considered for their fillet meat (being too difficult to penetrate with a regular knife). That's not the case anymore. Triggerfish are a delicacy in these parts now. They merit plenty of money per pound over the retail counters and are served at restaurants along the Gulf Coast and around the country.

The clean white meat carries a uniquely sweet flavor and is considered some of the finest fish along the Florida and Alabama coast, whether grilled, baked, broiled, or panfried. Here is my grand prize–winning recipe from the Apalachicola Seafood Recipe Contest in 1990.

(SERVES 4)

For the roasted peppers

2 medium red sweet peppers

2 tablespoons extra-virgin olive oil

For the seasoned croutons

8 slices white bread, crust removed

⅛ cup olive oil

To make the roasted peppers

Preheat oven to 450°F. Rub peppers with olive oil and place the whole peppers in a baking dish. Bake for 30 minutes or until the skins are completely wrinkled and peppers are charred, turning them twice during roasting. Remove from the oven and immediately transfer to a large ziplock bag. Seal the bag and set aside for 30 minutes or until the peppers are cool enough to handle and the skins are blistered.

Remove the stems and split each pepper in half. Lay them flat on a cutting surface and scrape with a knife to remove skin and seeds.

Discard the stems, peels, and seeds and chop the peppers into ½-inch pieces.

To make the croutons

Turn oven down to 350°F. Using a serrated knife, cut the bread into 1-inch squares. Place bread, olive oil, garlic, oregano, and thyme into a medium-size mixing bowl and lightly season with salt and pepper. Transfer onto baking pan and spread out to fill the pan. Bake for 10 minutes, using a spatula to turn the croutons once. Bake for another 10 minutes, or until light brown and toasted.

To make the triggerfish

Remove stems from basil. Roll leaves tightly like tobacco and cut into thin threads. Set aside. Pour and divide heavy cream into individual gratin dishes. Place each fillet into the cream and surround with the peppers. Sprinkle with fresh basil threads.

Preheat oven to 375°F. Coarsely chop the croutons and scatter over the top of each fillet. Divide and scatter chopped green onions over each fillet. Bake for 8–10 minutes, until they turn golden brown, the cream thickens slightly, and fish is firm. Place onto individual plates and serve.

1 tablespoon minced garlic

½ teaspoon dried oregano

½ teaspoon dried leaf thyme

Pinch of kosher salt

Dash of freshly ground black pepper

For the triggerfish

8 large fresh basil leaves

1 cup heavy cream

4 (6- to 8-ounce) triggerfish fillets

Pinch of kosher salt

Dash of freshly ground black pepper

4 tablespoons coarsely chopped green onion (whites and greens)

Mahi-Mahi with Cumin & Coriander Rub

Anna and Joe Patti started selling fish from their front porch on Devillier's Street in Pensacola before opening Joe Patti's Seafood dockside on South B Street on the bay. In these parts, the Patti name is synonymous with fresh seafood, earning its claim to fame around the country for over seventy-five years. Fresh seafood—oysters, a wide variety of shrimp, other shellfish, mahi-mahi, amberjack, flounder, grouper, snapper, catfish, salmon, swordfish, tuna and scamp—arrives at Joe Patti's Seafood on a daily basis from both local waters and around the country. Those are just a few reasons why the retail counter at Joe Patti's Seafood is the longest in the Panhandle.

On any given day the legendary Frank Patti himself can be spotted calling out numbers, shoveling ice, grading and weighing fish and shrimp, and personally serving customers. How's that for service in the twenty-first century? Joe Patti's Seafood Market is easily identified by its iconic roadside, neon-lighted shrimp and red snapper signs sitting on top of one another. It is also hard to miss the enormous American flag that flies just outside the entrance on West Main Street.

Mahi-mahi, or dolphinfish, is caught just offshore in the Gulf of Mexico's open waters. One of the most brilliantly colored fish when caught, its fillet meat is highly sought after for purchase in the Panhandle. The meat is large-flaked, uniquely sweet, moist, and fantastic when grilled over briquettes or with wood chips. This recipe features a simple, delicious, spice rub and herb combination that adds a southwest flavor to the tender meat.

(SERVES 4)

For the spice rub

1 poblano pepper

1 tablespoon minced garlic

2 tablespoons chopped cilantro

1 teaspoon ground cumin

1 teaspoon ground coriander

1 tablespoon chili power

½ teaspoon kosher salt

To make the spice rub

Preheat the grill to medium. Place the poblano pepper on grill grates and turn every 5–7 minutes until skin is completely charred all over (about 20 minutes total). Place pepper directly into a ziplock bag, seal the bag, and set aside for 30 minutes or until the pepper is cool enough to handle. Remove the stem from pepper and split it in half. Lay it flat on a cutting surface and scrape with knife to remove skin and seeds. Discard the stems, charred skin, and seeds.

Place the garlic, cilantro, cumin, coriander, chili powder, roasted pepper, salt, pepper, and olive oil in a food processor to make a paste.

To make the Mahi-mahi

Coat mahi-mahi completely with spice rub.

Start a charcoal fire or preheat the grill to medium-high heat. Rub the grill grates with a kitchen towel dipped in oil. Gently place the spice-rubbed mahi-mahi onto grill over open fire for 7–8 minutes on each side, depending on the thickness of the mahi-mahi fillet. Mahi-mahi is a tender and large-flaked meat, and will turn white when cooked.

Place grilled mahi-mahi onto a platter or individual plates. Serve with fresh lemon wedges, your favorite homemade salsa, fresh cilantro leaves, and a drizzle of extra-virgin olive oil.

Dash of freshly ground black pepper

4 tablespoons extra-virgin olive oil

For the Mahi-mahi

4 (6- to 8-ounce) skinless fillet sections

Extra oil for the grill grates

For the garnish

2 lemons cut into wedges

Extra-virgin olive oil for drizzle

Whole cilantro leaves removed from stem

Salsa

Grouper Cheeks with Lime–Dijon Mustard Sauce

Grouper cheeks are equally as famous to local "sea foodies" as snapper throats and mullet roe (and a favorite indulgence of many). Within the large head of the grouper you'll find the prized cheek meat, which has become a delicacy from coast to coast. It's a special day when someone shares a bag of fresh grouper cheeks. The best come from gag, black, snowy, and yellow-edge groupers that are less than ten pounds, providing quarter- to half-dollar-size cheek meat.

There are only two cheeks per fish (makes sense). The fishmongers will cut cheeks as they process fresh grouper for wholesale and often bag them for retail. They hand-select the perfect size grouper for cutting cheeks and often freeze them as they go in order to accumulate a significant quantity for restaurants. Most likely you will not see grouper cheeks iced-down on the fish retail counter on a regular basis. They get scooped up by the fish cutters, employees, locals in the know, and chefs on the hunt. I know this because I check regularly. One other thing: Be aware that frozen grouper cheeks adopt a chewy texture if overcooked, similar to large scallops. Fresh is best, but frozen is a viable option.

Pan-searing or my favorite, skillet-frying, are ideal ways to cook tender, fresh-cut cheeks. But it's hard to beat quick-fried grouper cheeks, especially with a simple and zesty mustard sauce to accompany it.

(SERVES 4–6)

For the mustard sauce

3 tablespoons Dijon mustard

1 tablespoon minced shallots

1 teaspoon minced garlic

1 tablespoon finely chopped parsley

1 tablespoon lime juice

¼ cup olive oil

½ cup sour cream

½ teaspoon ground coriander

Dash of hot sauce (Ed's Red XX brand preferred)

Pinch of kosher salt

Dash of freshly ground black pepper

To make the mustard sauce

Place the mustard, shallots, garlic, parsley, and lime juice in a food processor. Pulse to process. Keeping the processor running, drizzle in the olive oil in a slow, steady stream until all is used up and the mayonnaise is creamy thick. Transfer the mayonnaise to a small bowl, stir in sour cream and coriander, and add hot sauce, salt, and pepper to your liking. Cover and refrigerate until ready to serve.

To make the cheeks

Pour buttermilk into a mixing bowl. In a separate mixing bowl, place flour, cornmeal, cracker meal, cayenne pepper, and salt and blend with a fork or whisk.

Heat frying oil to 360°F in a deep skillet.

Dunk grouper cheeks into the buttermilk, then dust them with the flour mixture. Let sit for 1 minute, then drop them into the hot oil a few at a time. Skillet or deep-fry the breaded cheeks for 2–3 minutes (depending on their size), or until golden brown.

Transfer fried cheeks to paper towel–lined plate to drain. Place onto individual plates for first course or main course and serve with the lime-Dijon mustard sauce.

For the cheeks

2 cups buttermilk

½ cup all-purpose flour

½ cup yellow cornmeal

½ cup cracker meal

½ teaspoon ground cayenne pepper

1 teaspoon kosher salt

24 grouper cheeks

Oil, for frying (vegetable or peanut)

How to remove grouper cheeks

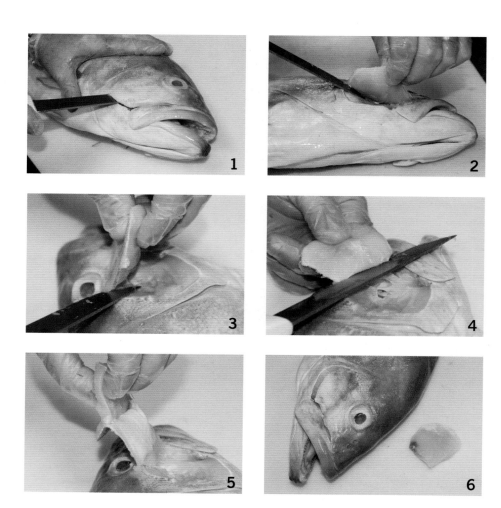

Mediterranean-Style Grouper

Grouper is one of Florida's most popular fish. Its season is during the warm-water months of April through October. Of the fifteen or so species, all are excellent for eating and most are easy to find, with the exception being Goliatho and Nassau, which are protected species. My favorite varieties are yellowedge, caught easily just off the coast; gag grouper; and scamp, the prized catch of the deep waters. A close cousin to groupers are golden tilefish, which are actually more of an East Coast favorite but are occasionally caught along this coast.

Fresh grouper is almost always available on the menus of local restaurants throughout the Redneck Riviera. But be careful when and where you buy grouper in chain restaurants along this region—you don't want to settle for frozen. In particular, I avoid frozen red grouper, as they lack luster and tender texture, and are watery when cooked.

In my kitchen the mild and subtle flavor of this championed fish lends itself to most any form of cooking, including baking, grilling, steaming, sautéing, deep-frying, or panfrying. A simple preparation for this fish is entirely acceptable, but for a dramatic alteration to the texture and flavor try crusting the fish instead. This is a fantastic way to cook white-meat fish such as grouper or snapper.

Here is one of my favorite Mediterranean-inspired recipes for this worldwide-celebrated fish.

Place all ingredients in a food processor and pulse until just blended and resembling tiny meal. Set aside.

To make the oven-roasted plum tomatoes
Preheat the oven to 325°F. Rinse and dry tomatoes. Slice them in half lengthwise and place them, cut side up, on baking pan. Spoon the olive oil over the tops of the tomatoes and brush or rub it evenly over them. Season with salt and pepper and bake for 2 hours.

(SERVES 2–4)

For the crust

1½ cups panko bread crumbs

3 ounces goat cheese, crumbled into pieces

3 tablespoons extra-virgin olive oil

For the oven-roasted plum
tomatoes

4 small plum tomatoes

**4 tablespoons extra-virgin olive
oil**

Pinch of kosher salt

**Dash of freshly ground black
pepper**

For the roasted red sweet
peppers

2 medium red sweet peppers

For the garlic confit

16 garlic cloves, peeled

¼ cup olive oil

For the vinaigrette

½ cup fresh basil leaves

⅛ cup lemon juice

¼ cup extra-virgin olive oil

Pinch of kosher salt

**Dash of freshly ground black
pepper**

For the grouper

**4 (6- to 8-ounce) skinless
grouper fillets, tiny fillet bones
cut away**

**6 tablespoons reserved garlic
oil**

Pinch of kosher salt

Freshly ground black pepper

Vegetable oil for grilling

For the finished dish

**3 tablespoons sliced pitted
niçoise or kalamata olives**

To make the roasted peppers

Preheat oven to 450°F. Place whole peppers in a baking dish and
bake for 30 minutes or until skins are completely wrinkled and
peppers are charred, turning them twice during roasting. Remove
from the oven and immediately transfer the roasted peppers to a large
ziplock bag. Seal the bag and set aside for 30 minutes or until the
peppers are cool enough to handle.

Remove stems from each pepper and split peppers in half. Lay them
flat on a cutting surface and scrape with knife to remove skin and
seeds. Discard the stems, peels, and seeds. Chop the peppers into
½-inch pieces.

To make the garlic confit

Place a small saucepan over medium heat and add the peeled garlic
and olive oil. Cook for 10 minutes, then reduce heat to low and
simmer for another 20 minutes. Garlic will become soft and still hold
its shape. Strain and reserve both the garlic and the oil separately.
Let cool completely.

To make the vinaigrette

Remove stems from basil, roll leaves tightly like tobacco and cut into
thin threads. Chop basil fine, and then place a separate bowl. Whisk
together with lemon juice and olive oil and then season with salt and
pepper.

To make the grouper

Preheat grill to medium high. Rub the fish fillets with garlic oil, salt,
and pepper. Rub the grill grates with a kitchen towel dipped in oil.
Gently place fish fillets onto grill over open fire for 3–4 minutes each
side. Remove fish from the grill and place, cut side up, in a baking
pan. Press crust evenly on top of the fish fillets, about ¼-inch thick.
Bake in oven for 6–8 minutes until grouper is moist and cooked and
crust is light brown.

To assemble

Reheat roasted tomato wedges, diced roasted peppers, sliced olives,
and garlic confit in the oven. Using a wide spatula, remove the
fish from the pan and place it onto individual plates. Arrange the
warm topping around and on the crusted grouper and drizzle with
vinaigrette.

Golden Fried Fish Backs

One of my local favorite seafood markets in Pensacola is Maria's Seafood Market. Their store is right on my way to work, so I stop frequently to talk to General Manager Ray Boyer and Manager Charlie Knodt about local seafood items and their whereabouts. One day while watching counter workers restock the usual varieties of shrimp, crab, fish, and shellfish, I observed fish cutters selling bags of "fish backbones." I asked Ray, "What do they use them for?" He smiled and explained, "I can't keep up with them! They fly out of here. Some locals can't always afford fresh fish fillets and low-income families like to snag these up for frying." In addition Ray claims, "They're a great value and have sweet meat on the bones."

To acquire backbones, a fish cutter fillets a fresh, small or medium white meat fish, and cuts off the remaining head, tail, fins, and belly with a heavy-duty cleaver, leaving a backbone with all its spiny bones attached, including the sweet meat in between. Charlie explains, "Local Asian cooks often steam or smoke backbones for fish cakes and dips." Chefs everywhere know that meat of any kind always has more intense flavor when it's cooked with the bone intact.

Here is a simple recipe for finger-licking-good fried snapper, grouper, or triggerfish backbones.

Place buttermilk into a mixing bowl. Place flour, cornmeal, cracker meal, and cayenne into a separate mixing bowl and blend with a fork or whisk. Place backbones into the buttermilk, then dust them with the flour mixture. Let sit for 1 minute before cooking.

Heat oil to 360°F in a deep skillet. Carefully drop floured backbones into the hot oil one at a time and cook for 3–4 minutes (depending on their size) or until golden brown. Drain well and transfer backbones to a paper towel–lined plate to drain. Taste and adjust seasoning with salt and pepper. Place onto platter or individual plates. Serve plain or with tartar sauce.

CHEF'S TIP: Be aware and very careful when eating these delicious backbone morsels. I like to lay them flat on a plate and use two forks—one to hold the fried backbone in place and the other to pull the cooked meat from in between the bones. The spiny bones are tiny and cannot be swallowed! I suggest carefully placing the meat in your mouth and biting down through all the meat to make sure there are no bones before swallowing.

(SERVES 4–6)

2 cups buttermilk

1 cup rice flour

1 cup yellow cornmeal

1 cup cracker meal

1 teaspoon cayenne

12 medium backbones (snapper, grouper, or triggerfish)

Pinch of kosher salt

Freshly ground black pepper

Oil for frying (vegetable or peanut)

Swordfish with Summer Salsa

Swordfish is perhaps one of the most underrated, delicious, and affordable long-line-caught fish species to frequent local seafood markets. In these parts, seafood mongers only handle young or small dressed swordfish. Large swordfish move offshore to deeper water off the continental shelf of the Atlantic down to Cuba (sometimes reaching 1,000 pounds) and do their foraging at depths exceeding 150 fathoms (900 feet).

The Gulf Coast grayish-blue and black-skinned swordfish yield firm white sides when cleaned, and can be cut into steaks or medallions. Their dense texture makes them perfect for grilling and allows for varying cooking temperatures, just like with a filet mignon. It's also perfectly suited for grilling with the skin on since the skin adds additional flavor and can easily be peeled off before eating.

I rarely recommend freezing any fish. However, I can comfortably say that freezing individual swordfish steaks works very well. If it is thawed properly in a refrigerator overnight, it's hard to tell the difference when cooked. I recommend serving juicy, grilled swordfish steaks with seasonal, refreshing, and easy-to-source ingredients in an exotic summer salsa.

(SERVES 4)

For the spice rub

1 teaspoon smoky paprika (La Chinata brand preferred)

1 teaspoon guajillo chile powder (or other hot chile powder)

¼ teaspoon cayenne pepper

1 teaspoon allspice

1 tablespoon ground cumin

1 tablespoon ground coriander

¾ teaspoon fine sea salt

6 tablespoons extra-virgin olive oil

For the salsa

1 tablespoon finely chopped red onion

1 cup cubed mango

1 cup cubed red seedless watermelon

2 tablespoons finely chopped cilantro

1 teaspoon finely chopped serrano peppers (add seeds for additional heat)

1 tablespoon extra-virgin olive oil

2 tablespoon lime juice

½ cup coarsely crumbled feta cheese

For the swordfish

8 (4-ounce) skin-on or skinless 1-inch-thick swordfish steaks

Vegetable oil as needed for grilling

To make the spice rub
Place all ingredients in a small mixing dish and use a fork or whisk to blend together. Set aside.

To make the salsa
Place onion, mango, watermelon, cilantro, peppers, olive oil, and lime juice into a mixing bowl. Stir to blend well. Add crumbled feta and stir. Set aside.

To make the swordfish
Preheat grill to medium high. Drizzle all the olive oil over the swordfish steaks and then massage the spice rub in. Rub the grill grates with a kitchen towel dipped in oil. Gently place fish steaks onto grill over open fire for 5–7 minutes per side.

Place grilled swordfish steaks onto a platter or onto individual plates. Spoon salsa over and serve.

Cobia with Deep South Spice Rub & Farm Slaw

Along the Gulf Coast the art of cobia fishing was passed down by the late Frank Helton, who is considered the father of cobia fishing. True cobia fishing is endeared by fishermen as one of the few boat methods in which they can still spot the fish from the boat tower, cast into them, and set the hook using a jig or live bait. Cobias often run in packs, and since the water has a brilliant emerald-green color, they're not usually too difficult to see, especially since they can be quite large. A record was set when a 100-pound-plus cobia was caught.

The best fishing in the world is found right here along our Gulf Coast. More than thirty years ago, local legend Charles Morgan of Harbor Docks Restaurant started the Cobia World Championships. The annual competition begins in March and ends in May, during which time the cobia migrate to our beautiful Emerald Coast from South Florida.

Cobias are powerful swimmers, rugged fighters, and one of the finest fresh wild-caught fish you will ever put in your mouth. If chefs aren't fishing and catching cobia for themselves, you'll catch them cooking it all season long. My favorite way to prepare cobia is to season and grill it over an open fire. A good spice rub and a hot grill are all you need. Here's a farmers' market–inspired slaw recipe to accompany the cobia steak medallions.

(SERVES 4)

For the spice rub

3 tablespoons olive oil

2 tablespoons fresh lemon juice

1 tablespoon freshly ground black pepper

1 tablespoon granulated garlic

1 teaspoon sea salt

1 teaspoon chili powder

1 teaspoon brown sugar

1 teaspoon cumin

½ teaspoon sweet smoked paprika

½ teaspoon cayenne pepper

For the farm slaw

Pinch of kosher salt

1 cup kale

1 cup julienned zucchini

2 cups shaved white cabbage

1 cup shaved red cabbage

1 medium carrot, grated

1 small green bell pepper, seeded and julienned

½ cup thin-sliced Vidalia onion

1 tablespoon granulated sugar

⅛ cup cider vinegar

⅛ cup extra-virgin olive oil

¼ teaspoon celery salt

1 teaspoon brown mustard seeds

Dash of freshly ground black pepper

For the cobia

8 (4-ounce) skinless cobia steak medallions

6 tablespoons spice rub

Oil for the grill grates

2 lemons, cut into 8 wedges

To make the spice rub
Place all ingredients into a shallow dish and blend with a fork. Set aside.

To make the farm slaw
Fill a 2-quart pot halfway with water and place over medium-high heat to boil. Add a generous pinch of salt. Add kale leaves and simmer for 2 minutes to blanch, then drain and cool. Cut kale crosswise into thin strips. In a medium-size mixing bowl combine kale, zucchini, cabbages, carrot, bell pepper, and onion. Place the sugar, vinegar, oil, celery salt, and mustard seeds in a separate mixing bowl and whisk together to blend. Pour over the vegetables and toss to coat the slaw evenly. Season with salt and pepper.

To make the cobia
Preheat grill to medium high. Rub each medallion with 1 teaspoon of spice rub. Rub the grill grates with a kitchen towel dipped in oil. Gently place medallions on grill over open fire for 3–4 minutes per side.

To assemble
Place slaw on a platter or divide among individual plates. Shingle 2 cobia steak medallions over the slaw on each plate. Serve with fresh lemon wedges.

Tuna with Spinach & Sesame Dressing

The first tuna caught (on record) off the Gulf Coast was in the early 1900s. The big prize in Southwest Florida waters in those days was the tarpon, often considered the "glittering silver king." But once sport anglers discovered hook-and-line tuna fishing with the advent of the star drag reel, attentions shifted to reeling in the mega fish. The area soon became the birthplace of big game fishing.

Yellowfin tuna is caught Gulf-wide from Florida to Louisiana, mainly during the summer months, but also the shoulder seasons. It is regularly brought up from South Florida and the Caribbean to help fill demand. Often marketed as ahi tuna (the name given to Hawaiian Big-Eye tuna), the closely related sushi-grade tuna has become a phenomenon throughout the country.

Yellowfin tuna became an excellent "food fish" from the Gulf of Mexico decades ago. It has long been sought after for its brilliant, deep-pink-to-red-color and fresh meaty flavor. One of my favorite ways to prepare tuna is simply to pan-sear and then slice it. Tokyo-born and trained sushi chef (and my friend) Yoshi Eddings from Harbor Docks Restaurant in Destin shared this recipe for simple sweet black sesame dressing with me years ago. It's great with this tuna.

To make the blanched spinach with sesame dressing
Finely grind sesame seeds in a grinding bowl (mortar and pestle). Transfer to a small mixing bowl and add sugar, soy sauce, and sesame oil if desired. Whisk to blend well. Steam or boil the spinach for 1 minute (until wilted) and then squeeze well to drain. Place drained spinach in a medium-size mixing bowl and toss with the dressing to coat well.

To make the tuna
Place a skillet over medium-high heat and coat with olive oil. Season the tuna generously with salt and pepper. Lay tuna in the hot oil and sear for 1 minute on all 4 sides to form a slight crust. Remove tuna from heat. Using a very sharp knife, slice the tuna ¼-inch thick until all has been sliced. In a small bowl whisk vinegar, soy sauce, cilantro, and olive oil to blend. Drizzle over the tuna and serve with the sliced avocado.

(SERVES 2)

For the blanched spinach with sesame dressing

4 tablespoons black sesame seeds

2 tablespoons granulated sugar

1 tablespoon soy sauce

¼ teaspoon sesame seed oil (optional)

3 cups tightly packed spinach

For the tuna

2 tablespoons olive oil

1 (12-ounce) block ahi tuna loin

Salt and black pepper to taste

1 tablespoon rice vinegar

1 tablespoon soy sauce

1 teaspoon chopped cilantro

3 tablespoons extra-virgin olive oil

1 ripe avocado, halved, peeled, pitted, and sliced

Chapter 6

Barbecue, Red Meat, and White Meat

Barbecuing and grilling are perhaps the world's most universal cooking methods. This basic form of heating food with fire originated early in human history, and barbecuing is the more modern adaptation for making the meat taste better. The most popular meats for barbecue include pork ribs and shoulder, beef brisket, chicken, whole pig, and game. Barbecue is characteristic of many things in the South (warmer weather comes to mind), and in the Florida Panhandle it is tied together by coastal geography. Town by town, from backyard to backyard, no two methods are exactly alike.

Almost every state in the country claims to have the best barbecue. Around these parts, cooks cherish it as a uniquely Southern thing and are more than happy to show off their techniques. In Pensacola, a prime example of this can be found by driving your car along 12th Avenue in East Hill. On the corner at City Grocery, on any given day, you will more than likely pass through a billowing cloud of smoky goodness pouring from their large barbecue smoker. How can any carnivore not stop to grab a bite? This is local barbecue done right.

To me, barbecued food binds the tastes of all socio-economic classes. Tell a group of your friends that you're having a barbecue and it's universally understood what is taking place. It appeals to almost everyone. It doesn't matter what the method is or whether you succeed. The only thing that does matter is that you do it. There is no science involved; it's just human nature.

I am somewhat amazed by the efforts people take to get their outdoor, low and slow, smoky cooking going, especially in the sizzling hot and humid days of summer. It's my view that many of us are too busy to take the time to properly fire up the outdoor smoker-barbeque to reach that dynamic ratio of red-hot coal to ash balance for optimum cooking. So as a result of this, I have adapted both indoor and outdoor cooking techniques to get great results for ribs and brisket.

Barbecuing is the opposite of grilling. Barbecuing is long and slow, with indirect low heat cooking from wood or coal. It is ideal for both small meat cuts with lots of connective tissue (ribs, brisket, and butts) and small whole pigs. Some of my favorite wood chips for barbecue smoking include oak, hickory, apple, pecan, cherry, laurel, and orange.

Grilling, a close relative of barbecuing, is done over high-heat on direct fire, and is ideal for quick-cooked individual classic cuts of meat such as filet mignon and chops. Marbled cuts (such as rib eye and New York strip) and flat cuts (such as flat iron, flank steak, and hanger steak) can be grilled sliced across the grain before serving. Fish fillets and fish steaks are good candidates for grilling as well. Great grilling can often be achieved on a well-seasoned gas grill. Another tasty and timely treatment is to add a bit of smoke to the grill by using soaked, smoldering wood chips.

Outdoor Barbecue Pork Ribs

For baby back (loin back) pork ribs or pork spare ribs, lay the ribs flat with the underside up. Use a kitchen towel to grab the corner of the very thin layer of fat that is on the underside and pull swiftly to remove. It should come off in one swipe. Getting rid of this fat barrier will allow better marinade absorption and more tender ribs. This process will also expedite absorption of the spice rub flavor.

Make or purchase your favorite spice rub. Salt, pepper, and granulated garlic and onion work well, as does a quality prepared dry spice brand. For thicker cuts, apply the spice rub liberally on both sides of the meat. Let meat marinate for a minimum of 3 hours. Prepare a barbecue grill to 225°F, using wood, coal, gas, or any combination thereof. Place marinated ribs on grill rack over indirect heat. Brush with a basting sauce: a lemon or vinegar mixture and any special flavoring of choice to add freshness. Let ribs cook over indirect heat for 1 hour. Turn and baste again. Cook for the second hour and baste again. Cook for the third hour and baste again. Ten minutes before serving, transfer meat to a cutting board and cut between the bones to make your portions. Coat liberally with more barbecue sauce and serve immediately.

Indoor Barbecue Pork Ribs

Through the years I have dabbled in basting, mopping, brining, and stovetop smoking to conjure up alternative indoor barbecue and smoking methods, ultimately adding flavor dimensions to cheeses, fish, chicken, pork, and beef.

For indoor and brisket cooking, preheat the oven to 300°F. Apply spice rub of your choice to the meat and let marinate for a minimum of 3 hours. Place the meat on a wire rack over a baking pan and apply a cooking liquid such as beer or water to the pan under the rack to catch all the flavored meat drippings.

Cover your meat tightly with foil, and cook slow at a low temperature for 3 hours. Throughout the cooking process, uncover and baste the meat 3–4 times with a lemon or vinegar mixture and special flavoring of your choice to add freshness. Always rewrap the meat to keep cooking.

Make your favorite barbeque sauce and have ready. Ribs will expose themselves by ¼–½ inch when the meat is completely tender. Let the ribs rest for 15 minutes in the sealed foil. Most people are shocked when I tell them that I did not use a barbeque grill to prepare them. Peel back or unfold the foil around the ribs. Turn oven off, and place ribs back in the oven for holding. Ten minutes before serving, transfer meat to a cutting board and coat with barbeque sauce and cut between the bones to make your portions. Coat between the bones liberally with more barbecue sauce and serve immediately.

CHEF'S NOTE: If you want to lightly char the ribs on the outdoor barbecue, keep them in the foil and place over indirect heat to avoid burning.

Adding Smoke Flavor

It's easy to infuse your basic outdoor grill with smoky goodness using a 15-minute smoker-setup. Here are a few tips: Soak your wood chips a minimum of 2 hours or overnight. Just before using, wrap them with tin foil with holes poked through it and place them into a smoking platform on your outdoor grill grates (or place a perforated smoker box directly onto the burner or ceramic briquettes) and crank up the grill. I often scatter the soaked chips directly onto the grill grate in a hot spot. Either way, in a few minutes you'll have some intense smoke.

To add smoky flavor, place the slow-cooked meat onto a foiled grill grate over indirect heat or leave ribs on a baking pan for easier handling. I like less mess to clean up so I form foil into a flat and shallow pouch to fit snugly around each rib, leaving the top exposed. The pouch makes for easier rib containment of the juices, and for easier and quick transferring between indirect heat and direct heat. The pouch formed this way leaves plenty of exposed surface area for the smoke to penetrate. Do not place the wrapped meat over direct fire! Slather the meat with barbecue sauce 10 minutes before serving.

North Florida Mustard Sauce

Seasonal Florida: A Taste of Life in North Florida, self-published in 1994 by Jo McDonald Manning, is a one-of-a-kind family cookbook from our neck of the woods. Manning compiled family-shared and regional-inspired stories and recipes and sold more than 10,000 copies from the trunk of her car. Her family has been located in Walton County, Florida, for five generations. Manning grew up with eight brothers and sisters in historic DeFuniak Springs, Florida. "Like most folks in my community, my family kept milk, cows, chickens, pigs, and horses, and we had our own vegetable garden," she recalls. "Family gatherings were large events, and cooking often brought the family together."

Manning further explains, "The first serious cooking in North Florida has been attributed to the Indians who populated the state prior to the 1500s. These Indians perfected the art of barbecuing and grilled their game and seafood over hot coals."

I am delighted to share several of Manning's recipes and pay tribute to her effort in sharing the food customs of the Florida Panhandle. Her recipe for Mustard Sauce, which I have updated and adapted to my taste buds, is a soulful and simple sauce for ham, chicken, and pork ribs of any kind.

Melt butter in a heavy-duty saucepan over medium-low heat. Add remaining ingredients, reduce heat, and simmer for 10 minutes. Refrigerate until ready to use.

(MAKES ABOUT 3 CUPS)

2 sticks (8-ounces) unsalted butter

2 lemons, sliced thin

12 ounces yellow or Dijon mustard

1 cup apple cider vinegar

1 tablespoon freshly ground black pepper

Pinch of kosher salt

Dash of cayenne

6 tablespoons granulated sugar

Florida Dry Rub

This recipe is adapted from Manning, who maintains that "pork is the preferred barbeque meat in the South and ribs are my favorite cut. There are three types of pork ribs: spare ribs, back ribs, and country-style. All are good barbequed."

"Every serious barbeque chef has their favorite rub, marinade, and sauce," Manning explains. "Dry rubs . . . this is simply a mixture of spices rubbed into the meat prior to cooking. Dry rubs are easy to make and add flavor to food without altering texture. We use them on fish and seafood as well as some pork and poultry."

(MAKES 1½ CUPS)

½ cup brown sugar

¼ cup table-ground black pepper

¼ cup smoked paprika (La Chinata brand preferred)

2 teaspoons grated orange zest

¼ cup chili powder

⅛ cup dry mustard (Coleman's brand preferred)

2 teaspoons kosher salt

½ teaspoon cayenne

Mix ingredients together and rub on meat 1 hour prior to cooking.

Florida Sweet Rib Sauce

Manning says it best: "Every serious barbeque chef has his or her own original sauce. The ingredients can vary and can include just about everything in the kitchen, except the sink, which can be used to mix it. Serious chefs are always looking for new ingredients to make their sauce unique. Most include some type of pepper for hotness and other ingredients from beer to cough syrup. These sauces are typically based with tomato, mustard, or vinegar, and other secret ingredients are added for unique flavors."

I'm excited to share Manning's no frills North Florida–style barbecue sauce, albeit adapted to fit my own taste buds, using the exact same ingredients provided in her book. I'm particularly fond of this formula because of its sweet regional honey, dry mustard bite, easy-to-find ingredients, and simplicity of preparation.

Heat oil in a heavy-duty saucepan over medium-low heat and add onion and garlic. Stir and sauté until softened, about 5 minutes. Add remaining ingredients, bring to a boil, reduce heat, and simmer for 5 minutes. Use directly or transfer to a tightly sealed container and store in the refrigerator for up to 2 weeks.

(MAKES ABOUT 5 CUPS)

¼ cup olive or vegetable oil

¾ cup chopped onion

2 teaspoons minced garlic

¾ cup tupelo honey (or artisan honey)

1 cup ketchup (Heinz brand preferred)

¾ cup red wine vinegar

¼ cup Worcestershire (L&P brand preferred)

2 tablespoons dry mustard (Coleman's brand preferred)

2 teaspoons kosher salt

½ teaspoon dried oregano leaves

½ teaspoon dried thyme leaves

1 teaspoon freshly ground black pepper

1 tablespoon lemon juice

Korean Barbecue Sauce

Fish and shellfish are as important to the coastal areas of Korea as they are to the coast of the Florida Panhandle. On the other hand, pork is a staple food utilized by the Korean people in a much different and more thorough manner. In Korean cuisine, all parts of the pig are used, including the head, intestines, liver, kidney, and other internal organs, which are either steamed, stewed, smoked, or used in sauce making.

One of Korea's main fermented spice blends is a condiment called gochujang. It's a moist hot pepper paste used in almost everything and found in most Korean markets. I use it here in my version of Korean barbecue sauce—a spicy, sweet sauce great for slathering on (or dipping) pork, chicken, or beef.

(MAKES ABOUT 2 CUPS)

1 teaspoon toasted sesame oil

1 teaspoon vegetable oil

½ cup coarsely chopped green onion

1 tablespoon minced garlic

⅓ cup gochujang

⅛ cup packed light brown sugar

3 tablespoons low-sodium soy sauce

3 tablespoons unseasoned rice vinegar

1 cup water

Heat sesame and vegetable oils over medium-high heat in a heavy-bottomed medium saucepan. Add the green onions and garlic, and cook until soft, about 5 minutes. Whisk in gochujang, brown sugar, soy sauce, vinegar, and water and cook over low heat until smooth and slightly thickened, about 30 minutes. Apply the barbeque sauce over ribs 10 minutes before serving. This sauce can be used directly or transferred to a tightly sealed container and stored in a refrigerator for up to 2 weeks.

Smoky Barbecue Sauce

I developed this recipe as an alternative to concentrate and distilled liquid smoke as a way to infuse smoky goodness into sweet barbecue sauce. This is my way of keeping quality without taking shortcuts when crunched for time. For this recipe, I recommend using rich in-smoke bacon from Benton's Country Ham or a small piece of smoked pork belly or jowl that can be chopped up large and easily removed before using. Sometimes there's just not enough time in every day.

Place a medium sauce pot over medium heat. Add bacon (chop if you like or use whole smoked bacon slices if you prefer to remove them later). Sauté for 5–7 minutes, stirring bacon to evenly cook without browning. Add the Sweet Florida Rib sauce, chipotle puree, molasses, soy sauce, paprika, and water, and simmer for 30–40 minutes. This sauce can be used directly or transferred to a tightly sealed container and stored in a refrigerator for up to 2 weeks.

(MAKES ABOUT 2 CUPS)

6 slices smoked bacon or chunked smoked pork belly or jowl

2 cups Sweet Florida Rib sauce (see recipe in this chapter)

1 teaspoon chipotle puree (from chipotle in adobo)

2 tablespoons molasses

2 tablespoons soy sauce

1 teaspoon smoked paprika (La Chinata brand preferred)

¼ cup water

Panhandle Peanut Barbecue Sauce

What makes slow-cooked pork taste so good? The answer is spice rubs, basting sauces, and signature barbecue sauces. Here's my unique recipe for traditional Thai-style peanut sauce, transformed into a spicy southern-inspired and non-traditional barbecue sauce to slather on pork ribs and chicken. Dry roasted peanuts add a crunchy texture to the sauce when added last.

(MAKES ABOUT 5 CUPS)

For the sauce

3 tablespoons peanut or vegetable oil

1 cup coarsely chopped yellow onion

4 tablespoons minced garlic

1 cup smooth peanut butter

4 tablespoons soy sauce

2 tablespoons water

1 cup hoisin sauce

¼ cup ketchup (Heinz brand preferred)

½ cup dark brown sugar

1 teaspoon sesame oil

3 tablespoons fresh grated ginger

1 fresh hot pepper, Thai chile or serrano (add seeds for extra heat), chopped

3 tablespoons fish sauce

¼ cup fresh lime juice

¼ cup chopped cilantro

Pinch of kosher salt and freshly ground black pepper

1 cup chopped dry roasted peanuts

2 tablespoons artisan honey

Heat the oil over medium-high heat in a heavy-bottomed medium saucepan. Add the onions and garlic and cook until soft, about 5 minutes. Use a whisk and blend in half of the peanut butter until smooth. Add the soy sauce and water and blend in remaining peanut butter until smooth. Add hoisin, ketchup, sugar, sesame oil, ginger, hot pepper, fish sauce, lime juice, and cilantro and blend until smooth. Lightly season with salt and pepper and whisk over low heat until thickened, about 30 minutes. Add peanuts and drizzle in honey. Apply the barbecue sauce over the ribs 10 minutes before serving. This sauce can be used directly or transferred to a tightly sealed container and stored in a refrigerator for up to 2 weeks.

Smoked Mullet Dip

Florida is synonymous with seafood, and smoked mullet is noted as a cultural marker for the Florida Panhandle. American journalist and fellow southerner John Egerton, whom I had the pleasure of knowing, ate his way through Florida in the 1980s and wrote of his affection for this coastal fish in his book *Southern Food: At Home, on the Road, in History.*

Mullets have also served as an important source of food in Mediterranean Europe since Roman times. Today it is mullet roe that is prized around the world. In Spain, a regional preparation process known as bottarga (cured and dried mullet roe) is often referred to as "Mediterranean caviar" by aficionados. Mullet roe is a regional delicacy here in Florida, too. In Cortez, Florida, along the central Gulf, Seth Cripe, owner and founder of Anna Maria Fish Company, uses a similar process for salting, pressing, and drying the golden roe of striped grey mullets, which are hand-harvested locally by sustainable fisherman. The roe is perfect for shaving with a micro plane over pasta or grits, or smoked or sautéed with eggs for breakfast.

In West Pensacola, Florida native Roger Cleckler prepares pecan-wood-smoked mullet and his version of a Panhandle bottarga. Roger uses locally caught black mullet for smoking year-round and in the spring and fall he smokes the roe. The freshly netted mullet are caught when they are running. For smoking, Roger dresses them and then adds his personal seasoning recipe. When they are finished, the smoked mullet are sold roadside for their smoky-flavored fillet meat and roe at Welding Shop BBQ on Gulf Beach Highway. The smoked fillet meat works perfectly for this recipe.

As fisherman and good cooks know, the best way to use fish in abundance is in dips, spreads, and patties. There are as many recipes for smoked-fish dips as there are fish. Whichever coast is nearest to you, other fish suitable for smoking are mackerel, marlin, amberjack, sailfish, haddock, trout, and a number of other saltwater species. When smoked properly, the meat is smoky-rich, mild, and so tender that it falls right off the bone.

If you're ambitious, here's my recipe using a standard outdoor gas grill with an easy one-hour smoking technique, producing a mouth-watering smoked mullet for dip. It's ideal as a first-course for any coastal gathering.

For the brining

3–4 pounds fresh mullet

1 gallon cold water

⅓ cup salt

1 cup brown sugar

1 tablespoon whole black peppercorns

4 bay leaves, crushed

2 garlic cloves, smashed

For grill smoking

1–2 cups wood chips covered with water

4 tablespoons vegetable oil for the grill grates

4 tablespoons olive oil for brushing grill and fish skin

For the dip

1½ cups fresh flaked smoked mullet

1 cup bacon cream cheese

¾ cups mayonnaise (such as Duke's brand)

4 tablespoons chopped green onions

1 teaspoon minced garlic

1 teaspoon minced jalapeño (add seeds for additional heat)

2 teaspoons Worcestershire (L&P brand preferred)

2 tablespoons Creole mustard

1 tablespoon Old Bay Seasoning

1 tablespoon fine chopped parsley

1 tablespoon lemon juice

2 teaspoons hot sauce (Louisiana brand preferred)

Pinch of kosher salt

Dash of freshly ground black pepper

To prepare the mullet

Use a sharp knife to remove the head. From the outside, cut the fish completely open along its backbone. Remove the backbone and leave the belly intact, butterflying the fillet so it's flat with the skin facing down. Lay it open, remove guts, and rinse well. Place water, salt, and sugar in a large plastic bowl or pail and stir until salt and sugar are dissolved. Add peppercorns, bay leaves, garlic, and mullet (turn the mullet skin side up so its flesh is submerged), making sure all surfaces are covered. Cover and refrigerate for 2 hours.

For grill smoking

Dump the wood chips into a separate large plastic bowl or pail, cover with water, and soak for at least 20 minutes. Preheat covered gas grill to medium. Close the lid for 10 minutes. Drain the wood chips and place them directly onto briquettes or into a foil pouch. Poke several pencil-thick holes in both sides of the foil pouch to ventilate. Place close to a burner on the grill.

Lift fish from brine and rinse under a slow stream of cold water for 10 seconds. Place fish, skin side down, on several layers of paper towels. Blot to absorb excess water, then let air dry, uncovered, at room temperature for 30 minutes. Place fish, skin side down, on a well-oiled grill 4–6 inches from the smoking fire. Close the grill all but a crack to keep the smoke and air circulating. Smoke fish for approximately 1 hour at 150°F–175°F or for 30–45 minutes at 200°F. The fish is done when the cut surface is golden brown and the flesh flakes easily when tested with a fork.

To make the dip

Place all the ingredients into a food processor and blend well. Transfer to a small bowl and seal with plastic wrap. Place in refrigerator for 4 hours. Serve with bacon hushpuppies as shown in the photo (see recipe on p. 235) or with your favorite crackers.

CHEF'S NOTE: Most any kind of fruitwood chips will work, but I suggest pecan, laurel, or hickory.

Byron's Smoked Brisket

Few chefs find their niche in an industry notorious for burnout and job hopping, but Santa Rosa Beach barbecue master and grand champion Byron Chism sure did. I first met the Texas native while I was chef at Bud and Alley's Restaurant in Seaside along Santa Rosa Beach. This young man made his way into my kitchen as a cook, fresh from the well-known Criolla's Restaurant just a few miles down the road in Grayton Beach.

A few years later Byron made his way to the Culinary Institute of America in Hyde Park, New York, and, upon graduating, worked under famed American Chef Larry Forgione. When opportunity came knocking, Byron traded in his fine dining menus for pork ribs, apple juice, and wood chips, and then buried himself in the barbecue market.

Byron has attended over two hundred events in twenty-one states, and four countries (the United States, Switzerland, England, and Holland) and has been featured on the Food Network. Not only is he "high on the hog," but he rules the barbecue industry in all categories, including chicken, ribs, pork and brisket. He is also the creator of Bad Byron's Butt Rub® Barbecue Seasoning.

Here, Byron has shared his expertise for cooking brisket and pork spare ribs, two of the region's favorite backyard foods.

(SERVES 10–12)

1 (8- to 12-pound) whole brisket, first and second cut intact

½ cup Worcestershire sauce

Pinch of kosher salt and freshly ground black pepper

Wood chips/chunks (oak, pecan, hickory, or combination thereof), soaked overnight in water

½ cup beef stock

1 Vidalia or sweet onion, sliced

3 tablespoons minced garlic

Season brisket on both sides with half of the Worcestershire sauce. Rub it in all over and into the sides and corners. Season the brisket generously with salt and pepper. This can be done up to 24 hours ahead. Remove from refrigerator and allow marinated brisket to sit at room temperature at least 2 hours before cooking.

In an offset or standard barbecue grill, prepare a charcoal fire using 8–10 pounds of charcoal. Burn until the coals are completely covered with a thin coating of gray ash, 30–40 minutes. Spread the coals evenly and have a steady thermometer reading between 225°F and 240°F. Place brisket, fat side up, over indirect heat. Add a handful of soaked wood chips or chunks to the coals every hour for the first 3 hours. At 225°F–240°F, a brisket should cook at approximately 1½ hours per pound. After five hours, turn brisket over (fat side down) and continue cooking.

When the internal temperature of the meat reaches 170°F, remove to two oversized layers of aluminum foil. Pour the beef stock, remaining Worcestershire sauce, onion slices, and garlic over the brisket. Re-season with salt and pepper. Seal aluminum foil tightly. Return to the grill or indoor oven heated to 225°F for 2–3 hours. When brisket reaches 200°F internal temperature, remove from heat and allow to rest in foil for at least 1 hour. Remove from foil and slice across the grain. Save all juice from the foil to brush onto the slices.

Byron's Santa Rosa Beach Spare Ribs

(SERVES 4–6)

To make the vinaigrette

Place ingredients in small mixing bowl and whisk to blend well.

To make the ribs

Prepare a charcoal or gas grill to 225°F. Turn baby back ribs underside up. Using the point of a metal skewer, lift the thin membrane and grab the end with a towel. Pull firmly and remove.

Place the oil and barbeque seasoning into a small mixing bowl and whisk to blend. Brush or hand massage the mixture into the ribs until all used. Add a handful of soaked wood chips to the coals or briquettes and place ribs, meat side up, away from the direct heat. Cook for 1 hour. Add another handful of wood chips, turn ribs to meat side down, and cook for another hour.

When ribs have reached amber brown color, remove and individually wrap each slab with 3 layers of heavy-duty foil to prevent tearing and leaking. Add the vinaigrette and apple juice and fold like an envelope to seal the foil. Continue cooking meat in the foil at 225°F over indirect heat for 1½ hours, making a total of 3½ hours cook time.

Remove ribs and allow them to rest for 30 minutes before opening the sealed foil. Place on platter and brush with tupelo honey. Turn over to see ribs and cut into portions. Brush with honey one more time in between the cuts and serve.

For the Italian vinaigrette

⅔ cup olive oil

1 teaspoon minced garlic

2 teaspoons finely chopped shallots

1 teaspoon chopped fresh chives

1 teaspoon fresh thyme leaves, stems removed

8 tablespoons red wine vinegar

1 teaspoon granulated sugar

Pinch of kosher salt

Dash of freshly ground black pepper

For the ribs

2 slabs (3½–4 pounds) baby back ribs (loin back ribs)

6 tablespoons canola oil, divided

2 tablespoon Bad Byron's Butt Rub® Barbeque Seasoning

2 cups soaked wood chips (hickory, apple, pecan, or combination thereof)

⅔ cup Italian vinaigrette (recipe above)

⅔ cup apple juice

¼ cup tupelo honey

Baby Back Ribs with Star Anise Barbecue Sauce

One of the great things about barbecue sauce is that it's very forgiving in its preparation and exactness. With barbecue sauce basics intact, new flavors can easily be transformed by swapping out or adding a few key ingredients. This recipe is a perfect example of major swapping. I substituted vinegars, added Chinese five spices to a basic dry rub, and then added plum sauce, hoisin sauce, red chili garlic paste, and licorice flavor. I altered a basic barbecue sauce to create a finger-licking good, Asian-inspired barbecue sauce!

(SERVES 8–10)

For the dry rub

1 tablespoon Chinese five spices

2 tablespoon granulated garlic

2 tablespoon kosher salt

2 tablespoon freshly cracked black pepper

For the basting sauce

1 cup ginger beer

1 cup seasoned rice wine vinegar

3 tablespoons lemon juice

For the barbecue sauce

2 cups ketchup (Heinz brand preferred)

1 cup light soy sauce

1 cup light brown sugar

1 cup plum sauce

½ cup water

½ cup molasses

½ cup seasoned rice wine vinegar

½ cup hoisin sauce

¼ cup peeled and grated ginger

3 tablespoons red chile garlic sauce

1 tablespoon minced garlic

2 star anise

For the ribs

4 baby back (loin back) pork ribs (7–8 pounds)

To make the dry rub

Add spices to a small mixing bowl and whisk to blend well.

To make the basting sauce

Combine all ingredients in a small mixing bowl.

To make the barbecue sauce

Combine all ingredients in a heavy-bottom saucepot. Increase heat to boil, then reduce to a gentle simmer. Let simmer 30 minutes, whisking frequently. Set aside.

To make the ribs

Preheat oven to 300°F. Turn baby back ribs underside up and remove the thin membrane by holding the end with a kitchen towel and pulling. Generously coat both sides of ribs with the dry rub and let marinated ribs sit for a minimum of 1 hour.

Place spice-coated ribs on a rack over a drip or roasting pan, add 6 cups of water, and cover lightly with foil. Let slow roast for 3½ hours, pouring over or brushing on the basting sauce twice while roasting. Remove from oven when done. Let sit covered for 15 minutes to rest. Uncover and then baste one more time.

If your barbecue sauce becomes too thick, spoon some pan juices from the roasting pan into the prepared barbeque sauce. Whisk barbecue sauce well, and then brush over the ribs 10 minutes before serving.

Baby Back Ribs with Ginger-Blackberry Barbecue Sauce

Here's a recipe from my cooking class days at Jackson's Steakhouse. Inspired by Indian flavors, this aromatic mix combines homemade curry with a spicy ginger beer sauce for basting the baby backs. It is counterbalanced with brown sugar and fresh blackberries, making for a unique, fruit-enriched, one-of-a kind barbecue sauce.

To make the curry spice blend
Place whole spices into a small sauté pan over medium heat and shake pan for 1 minute. Heating will release oils from the whole seeds and maximize the spice flavor before grinding. Let cool then place into coffee grinder. Process until pulverized, about 10 seconds. Transfer to a small mixing bowl and combine with remaining spices. Store in a tightly sealed container.

To make the dry rub
Combine all ingredients in a small mixing bowl. Set aside.

(SERVES 8–10)

For the curry spice blend

2 tablespoons cumin seed

2 tablespoons coriander seed

1 tablespoon turmeric

1 tablespoon chili powder

½ teaspoon cinnamon powder

1 tablespoon fenugreek

½ tablespoon ginger powder

¼ teaspoon brown or yellow mustard seed

¼ teaspoon ground cardamom

¼ teaspoon black peppercorns

For the dry rub

1 tablespoon curry spice blend

2 tablespoons granulated garlic

2 tablespoons kosher salt

2 tablespoons fresh ground black pepper

For the ginger basting sauce

1 cup ginger beer or juice

1 cup seasoned rice wine vinegar

3 tablespoons lemons juice

For the barbecue sauce

1 pound fresh ginger, peeled

2 tablespoons peanut oil

1 cup Vidalia onions, diced

2 cups fresh blackberries, rinsed

2 tablespoons cornstarch

1 teaspoon curry spice blend (recipe above)

2 cups ketchup (Heinz brand preferred)

1 cup light soy sauce

1 cup dark brown sugar

1–2 cups water

½ cup molasses

½ cup seasoned rice wine vinegar

3 tablespoons red chile garlic sauce or sriracha sauce

1 tablespoon garlic, chopped fine

2 tablespoons artisan honey

Pinch of kosher salt

Dash of freshly ground black pepper

For the finished dish

4 baby back pork ribs (7–8 pounds)

1 cup fresh blackberries, rinsed

To make the ginger basting sauce

Add ingredients to small mixing bowl and whisk well to bend.

To make the barbecue sauce

Grate the ginger using a ginger grater, then push remaining fibers through a small-mesh strainer over a small bowl to collect all the juice; discard pulp. Pour peanut oil into a medium-size saucepot over medium heat. Add diced onions and sauté for about 3 minutes or until they become translucent.

In a small bowl toss the blackberries with the cornstarch. Add berries to the onions in the saucepot along with the curry spice. Stir to blend well, then add ketchup, soy sauce, brown sugar, water, molasses, vinegar, red chile sauce, garlic, honey, grated ginger, and ginger juice. Bring to a boil, then reduce heat to a simmer. Stirring frequently, simmer gently for 1 hour. Place in a blender and pulse to blend; sauce should be slightly thick and not runny. Taste, and adjust seasoning with salt and pepper

For the finished dish

Preheat oven to 300°F. Turn baby back ribs underside up and remove the thin membrane by holding the end of the membrane firmly with a kitchen towel and pulling. Generously coat both sides of ribs with the dry rub. Let marinated ribs sit for a minimum of 1 hour.

Place spice-coated ribs on a rack over a drip or roasting pan. Add 3 cups of water to the roasting pan. Cover ribs lightly with foil and let slow roast for 3½ hours. Pour over or brush on the basting sauce twice while roasting. Remove from oven when done and baste once more. Pour remaining pan juices into the prepared barbeque sauce to thin if necessary. Whisk barbecue sauce well, and then brush over the ribs 10 minutes before serving. Garnish servings with fresh blackberries.

New York Strip with Zinfandel Mustard Sauce

Jackson's Steakhouse has been Pensacola's landmark restaurant for more than sixteen years. It's the original restaurant concept and has been recognized as significant in the resurgence of historic downtown Pensacola since 1999. Jackson's Steakhouse occupies the ground floor of the revitalized 1860s-era building that originally housed H. Pfeiffer & Company Mercantile and was later occupied by Peaden's Office Supply. The near complete renovation was the brainchild of architect and entrepreneurs Brian Spencer and his wife Crystal, along with partners Dr. Roger Orth and his former wife Ruth.

As the restaurant's founding executive chef (and a carnivore), I procure the finest wet-aged, corn-fed beef from the Midwestern Corn Belt for our mainstay beef cuts. Jackson's Steakhouse has been cooking steaks with the original kitchen broiler and grills since opening. I knew using the best quality meats combined with well-seasoned grills, year after year, would create the unique, mouthwatering flavors of our one-of-a-kind steaks.

If you don't have a great seasoned grill, another excellent way to prepare fine cuts of beef is to pan-sear them in the French manner, and make a quick pan sauce to adorn. Here is an outstanding pan sauce recipe for a New York strip, which could easily be swapped out for filet mignon.

2 (12- to 14-ounce) New York strip steaks

Pinch of kosher salt

Dash of freshly ground black pepper

3 tablespoons olive oil

1 tablespoon minced shallots

1 teaspoon minced garlic

2 ounces red zinfandel wine

1 tablespoon whole grain mustard

½ teaspoon chopped fresh rosemary

½ teaspoon fresh thyme leaves, removed from the stem

1–2 ounces demi-glace (store-bought)

2 tablespoons unsalted butter, chilled

Lightly season steaks with salt and pepper. Pour oil into a sauté pan over medium-high heat. Add seasoned steaks to the pan and sear each side about 3 minutes. Place a lid on the pan, reduce heat, and cook 3–4 additional minutes. When cooked to desired doneness, remove from pan. Transfer steaks to a plate to let rest as you prepare the sauce.

Turn the heat back up to medium high and add shallots, garlic, wine, mustard, and fresh herbs. Reduce heat to medium low and simmer for 2 minutes. Add demi-glace and simmer for another 2 minutes to make a smooth sauce. Whisk in chilled butter. Taste and adjust seasoning with salt and pepper.

Place the steaks on individual plates, drizzle with sauce, and serve.

Lamb Lollipops with Goat Cheese Crust & Balsamic Caramelized Vidalia Onions

Still echoing in my memory is the weekend of October 19, 2008. Celebrity Chef Jacques Pepin arrived in Pensacola to serve as the guest chef for the twentieth WSRE Wine and Food Classic at the former Pensacola Civic Center to support public television. As an internationally recognized French chef, television personality, and author, Pepin's appearance lent credibility to the event.

Since this event was a "Tour the World" wine and food event, I chose to compete in the French division. At that time, I had no idea Jacques Pepin would be judging my food. The day of the competition, Jackson's Chef de Cuisine Jason Perry and I prepared a French lamb dish (and won first place!). We took center stage with Jacques to receive our award. I was thrilled and honored to spend time with one of the kindest and most talented chefs in the industry. Chef Pepin shared stories with us about working with Julia Child, about his daughter Claudine, and reminisced about his numerous cooking series.

I have always had a special place in my heart for French country cooking. French food was my passion back in the early days, as I had served as chef for two local French restaurants in this region. Here's a simple technique and recipe for baby rack of lamb. Whether your lamb is from New Zealand, Colorado, Australia, or, better yet, from a Gulf Coast farmer, this recipe will be a winner, too.

Place garlic and olive oil in a small saucepan over medium heat and cook for 10 minutes. Reduce heat to low and simmer for another 20 minutes. Garlic will become soft and still hold its shape. Strain and reserve both the garlic and the oil separately. Let cool completely. Place soft garlic in a food processor and pulse to purée. Use a rubber spatula to remove and transfer puree to a small dish. Set aside.

Place a small sauté pan over medium heat, add butter and sliced onions, and stir occasionally until light brown in color, about 10 minutes. Add the balsamic vinegar and simmer until it evaporates, an additional 5–7 minutes. Taste, and adjust seasoning with salt and pepper.

Combine bread crumbs and goat cheese in a food processor. Pulse in short bursts, about 5 times to blend to meal consistency. Transfer mixture to a baking pan and brown mixture in oven for 5–7 minutes, then turn the mixture with a flat kitchen spatula and continue to brown for an additional 5 minutes.

(MAKES 14 LOLLIPOPS)

- 24 peeled garlic cloves
- ⅓ cup olive oil
- 2 tablespoons butter
- 1 large Vidalia onion
- ⅛ cup balsamic vinegar
- Pinch of kosher salt
- Dash of freshly ground black pepper
- 1 cup panko bread crumbs
- 1 (4-ounce) goat cheese log
- 2 racks of baby lamb
- 1 tablespoon chopped fresh rosemary
- 4 sprigs fresh rosemary for garnish

Preheat oven to 400°F. Rub lamb rack with about 4 tablespoons of the garlic olive oil, the rosemary, salt, and pepper. Preheat a large heavy-duty skillet to medium high. Add 3 tablespoons garlic oil to the pan, wait 2 minutes, and then place the lamb, meat side down, in the pan and sear for 3 minutes. Turn it over, place it in the oven, and bake for 12–15 minutes or until medium rare (130°F on a meat thermometer). Remove and let rest for 5 minutes before slicing into individual lollipop chops.

Spoon the balsamic caramelized onions onto a platter or among individual plates. Smear the garlic purée over top of each individually sliced lamb lollipop. Dip the garlic-puree-coated lamb lollipop into the bread crumb mixture and place, crumb side up, onto the plate. Serve with fresh rosemary sprigs.

Dressed Flat Iron Steak

Chef Emeril Lagasse is one of the most iconic chefs from this region, and, according to many, the most well known in the country. All you have to do is mention "Emeril," and, without any mention of profession, people will generally know who you're talking about. In his heyday Emeril spent two decades reaching national celebrity status from his cooking show. His trademark "Bam!" when putting his stamp on a finished dish is hard to forget. His entertaining achievement carried country-wide recognition for the culture of the Gulf Coast, and still does to this day.

In 2013, Emeril's Florida became the first on-location television food show for the Sunshine State, highlighting top restaurants and Florida destinations. Jackson's Steakhouse in Pensacola, along with historic Columbia Restaurant in Tampa, were included in the "Viva Florida" episode, which included history highlights and several of my favorite dishes. I prepared oysters, grits, collard greens, debris gravy, and an out-of-the-ordinary meat dish using inexpensive flat iron steak.

One day, during a break from production, we prepared some just-caught triggerfish for Emeril and his crew. Emeril is passionate about Gulf Coast seafood, Florida agriculture, and Gulf fishing and was thrilled.

Here's the recipe I prepared for the episode using the flavorful beef shoulder or blade cut that is most tender when sliced across the grain.

(SERVES 2)

To make the kale chips

Preheat oven to 325°F. Rinse and remove stem at the base. Drizzle some olive oil onto your hands and gently rub each leaf lightly with the oil. Lay the leaves flat on a baking tray and bake for 30–40 minutes or until lightly toasted. Remove from oven and let cool.

For the kale chips

6 large leaves Florida kale

2 tablespoons olive oil

To make the herb chimichurri sauce

Place all ingredients in a food processor and pulse to thoroughly blend. Transfer to a container, cover, and allow the mixture to rest for at least 2 hours before use. You can prepare chimichurri the day before and store in the refrigerator. Remove sauce from the refrigerator and bring to room temperature before using.

For the herb chimichurri sauce

½ cup extra-virgin olive oil

¼ cup red wine vinegar

¼ cup packed fresh basil leaves

¼ cup flat-leaf parsley leaves

1 tablespoon dried oregano

½ cup chopped yellow onion

2 teaspoons minced garlic

½ teaspoon red chile flakes

Pinch of kosher salt

Dash of freshly ground black pepper

To make the beef

Preheat a gas grill to medium high. Preheat the oven to 350°F. Pour ¼ cup olive oil over steak, smear with the garlic, and marinate for 1 hour. Remove meat from the marinade and season with salt and pepper. Place the meat over open fire and sear on all sides. Grill for

For the beef

½ cup extra-virgin olive oil, divided

1 pound certified Angus beef flat iron steak, cleaned and trimmed

2 teaspoons minced garlic

Pinch of kosher salt

Freshly ground black pepper

For the salad

1 cup broccoli florets

2 tablespoons white pearl onions, peeled and blanched

2 tablespoons olive oil

3 Florida baby heirloom or cherry tomatoes

2 cups Florida baby arugula, rinsed and lightly packed

Splash of hot pepper vinegar (optional)

Kosher salt and fresh-cracked black pepper to taste

7–8 minutes each side. Place the meat in the oven and roast for 5–7 minutes or until medium rare. Remove from oven and let rest for 5 minutes. Slice steak against the grain into ⅛-inch-thick slices for two portions.

To make the salad

Prepare a 1-quart ice bath by adding equal amounts of ice and water in a medium-sized bowl. Bring a small pot of water to a boil over high heat, drop in broccoli florets for 3 minutes, then shock in an ice bath to blanch. Remove, let drain, and set aside.

Use a paper towel and pat the pearl onions dry. Place olive oil in the skillet and turn up heat to medium-high. Add the onions and shake pan to roll and brown all over, about 2 minutes. Remove them to drain.

Rinse and slice the tomatoes in half and set aside.

In a medium-size mixing bowl add the sliced steak, arugula, cut tomatoes, caramelized pearl onions, broccoli florets, and 2–3 tablespoons of chimichurri sauce. Add a splash of hot pepper vinegar, and season the mixture with a pinch of salt and fresh-cracked pepper. Use a pair of tongs and toss well, adding any beef drippings back into the mixture before plating.

To assemble

Arrange the kale chips to cover the bottom of two plates with the crispy kale chips flat in the center with the ruffled ends facing out. Divide the dressed steak and salad mixture over top of the kale and serve.

Grass-Fed Steak

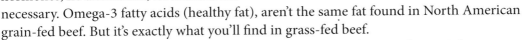

Grass-fed cattle graze freely throughout their lives, eating the all-grass diet that nature intended, to become robust and healthy. No hormones, no antibiotics, no steroids are necessary. Omega-3 fatty acids (healthy fat), aren't the same fat found in North American grain-fed beef. But it's exactly what you'll find in grass-fed beef.

For me, fifth-generation and life-long Missouri farmer John Woods says it best: "Sustainable practices not only produce the healthiest, best-tasting grass-fed beef, they keep our farms and planet strong, too. Our grass isn't dependent on imported oil and fertilizer, and it helps absorb carbon rather than produce it. The cattle eat right and so can you! We raise cattle throughout the south and have over 500 grass-fed cattle between Fairhope and Loxley, Alabama, all south of I-10 in Baldwin County."

Grass-fed beef is naturally lean with little marbling and apt to have a bit more chew than grain-fed beef. It's important to remember, grain-fed cattle are raised on starch, which produces Omega-6 fat. These fats are void of the natural compounds found in the grass-foraged diet.

For US Wellness Meats' Grassland Beef, thirty-day, wet-aging is an essential practice for tenderness and flavor maturity. Here is my simple recipe for a steak that does not require much more than an excellent char, sweet earthy garlic, olive oil, salt, and pepper.

Place a small saucepan over medium heat. Add the peeled garlic and olive oil and cook for 10 minutes. Reduce heat to low and simmer for another 20 minutes. Garlic will become soft and still hold its shape. Strain and reserve both the garlic and the oil separately, let cool completely.

Preheat gas grill to medium high. For optimum results, prepare a hardwood or charcoal grill. Allow coals or hardwood to reach an equal ratio of red-hot coal to ash for optimum direct cooking. Spread them out evenly over the bottom of the grill.

Place steaks in a baking dish and pour the reserved garlic oil over them. Let sit at room temperature for 45 minutes, turning once after 20 minutes. Remove steaks from the oil and place on wire rack to drain. Season each steak generously with salt and pepper. Place steaks on grill over direct heat for 5–7 minutes per side to cook them medium rare. When done, remove to a deep serving platter to rest for 8–10 minutes before serving.

Place grilled steaks onto individual plates, add 2 or 3 cooked garlic cloves to each steak, and serve. If desired, drizzle 1 ounce of demi-glace over each steak.

(SERVES 4)

4 garlic cloves

¼ cup olive oil

4 (14-ounce) grass-fed rib eye steaks or New York strips, preferably center-cut (about 1-inch thick)

Pinch of kosher salt

Dash of freshly ground black pepper

4 ounces demi-glace (store-bought), optional

Desoto Canyon Surf Burger

Pensacola is home to the Spencer family and late, legendary surfer, Yancey Spencer III. Yancey not only enlightened the state of Florida on Gulf Coast surfing, but also entire surfing communities from coast to coast. It was Yancey who brought his surfer comrades from the East Coast, West Coast and the Islands to the Panhandle beaches and Alabama point surf breaks. Once here, they experienced, first hand, our respected, yet infrequent large surf, common wind swells, and occasional groundswells. In 1996 he was inducted into the East Coast Surfing Hall Of Fame.

Eldest son of the surfing family, Yancey Spencer IV, once requested that I create a recipe for a surf burger using two of his dad's favorite ingredients: chili-spiced beef and fresh pineapple. Long board surfing has always been part of my adulthood along both the East and Gulf Coasts, so the idea was fitting and I gladly agreed. As chef, I work diligently dreaming of one day making our unsung Panhandle cooking as memorable as Yancey III made Panhandle surfing for Florida and around the country.

I named my creation the "Desoto Canyon Surf Burger" after the deep underwater canyon that begins just off our coast in the Gulf of Mexico. This trench is beneficial not only to our fisheries, but our surf too. I'm excited to share my version of this homespun surf burger with smoky grilled slaw along with a regional Florida sweet rib sauce. Finding the perfect bun can be a challenge. However, good fresh baked onion, potato, Parmesan, Semolina or brioche buns are ideal.

(SERVES 4)

For the smoky grilled pineapple slaw

1 cup hickory chips (or your favorite wood chips)

½-inch slab of red cabbage (1 cup chopped)

½-inch slab of white cabbage (1 cup chopped)

½-inch slab cored pineapple (1 cup chopped)

1 medium carrot, grated

4 tablespoons chopped red onion

4 tablespoons cider vinegar

¼ cup extra virgin olive oil

¼ teaspoon celery salt

1–2 teaspoons sugar

For the smoky grilled pineapple slaw
Soak the wood chips in water for 2 hours. Drain well.

Prepare a hard wood, charcoal or gas grill. Allow coals or hard wood used to reach a ratio of red hot coal to ash for optimum indirect cooking. Spread them out evenly over the bottom of the grill. Sprinkle the soaked wood chips onto the coals. While waiting for the chips to begin smoldering, arrange the red and white cabbage, and pineapple on the grill grate. Cover the grill and smoke for 15–20 minutes, turning cabbage and pineapple once.

Remove the cabbage and pineapple rack from the grill and cool to room temperature (should be slightly charred on the surface and edges). Remove core before chopping.

The ripe pineapple core is fine to chop for the slaw. Hands chop the cabbage and pineapple into to spoon size and then add red onions, carrot, cider vinegar and olive oil. Adjust the seasoning with sugar, salt and pepper, and blend well. Cover with plastic wrap and set refrigerate until needed.

Chili-spice mix

Place all spices and seasonings in a small bowl and blend well with a fork. Set aside until needed.

For the caramelized onions

Grate or thin slice onions. Preheat a wide sauté pan over medium-high heat. Add the onions and stir occasionally for even browning, about 25 minutes. Turn off heat and let cool until needed.

For the burger

In a large mixing bowl combine the ground beef, caramelized onions, peppers, garlic sand Worcestershire and by hand to blend well.

Divide the mixture by half, and then divide each half into half, creating 4 beef portions. Shape the burger mixture into 4 (1½-inch) thick burgers. Re-shape the center using you thumb to create a ½-inch depression, 1-inch wide, so the burger cooks evenly. Cover the burgers with plastic wrap and store in refrigerator.

To assemble

Season both sides of each burger with a generous pinch of the chili-spice mixture. Press spices into the meat. Grill the burgers over medium heat and cook to desired doneness, and then brush 2–3 tablespoons of barbecue sauce over each burger. Add the cheese to melt, and then remove burgers from grill. Toast the buns, cut side down on the grill for about 1 minute. Place burger on bottom bun and then top each burger with ½ cup of grilled pineapple slaw. Dress with top bun and serve right away.

Pinch kosher salt

Dash freshly ground black pepper

Chili-spice mix

1 tablespoons chili powder

½ teaspoon smoked paprika

½ teaspoon ground cumin

½ teaspoon ground coriander

½ teaspoon dried oregano

Pinch kosher salt

Dash freshly ground black pepper

For the burger

1½ pounds lean ground beef chuck

2 cups finely chopped yellow onions, caramelized

2 tablespoons fine chopped Serrano peppers (add seeds for additional heat)

1 tablespoon minced garlic

3 tablespoons Worcestershire sauce

To assemble

4 (1¼-inch) thick burgers

4 (1-ounce) slices of American or jack cheese

1 cup smoky grilled pineapple slaw

8 tablespoons Florida sweet rib sauce (see page 153)

4 potato rolls (or other favorite roll) cut in half

Creole-Spiced Pork Chops with Caramelized Shallots, Fig Preserves & Ham Hock Meat

The flavors of the Deep South are simple and dance on your palate in a comforting way. On my palate, there is rarely a better flavor combination than spicy, smoky, and sweet. Also revered in the South is the pig. From head to toe, there is no more essential protein for cooking than pork, and no one is more "high on the hog" than Roger and Pam Elliot, owners of Green Cedars Farm in Molino, Florida. You can find Roger at the Palafox Market in downtown Pensacola every Saturday morning selling his USDA-approved Hereford pork, as well as his ground lamb.

Pork chops are easy to find in most grocery stores, but I recommend you seek them out at the farmers' markets from local reputable farms closest to you. My preferred cuts are the pork chop, rib rack, loin, and shoulder. Break them down into portions or have your butcher cut bone-in chops that are perfect for speedy and direct cooking, as with this recipe.

Through the years I have engineered this recipe to be used primarily with pork chops. Pork on pork is not uncommon here. Smoky ham hocks are simmered, then the meat is pulled, and spicy flour is used for the pork and the sauce. In addition to that tasty visual image, shallots and preserved figs are added, caramelized, and blended with sweet syrup, making for a remarkable sauce. I'm salivating just writing about it!

The preserved figs are key. I gather them from J. W. Renfroe Pecan Company, a third-generation, family-owned business in Pensacola.

(SERVES 4)

For the ham hocks

2 ham hocks, boiled, meat removed from bone and chopped

1 cup ham hock broth

2 quarts water

For the pork chops

1 cup all-purpose flour

3 tablespoons Creole seasoning

4 tablespoons olive oil, divided

8 whole medium shallots, peeled

4 (8-ounce) bone-in pork chops

1 cup ham hock broth

To make the ham hocks
Place the ham hocks in a 4-quart soup pot and add the water. Bring to a boil over medium-high heat, reduce heat, and simmer for 1½ hours. Strain, reserving broth, and let ham hocks cool. When cool, remove all the meat from the ham bone and chop small.

To make the pork chops
Place the flour and Creole seasoning in a medium-size mixing bowl and set aside.

Place 2 tablespoons of oil in a heavy-bottom skillet over medium-high heat. Add the shallots and brown them all over, about 3 minutes. Turn off and cover for 10 minutes.

Remove the caramelized shallots from the pan and set aside.

Meanwhile, dust the pork chops in the seasoned flour, add remaining oil to the pan, and increase heat to medium. Place the pork in the pan leaving, 1 inch between each chop. Let brown for 4 minutes on each side, cover, and cook until meat thermometer reads 155°F.

Remove pork chops from the pan and whisk 2 teaspoons of the seasoned flour into the hot oil. Whisk over low heat for 1 minute to blend well and make smooth. Add ham broth and whisk until blended smooth. Add the figs and their syrup to sweeten the sauce. Add caramelized shallots and ham hock meat. Bring sauce to a boil and then let simmer until slightly thickened, about 5 minutes. Adjust seasoning with salt and pepper to your liking. Place pork chops onto plates, drizzle with sauce, and serve.

8 whole figs preserves in syrup (J.W. Renfroe Pecan Company)

4 tablespoons syrup from the fig preserves

Ham hock meat

Pinch of kosher salt

Dash of freshly ground black pepper

Chapter 7

Poultry, Waterfowl, and Game

Baked Chicken with Pepper Gravy

One of my favorite ways to prepare whole chickens is to split and then bake them. There's nothing quite as glorious as simple baked chicken. This recipe came about in the early 1990s when I started preparing it as a daily lunch feature for the menu at Bud and Alley's restaurant at Seaside on Santa Rosa Beach in Florida. It is as down-to-earth as cooking gets and I still use it today. The best, basic application is for split chicken cooked over vegetables and aromatics, and then combined with roux and milk in order to flavor the home-style white gravy. It's one of my much-loved comfort foods any time of the year!

(SERVES 4)

1 (3–4 pound) chicken, giblets and neck removed

Kosher salt and freshly ground black pepper

2 cups coarsely chopped onions

1 cup coarsely chopped celery

3 fresh thyme sprigs

2 cloves garlic, peeled

⅛ cup all-purpose flour

3 cups milk

1 bay leaf, crushed

1 teaspoon freshly ground black pepper

Pinch of kosher salt

Preheat oven to 375°F. Using a sharp boning knife, cut and remove backbone, then split the chicken in half completely. Season the chicken on both sides with salt and pepper. Place onion, celery, thyme, and garlic on a baking pan and spread them out level. Arrange the cut chicken, breast-side-up, on top of the vegetable mixture. Place the pan on the oven rack. Roast until the juices run clear when pierced at the thickest part of the thigh with a knife, 1¼–1½ hours.

Transfer the chicken to a cutting board, cover loosely with foil, and let rest in a warm place to allow the juices to redistribute, about 15 minutes. Transfer the cooked vegetables and drippings into a deep saucepot. Stir in the flour and cook over medium heat for 5–7 minutes. Add the milk and bay leaf and stir to blend well. Increase heat to medium high to bring to a boil, and then reduce and simmer for 12 minutes. Add measured ground black pepper. Taste and adjust seasoning with salt. Strain to remove vegetables (optional), and discard bay leaf.

Cut and divide the chicken into fourths. Arrange them onto individual plates with your favorite sides, such as rice and grilled vegetables. Drizzle with pepper gravy and serve.

Fried Chicken and Pumpkin-Bourbon Waffles

I first prepared this chicken recipe for the inaugural Slow Food Gulf Coast event held in Pensacola for the Florida Panhandle region. The Slow Food mission, in part, raises public awareness and encourages the enjoyment of foods that are local, seasonal, and sustainable. For this "Community Cooks" event, I used red ranger chickens that were raised on Green Cedar Farm in Molino, Florida, just 40 miles north of Pensacola. Most any store-bought chicken will work for the recipe, but these sustainably raised, free-range chickens are by far the most tender, juicy, and flavorful chickens I have ever put in my mouth.

Here is my recipe for tender and crispy fried chicken served over bourbon-flavored waffles, and crowned with local, raw pecan honey from East Hill Honey Company.

(SERVES 4–6)

To make the chicken

Combine flour, salt, pepper, garlic, and onion in a bowl and blend well. Rinse the chicken pieces in ice water, drain, and then place into buttermilk to soak for 15 minutes before frying. Remove chicken from buttermilk a couple of pieces at a time. Roll each piece in the seasoned flour. Place coated chicken pieces on a wire rack over a baking pan.

Heat lard in a skillet on medium high. Add 2 slices of bacon to the lard for smokiness if desired. Use an oil thermometer to monitor the temperature. When lard approaches 360°F, begin adding chicken pieces, a few at a time, being careful not to overload and drop the temperature below 350°F. Lard should rise halfway up the chicken in the pan. Cook each side to a golden color (10–12 minutes each side), turning frequently to evenly brown. When each piece is done, remove from pan, and let drain and rest on a wire rack for 15 minutes. Total cooking time is about 25–30 minutes.

For the chicken

3 cups all-purpose flour

3 teaspoons kosher salt

2 teaspoons fresh ground black pepper

1 teaspoon granulated garlic

1 teaspoon granulated onion

3–4 pound whole chicken, cut into 12 pieces

4 cups buttermilk

3 pounds lard for panfrying

2 thick slices smoky bacon per batch (optional)

To make the waffles

Preheat waffle iron. Mix all dry ingredients in a large bowl. In a separate bowl, whisk eggs to break them up, and then add pumpkin puree and bourbon. Mix till blended smooth. Make a well in the center of the dry ingredients and slowly mix in the liquid until batter is formed. Whisk to smooth. Pour or ladle the batter mixture onto the waffle iron and cook for 3 minutes or until batter sets and waffle is brown. Repeat.

Top each waffle with a piece of fried chicken. Spoon pecan honey over chicken and waffles, and serve.

For the waffles

2 cups all-purpose flour

1 teaspoon baking soda

½ teaspoon kosher salt

1 teaspoon cinnamon

1 teaspoon sugar

4 eggs

4 ounces pure pumpkin puree

2 ounces bourbon

1 teaspoon vanilla extract

1 teaspoon melted butter

1 jar pecan honey (East Hill Honey Company brand preferred)

Spanish–Style Sofrito Chicken

The *fond de cuisine,* or the foundation of classic French soup, sauce, and stock, usually begins with a vegetable mixture or *mirepoix* (onions, carrots, and celery) as the flavor base. Holy Trinity (onions, green peppers, and garlic) is the *mirepoix* of New Orleans–style Cajun and Creole cooking often used in étouffée, gumbos, and sauces. Sofrito or *sofregit* (as it is called in Catalonia) is deeply stewed onions, green peppers, and tomato. Garlic (in Catalonia garlic is often omitted) is the foundation of many Spanish dishes.

Enjoy this bold-flavored and colorfully stewed sauce with simple marinated and grilled chicken breast. It is perfect when accompanied by Spanish rice and a piece of crusted rustic bread.

(SERVES 4)

4 (6-ounce) boneless chicken breasts, skin-on optional

For the marinade

2 sprigs fresh rosemary

2 sprigs fresh thyme

6 cloves garlic, smashed

⅛ cup lemon juice

¼ cup Hojiblanca (Spanish olive oil) or high-quality extra-virgin olive oil

For the sofrito sauce

3 tablespoons Hojiblanca

1 cup chopped onions

½ cup small-chopped green bell pepper

½ cup small-chopped celery

1 cup peeled, seeded, and coarsely chopped tomatoes

1 teaspoon minced garlic

½ cup dry sherry

½ cup golden raisins

½ teaspoon sweet smoked paprika (La Chinata brand preferred)

½ teaspoon granulated garlic

¼ teaspoon granulated onion

¼ teaspoon cumin powder

¼ teaspoon fresh chilies, finely chopped

2 teaspoon chopped fresh chives

1 teaspoon fresh thyme, removed from the stem

½ cup sliced and toasted almonds

Pinch of kosher salt

Dash of freshly ground black pepper

To make the marinade

In a medium-size mixing bowl combine the rosemary, thyme, garlic, lemon juice, and Hojiblanca. Mix well, add chicken, and marinate for 2–3 hours in refrigerator. Remove chicken from the marinade and wipe off all the oil.

To make the sofrito

Place a heavy skillet or dutch oven over medium-high heat. Add Hojiblanca and onions and sauté for 15–20 minutes to caramelize; they should turn the color of dark brown sugar. Add bell pepper, celery, tomato, and garlic and stir in to cook for another 5 minutes or until tender. Add sherry, raisins, and spices. Simmer sauce over low heat until slightly thickened. Add chives, thyme, and almonds. Taste, and adjust seasoning with salt and pepper.

To make the chicken

Preheat griddle to medium high. Place chicken on griddle, skin side down (if using skin), and cook until golden, about 6 minutes. Turn to cook other side for another 6 minutes.

Slice the chicken breasts on a 45-degree bias and arrange on individual plates. Spoon sofrito over the chicken and around the plate. Serve with your favorite side such as Spanish rice.

Herb and Peppercorn Chicken with Roasted Plum Tomato and Fresh Basil Vinaigrette

What makes Steak au Poivre a timeless dish? Black peppercorns! True pepper steak, in the classic French way, is made by coarsely crushing black peppercorns. These tiny peppers buds are flavor-packed. Be careful though, if not pulverized finely enough and used in excess (which black peppercorns often are) they can be overpowering, even dangerous, perhaps resulting in a chipped tooth.

On the other hand, fresh green peppercorns, which are amazing right off the vine, would be the ideal pepper for this chicken dish. The next best option is soft-brined, whole green peppercorns, which are easy to spot at quality grocery stores and are the unripe berries of the same vine, picked before maturity. The combination of pepper and fresh herbs makes for a spicy and aromatic rub when applied to beef, chicken, pork, or lamb.

I have included my recipe for vinaigrette, which includes roasting plum tomatoes for intense flavor and combining them with fragrant, fresh, sweet basil, making the ideal sauce for this dish.

To make the vinaigrette
Preheat oven to 325°F. Rinse tomatoes and dry them with towel. Slice tomatoes in half lengthwise. Place them, cut side up, on baking pan. Spoon the olive oil over top of the tomatoes and brush or rub over evenly. Season with salt and pepper and bake for 1½–2 hours until the edges of the cut tomatoes begin to caramelize and turn light brown.

Peel the roasted tomatoes and place them in the food processor. Add the basil, vinegar, shallots, and garlic and pulse to blend. With the processor still running, slowly drizzle in olive oil and remaining extra-virgin olive oil until incorporated. Taste and adjust seasoning with sugar, salt, and pepper.

To make the marinade
Place all ingredients into a ziplock bag. Massage bag well and then place into a bowl and into refrigerator for 2–4 hours.

To make the peppercorns and herbs
Place the peppercorns, chives, and thyme in a mortar and pestle and pulverize to make pepper and herb mixture.

(SERVES 4)

For the vinaigrette

5 each small plum tomatoes

4 tablespoons extra-virgin olive oil, plus ¼ cup

Pinch of kosher salt

Dash of freshly ground black pepper

¼ cup packed sweet basil leaves

¼ cup red wine vinegar

2 tablespoons minced shallots

1 tablespoon minced garlic

¾ cup olive oil

Pinch of granulated sugar

For the marinade

2 sprigs fresh rosemary

2 sprigs fresh thyme

6 garlic cloves, smashed

3 tablespoons lemon juice

½ cup extra-virgin olive oil

4 (8-ounce) boneless, skinless chicken breasts

For the peppercorns and herbs

4 tablespoons green peppercorns, crushed

3 teaspoons fresh chives, chopped

1 teaspoon fresh thyme leaves, removed from the stem

To assemble

Remove the chicken from the marinade and wipe off. Preheat a medium-size, cast-iron skillet to medium heat. Place chicken in skillet and cook each side for about 6 minutes, or until juices run clear when poked with a skewer.

Spoon the room temperature or slightly warmed vinaigrette onto individual plates. Place chicken breast (sliced or whole) on the vinaigrette. Drizzle with herb and peppercorn mixture (also at room temperature or slightly warm). Serve right away.

Chicken with Butter Beans, Tomato & Marjoram

This tagine-inspired, summertime recipe came from a Moroccan cooking class I led one night at Jackson's Steakhouse. For this baked and uncovered recipe, I apply the same cooking steps used in tagine cooking, except for the steaming action provided by the teepee-style lid. To cook the chicken, a traditional cast-iron dutch oven is substituted for the tagine. The chicken is seasoned with a mixture of homemade Deep South spice rub, creating a fantastic chicken dish. The meat will begin to fall off the bone as it sits, so if you want it that way, just let it remain in the sauce for as long as you desire.

In a large ziplock bag, combine chile pepper, half the olive oil, garlic, and Deep South spice rub. Insert chicken thighs, seal bag, and massage well to coat thighs evenly. Let marinate 2–3 hours in the refrigerator.

Preheat oven to 400°F. Remove chicken from marinade and wipe off any excess with your fingers. Season chicken lightly all over with salt and pepper. Add remaining olive oil to the bottom of the dutch oven and increase heat to medium high. Place chicken thighs, skin-side down to brown the skin, in the dutch oven for 5–7 minutes. Remove thighs from oil and set aside. Add onions, potatoes, carrots, tomatoes, and stock. Stir in beans, add chopped marjoram, and stir in.

Place chicken back on top of the vegetables skin-side up. Place dutch oven over medium heat and bring to a boil, about 10 minutes. Reduce heat to medium-low, cover, and simmer on stovetop for 10 minutes. Place dutch oven in preheated oven, covered, for 40 minutes. To brown chicken and vegetables, remove lid and allow an additional 10–12 minutes. Make sure the beans are cooked tender.

When you're ready to serve, spoon vegetables and broth into individual bowls, add 2 thighs per person, and serve.

(SERVES 4)

1 medium chile, finely chopped

¼ cup extra-virgin olive oil, divided

1 tablespoon minced garlic

2 tablespoons Deep South spice rub (see recipe in Chapter 5)

8 skin-on, bone-in chicken thighs

Pinch of kosher salt

Dash of freshly ground black pepper

3 cups coarse-chopped yellow onions

3 cups coarse-chopped potatoes

2 cups coarse-chopped carrots

1 (16-ounce) can whole plum tomatoes and juice

2 cups vegetable or chicken broth

2 cups fresh white butter beans (lima beans)

2 tablespoons fresh marjoram or oregano, rough chopped

Duck with Papaya & Ginger Sauce

On occasion folks will ask about the Peking duck dish that's on my menu. Besides being the older English spelling for the city of Beijing in China, Peking is also the ancient Chinese preparation created in Beijing that involves fastidious preparatory steps taken with whole duck. It is air-dried and boiled, which enables the skin to separate from the meat so when it is roasted, the skin bubbles, thins, and crisps. But this kind of duck isn't the one I handle, that would be Pekin duck. It is quite easy to confuse Pekin duck with Peking duck, since they are almost spelled the same. It happens every year.

Let me clear up the confusion. "Long Island duckling," the familiar name used throughout the country, is American Pekin duck (a variety of mallard). This waterfowl is the most popular commercial duck breed in the United States. Nearly 90 percent off all the duck eaten by consumers is Pekin. These birds were imported to Long Island, New York, from China way back in 1873! Down in the South, we often use Muscovy duck, which is native to the region. This variety is the most common duck we find in the market place and grocery stores. In the South we often use Muscovy duck, a native fowl. Either bird will do, and what's best is you don't have to be a hunter to enjoy it!

Immodestly perhaps, but exuberantly, I wrote in my notebook for this recipe "Many rave reviews!!!" The first time I prepared it was in my early Destin days. This recipe is typical of one of the many sweet and spicy preparations for whole duck. This particular recipe resurfaced last decade and once again, recently, it graced a seasonal menu change at Jackson's Steakhouse in Pensacola.

(SERVES 2)

1 (5- to 6-pound) whole duck

½ teaspoon kosher salt

¼ teaspoon fresh ground black pepper

2 tablespoons dried leaf thyme

1 fresh navel orange, peeled and cut into quarters

1 (1-inch) piece ginger root, peeled and coarsely chopped

1 cup fresh orange juice

2 cups ripe papaya flesh, peeled, seeded, and split

Preheat the oven to 500°F. Trim the wing tips and neck fat from the duck and remove the giblets. Rinse duck under cold water, then pat dry with a paper towel. Rub the outside and inside with a mixture of salt, pepper, and dried thyme. Place the orange wedges and gingerroot inside the duck cavity. Place the duck, breast side up, on a rack inside a roasting pan and roast for 25 minutes.

Reduce the heat to 300°F and continue to roast for an additional 50 minutes. Skin should turn golden brown and the meat juices should run clear. Remove from oven, take out the orange and ginger, and place into small saucepot. Let the duck rest for 30 minutes and cover loosely with foil.

Place the saucepot with the orange and ginger over medium heat and add the orange juice and papaya. Reduce by one-third, about 25 minutes. Add the demi-glace and honey, return to a boil, then turn down and simmer an additional 10 minutes until slightly thickened. Push sauce through a fine strainer and the discard pulp. Reserve the sauce for plating.

With a sharp knife, split the duck completely in half lengthwise and remove breast meat from breast bone. Repeat for second side. Slice and keep the leg and thigh attached. Serve each person 1 breast, 1 leg, and 1 thigh. Slice the breast on a bias and arrange on plate around the leg and thigh. Serve with favorite sides such as wild rice and oven-roasted seasonal vegetables. Spoon sauce onto the plate around the duck and serve right away.

½ cup natural demi-glace or duck glace (store-bought)

1 tablespoon artisan honey

Vietnamese-Inspired Smoked Duck Breast

This exquisite, yet simple dish embodies the principles of Vietnamese cooking. It's light and healthy, yet rich in sensual pleasures. Resonating in my memory is my first stab at a chef's position, which came just a few months after relocating from San Antonio, Texas, to Destin, Florida. I was the newest and youngest chef from the multi-unit Universal Restaurants based in Dallas, Texas, to expand into the Florida Panhandle. The late corporate Chef Jean La Font required me to prepare *Canard Roti a l'idee du Chef,* which translated as "roasted duck prepared in a different manner each evening"; *Huitres a l' idee du Chef,* which means "oyster prepared in a different manner each evening"; and Soupe du Jour (no translation needed) for all of my seasonal menus. It was a test of my creativity, capabilities, and character.

Les Saisons is where I first began to gather knowledge of the numerous preparations for cooking duck. I merged global ingredients into my dishes. After those years, confit and smoking have become two of my favorite preparations. The results are as magnificent as the traditional searing and slicing, or roasting duck whole.

This recipe was inspired by a wonderful array of irresistible Vietnamese ingredients and is an especially memorable smoked duck recipe.

(SERVES 4)

For the duck

4 (9-ounce) duck breasts

¼ cup kosher salt

4 cups water

For the dressing

¼ cup fresh lemon juice

¼ cup chopped cilantro

1 teaspoon sesame oil

2 tablespoons low-sodium soy sauce

2 tablespoons chopped lemon grass

2 tablespoons minced serrano chiles

1 teaspoon black combined with 1 teaspoon white sesame seeds

To make the duck

Submerge the duck breasts into the mixture of salt and water and leave in the refrigerator overnight. In the morning, remove the duck breasts from the water and pat them dry. Set in a cool place for a few hours to dry out a bit before smoking.

Place duck breasts in your smoker with a drip pan underneath. Smoke between 200°F and 225°F over apple or hickory wood for 1 hour.

To make the dressing

Place the lemon juice, cilantro, sesame oil, soy sauce, lemon grass, chiles, sesame seeds, fish sauce, sugar, and pepper in a food processor. Use pulse button to blend well. With the machine on, drizzle in olive oil.

To make the salad

Place a small saucepot over medium-high heat and fill halfway with water. Snap noodles into short lengths, add to the pot, and cook for 3–4 minutes. Rinse under cold water, then drain and set aside.

In a medium-size bowl, combine spearmint, cucumber slices, bok choy, cabbage, tomatoes, onions, radish sprouts, and peanuts. Add in noodles and toss with dressing.

After the duck breasts have been smoked and cooled completely, slice them on a 45-degree bias into very thin slices. Arrange tossed salad onto individual plates, and then arrange the sliced meat around the salad. Serve immediately.

1½ tablespoons Thai fish sauce

2 tablespoons palm or light brown sugar

Dash of freshly ground black pepper

¼ cup vegetable oil

For the salad

7 ounces vermicelli rice noodles

⅛ cup fresh chopped spearmint

1 cucumber, skin on, seeds removed, and thinly sliced

1 cup thinly sliced bok choy

1 cup thinly sliced savoy cabbage

1 medium tomato, cut into very thin wedges

1 small red onion, thinly sliced

¼ cup chopped green onions

¼ cup daikon radish sprouts

2 tablespoons roasted peanuts

"The Mediterranean, the Caribbean and the Gulf of Mexico form a homogeneous, though interrupted sea."

—A.J. Leibling, *The Earl of Louisiana*

Buttermilk Fried Quail with Blackberry Dressing

Blackberries are one of the easiest fruits to grow, and are typically picked in the Florida and Alabama Panhandle regions in May and June. Blackberries may also be called dewberries in some areas. Boysenberries, Marion berries, and loganberries are other common names for blackberry varieties in Pensacola.

Quail are pint-sized, farm-raised game birds that are exceptionally simple to prepare. Just soak them in buttermilk and prepare them like "honest" fried chicken, dusted with seasoned flour and skillet-fried. Here is one of my favorite ways to prepare quail with a country-style corn bread dressing and some of those tasty, seasonally ripened blackberries. If you're foraging for berries yourself, be careful when picking them—many varieties have sharp thorns.

(SERVES 8)

For the corn bread

1 cup unbleached all-purpose flour

1 cup yellow cornmeal

1 tablespoon baking powder

1 teaspoon salt

2 cups buttermilk

5 tablespoons extra-virgin olive oil (or bacon fat), divided

3 eggs, well beaten

For the dressing

8 cups crumbled corn bread

1½ cups small-chopped andouille sausage

½ stick (2- ounces) unsalted butter

1 cup small chopped yellow onions

½ cup small-chopped celery with leaves

⅛ cup chopped fresh sage leaves

⅛ cup chopped parsley

½ teaspoon celery salt

To make the corn bread

Preheat oven to 375°F. Sift flour, cornmeal, baking powder, and salt together into a large mixing bowl and set aside. Mix buttermilk with 2 tablespoons of olive oil and the eggs. Add to the dry ingredients and stir briefly to combine.

Heat 2 tablespoons of olive oil (or bacon fat) in a skillet. Remove pan from heat and set aside until corn bread batter is ready. Heat a 10-inch round cast-iron skillet over a low flame and pour in the remaining 1 tablespoon of olive oil. Swirl the skillet around so the oil completely coats bottom and sides of pan. (If a cast-iron skillet is not available, oil an 8 × 8 × 2-inch or 1 × 7 × 2-inch glass baking dish well with the olive oil.)

Pour in the corn bread batter. Bake for 40–60 minutes or until a toothpick inserted into middle comes out clean and top is golden brown. Remove and let cool completely, then crumble into fine crumbs and place in a mixing bowl. (This can be made a day in advance and stored in a sealed container until needed.)

To make the dressing

Preheat oven to 375°F. Place crumbled corn bread into a large mixing bowl. Place a large skillet over medium-high heat and add the sausage. Sauté for 8–10 minutes until sausage is slightly brown on the edges. Use a slotted spoon and add the sausage with drippings to the crumbled corn bread.

Place the same skillet on medium heat and add the butter, onions, and celery. Stir vegetables occasionally until they become tender, 8–10 minutes. Add the sage, parsley, and celery salt and stir in to blend well. Pour all the cooked vegetables over the corn bread mixture and blend well.

In a small bowl whisk together the eggs and half the broth, and then pour into corn bread mixture. Gently fold in fresh blackberries to the dressing. Taste and adjust seasoning with salt and pepper. Coat a 9 × 13 × 2-inch pan with pan spray and pour in the casserole, forming it to the dish. Pour in remaining broth, cover with foil and bake at 350°F for 40 minutes.

To make the quail

In a medium bowl, combine flour, onion, garlic, paprika, black pepper, and cayenne and set it aside. Submerge quail into buttermilk for 15 minutes. Remove and dip each piece individually into the flour and spice mixture.

To make the bourbon blackberry sauce

Place the shallots, berries, maple syrup, bourbon, and wine in a pan over medium heat and let reduce by half, 20–30 minutes. Add the demi-glace and simmer another 15 minutes. Taste, and adjust season with salt if necessary. Sauce should be slightly thick. Strain and reserve.

To assemble

Heat frying oil in a heavy-duty skillet over medium heat to 350°F. Place coated quail into heated frying oil for 3–4 minutes. Remove and drain on a plate lined with paper towels. Season with salt while still hot. Place a large spoon or scoop of dressing onto individual plates. Place fried quail on top, strain, and spoon sauce over top of fried quail and around the dressing. Serve immediately.

2 eggs, whisked

2–3 cups chicken broth

2 cups fresh blackberries

Pinch of kosher salt

Dash of freshly ground black pepper

For the quail

2 cups all-purpose flour

2 teaspoons granulated onion

2 teaspoons granulated garlic

½ teaspoon smoky sweet paprika (La Chinata brand preferred)

1 teaspoon freshly ground black pepper

½ teaspoon cayenne

8 whole semi-boneless quail

2 cups buttermilk

For the bourbon blackberry sauce

1 tablespoon sliced shallots

1 cup fresh blackberries

¼ cup pure maple syrup

½ cup bourbon

½ cup ruby port wine

6 ounces demi-glace

Pinch of kosher salt

For the finished dish

1 quart vegetable or peanut oil for skillet frying

Kosher salt to taste

Spicy Orange Roasted Cornish Game Hens

A specific variety of orange, known as the Seville orange, took root in Historic Pensacola centuries ago. The Spaniards started to bring the seeds of this tart orange with them when the first explorers began to settle in the Americas. Northwest Florida's prolonged heat and humidity were ideal for this bitter seed to sew its permanency.

Florida is the largest orange-producing state in the country. Even though the state is mostly known for its oranges, it also produces a large number of other citrus fruit including grapefruit, lemon, and lime.

The following easy-to-prepare recipe is ideal for small birds, game birds, and waterfowl, such as *poussin* (small chicken), squab, and quail. Your kitchen fills with amazing aromas from the roasting and, as the sauces begin to reduce and caramelize, something magical happens to the blending of these ingredients. The evergreen-like orange and hen juices become a complex and luscious glaze, creating an everlasting dish.

SERVES (4–6)

4 (1¼–1½ pounds) Cornish game hens

4 cloves peeled garlic

2 (1-inch) pieces of peeled and coarse chopped ginger

½ teaspoon minced fresh rosemary

½ cup light soy sauce

3 tablespoons artisan honey

2 tablespoon olive oil

3 cups fresh orange juice

1 teaspoon minced orange zest

½ teaspoon crushed red peppers

Pinch of kosher salt

Dash of freshly ground black pepper

Rinse hens, trim off excess fat, and pat dry. Arrange the hens in a shallow roasting pan. Place garlic, ginger, and rosemary in a food processor and pulse to process. With machine running, add soy sauce, honey, oil, orange juice, zest, crushed red pepper, salt, and black pepper to blend well. Pour mixture over game hens, coating well. Refrigerate overnight, turning in marinade several times.

Preheat oven to 350°F. Place shallow roasting pan with the hens and marinade into the oven. Bake for 45 minutes covered, basting every 15 minutes. Uncover and bake another 15 minutes. Remove hens to serving platter. Place a saucepot over medium heat, pour in all the cooked hen marinade and juices, bring to boil, and simmer over low heat for 5 minutes or until the sauce thickens. Strain and pour over hens just before serving. Serve with your favorite side, such as rice or potatoes.

Pan-Seared Peppered Venison Chops

Wild venison has a reputation for being tough and gamey. To ensure mild game flavor, I suggest purchasing farm-raised venison from a well-respected farm that uses sustainable practices. Venison rack chops and back strap are two of my favorite cuts. I love to pair, with the venison chops in particular, a combination of maple syrup and black pepper. And not just any maple syrup, which is often cut with corn syrup, but 100 percent pure maple syrup.

To make the marinade
Combine onion, garlic, red wine, olive oil, and bay leaves in a bowl. Cut 4 sets of double-bone chops and place them in the marinade for 2–3 hours.

To prepare the chops
Preheat oven to 350°F. Remove chops from marinade and wipe off all the marinade. Sprinkle with fresh ground pepper and salt. Place oil in a heavy-duty skillet to coat the bottom. Turn heat up to medium high, add chops, and sear on both sides, about 2 minutes each, then turn heat down to low. Place the pan with the seared chops into the oven and cook 10–12 minutes or until temperature reaches 130°F.

To prepare pan sauce and serve
Remove pan from the oven and drain off excess oil. Remove chops from the pan and set aside. Place the pan over medium-high heat and add wine and maple syrup. Reduce heat to low and simmer for 5–7 minutes. Add demi-glace and simmer 5 more minutes, until slightly thickened, then pour over chops and serve immediately.

(SERVES 4)

½ cup chopped Vidalia onion

2 tablespoons minced garlic

½ cup red wine

½ cup olive oil, plus more for pan frying

2 bay leaves, crushed

1 (24-ounce) rack of venison

1 tablespoon black peppercorns, crushed

Pinch of kosher salt

4 tablespoons pure maple syrup

½ cup demi-glace (Provimi brand preferred)

2 tablespoons chopped fresh flat-leaf parsley

Chapter 8

Farm Vegetables and Sides

Farmers' Market Succotash

I grew up in the north, and up there succotash was one of the most popular and most traditional dishes served during the Thanksgiving season. Northeast Native Americans are said to have been the first to prepare this dish. The foundation for this tasty medley combines sweet corn, peppers, and tomatoes, which are plentiful throughout the state of Florida, year-round.

Succotash is one of my favorite go-to preparations for just-picked vegetables gathered from the local farmers' markets. It is a great celebratory representation of the simply cooked philosophy. The removal of the corn kernels from the cob and chop-prepping are a bit labor intensive, but the end result is a sauté pan filled with a wonderful blend of garden-fresh flavors, brilliant colors, tender textures, and soul-warming simmering goodness.

Succotash ingredients can be varied and elusive, but adding non-traditional succotash veggies like tiny cut green beans, zucchini, and squash allows for more flexibility in the event that the more traditional ones are not available. I'm a carnivore, so my blend often includes smoky bacon, chorizo, or andouille sausage. Here is my basic recipe for a Southern-inspired succotash. It's a great jumping off point, and I highly recommend having fun creating your own version. Be flexible!

(6 SERVINGS)

2 tablespoons unsalted butter

½ cup small chopped Vidalia onions

⅓ cup small chopped celery

1 teaspoon minced garlic

⅓ cup small-chopped green bell peppers

⅓ cup small-chopped red sweet bell peppers

1 cup fresh shucked white butter beans, White Acres peas, or pink-eyed peas

2–3 cups shaved sweet corn kernels (from 3 ears of corn)

1 cup small-chopped, vine-ripe tomatoes, seeded

1 cup small-cut fresh okra

1 cup vegetable broth

1 tablespoon fresh chopped parsley

Pinch of kosher salt

Freshly ground black pepper

Add butter to medium-size skillet and place over medium heat. Add onions, celery, garlic, peppers, and peas, stirring frequently until onions become translucent (about 5 minutes). Add corn, tomatoes, okra, and broth. Stir frequently to blend well. Increase heat to medium high and, once boiling, reduce heat to a low simmer. Cook 40 minutes uncovered and until peas are tender. Add additional broth if peas are not tender. Stir in parsley. Taste, adjust seasoning with salt and pepper, and serve.

Homemade Creamed Corn

Made fresh, this crisp and creamy dish bursts with the sunny flavor of corn right off the cob. Decades ago, when vegetarian cooking was sweeping across the nation, I discovered how to capture the deep flavors within the cob itself. I still cringe a bit when I see corncobs in the trash—what a waste. By simply simmering the cobs in milk, heavy cream, or broth, you can extract the corncob's rich flavor. The soul-satisfying liquor can be the foundation for any vegetable-based soup or sauce—cob stock if you will. It can be used to wilt greens or even in meat-based stews and soups.

I use lots of fresh corn year-round. I was so adamant about saving the flavor-packed corncobs that I stored them in ziplock bags in the freezer. Some of my cooks thought it was strange until I explained why there was a freezer full of corncobs. After making corncob jelly, broth, soup, and vegan-based dishes for what seemed like an eternity, I eventually began to part ways with the cobs.

When it comes to creamed corn, I like mine with lots of corn and very creamy. Keep the corn stock close at hand and adjust the creamed corn recipe to your liking. The thickness can be easily adjusted by simmering to thicken or by adding broth to thin the mixture.

Shuck and rinse the ears of corn. Cut the ends off the corncob so they are flat. Stand them upright and use a sharp knife to remove the kernels and scrape the milk from the cob. Set kernels aside. Place the cobs and into a 4-quart stockpot and cover with about 1 quart of water. Bring to boil and let simmer for 1½ hours. Strain and discard cobs.

Heat butter in a large saucepan over medium-high heat until foaming. Add onions and sauté the mixture for 3 minutes until it turns translucent. Add the corn kernels and season the mixture lightly with salt and pepper. Cook mixture for 5 minutes, stirring frequently. Sprinkle in flour and stir to blend. Add 1 cup of corn broth and cream and bring to a boil. Reduce heat to low and let simmer for 15 minutes or until corn is tender. Taste, and adjust seasoning to your liking with salt, pepper, and sugar.

(SERVES 4–6)

4 ears of corn

4 tablespoons (½ stick) unsalted sweet butter

½ cup small-chopped Vidalia onion

Pinch of kosher salt

Freshly ground black pepper

2 tablespoons all-purpose flour

1 cup heavy whipping cream

Pinch of granulated sugar (optional)

Old-Fashioned Yellow Grits

My good friends Cloyd W. (Brandy) and Dorothy Bruton began their home-ground grits business, C&D Mill, selling to a handful of local restaurants, at open markets, and to some local retailers. You might even spot the Brutons at the many local festivals in and around the downtown Pensacola area firing up the Hercules engine on their portable mill, grinding and packaging fresh grits (and cornmeal) on demand. The old school hit-and-miss engine is quite impressive. Their whole exhibit, including Brandy's overtly wide-brimmed straw hat, is truly a showstopper.

Unlike the mass-produced variety, the Brutons' grits have not yet been stripped of the heart (germ), which makes them true stone-ground grits. It also means a longer cook time than processed quick grits, ensures better nutritional value, and results in the traditional creamy-style variety. Many aficionados refer to these as dinner grits.

Brandy particularly favors the taste of yellow corn. "It just has more flavor," he says. So when he shops the nearby corn growers for dried-corn, he looks for the deepest and richest yellow kernels he can find.

(SERVES 4–6)

2 cups water

2 cups milk

¾ cup stone-ground yellow grits (C&D Mill brand preferred)

Pinch of kosher salt

2–3 cups grated medium cheddar cheese

4 tablespoons unsalted butter

Dash of freshly ground black pepper

Place water, milk, grits, and salt into a double boiler. Bring to a boil and reduce heat to a simmer. Cover and cook for 45–60 minutes. Stir frequently with a whisk or heavy-duty wooden spoon to avoid sticking and lumps. When grits are tender, add grated cheese, and stir until blended smooth. Stir in butter until completely melted, and season with salt and pepper to your liking.

CHEF'S TIP: If you prefer no cheese, substitute ¼ cup heavy whipping cream and stir in last to make creamy.

Seasonal Hash with Bacon & Pecans

In England, corned beef hash is a traditional, inexpensive, and quick dish dating back several score and many years ago. There are endless variations on the dish, but all consist of a base of mashed or coarsely chopped potatoes with onions and leftover meat. Hash doesn't always have to come from leftovers, but I'm certain that's how it came about. It's always been a fantastic way for me to utilize delicious leftovers, particularly after a holiday meal such as Thanksgiving. Eggs any style with hash is great for breakfast.

There are few foods more wonderful than a well-balanced hash: beautiful in color, texture, and flavor. I recommend using some variety of potato or even a hard squash, such as butternut. In this recipe, I use sweet potatoes. I also like meat in my hash. So instead of waiting for a holiday to come around with the usual large plates of leftover beef, turkey, or ham, I created this recipe for freshly gathered local ingredients for a Southern-style hash. I love the flavor of good smoky bacon for cooking potatoes and greens. Sweet potatoes are always plentiful and could easily be swapped out for russet potatoes in this recipe for breakfast, or as a supper side dish for any time of the year.

(SERVES 6)

6 slices smoky bacon (such as Benton's Smokey Mountain Country Hams)

5 cups peeled and small-chopped sweet potatoes

1 cup small-chopped yellow onions

2 cups coarsely chopped kale or Swiss chard

½ cup coarsely chopped pecans

Pinch of kosher salt

Dash of freshly ground black pepper

Preheat a 12-inch cast-iron skillet over medium heat, add bacon, and cook until almost crisp, 5–7 minutes, then remove. Chop the cooked bacon small and set aside. Pour off half the bacon fat from the skillet and add the sweet potatoes so they fill the bottom of the skillet. Increase the heat to medium high and cook the potatoes for 3–5 minutes or until edges become brown. Turn them once with a spatula. Stir in the onions and cook another 5 minutes. Add the greens and wilt. When potatoes are fork tender, add chopped bacon and pecans. To caramelize, let sit 3–5 minutes without turning just before serving. Taste, and adjust seasoning with salt and pepper. Serve right away.

Sicilian-Style Kale

Shueh-Mei Pong and her husband Charles Bush own and operate Dragonfly Farms, a 17-acre farm in Defuniak Springs, Florida. They cultivate some of the finest inland greens for the coastal Seaside region. The pair first met in the 1980s at the famed Paradise Café and later worked, along with Chef Johnny Earles, at Criolla's in Grayton Beach, and with me at Bud and Alley's in Seaside. They also used to own and operate Basmati's Asian Cuisine in Seaside, where Charles was the wine guru and Shueh-Mei the chef: a perfect team.

Shueh-Mei and I shared an adoration of just-dug foods, and we had a penchant for local ingredients prepared with tender loving care. This was always evident by the way we cooked our Seaside foods. The couple took to the earth to grow their own fields of green, a huge undertaking and commitment that few could endure. And now they are known for supplying greens varieties such as chard, curly kale, collards, baby pak choy, arugula, and spinach, along with strawberries and tomatoes. Their produce is sold at the Seaside Farmers Market and to local Santa Rosa Beach chefs.

Kale of any array, fresh from the farm, doesn't require a lot of embellishment. However, this unique Mediterranean preparation combines a sweet, salty, sour, and crunchy texture, making a typical Greek-inspired dish.

Heat olive oil in a large sauté pan over medium heat. Add the diced slab bacon and sauté until the fat renders and the bacon is browning, 2–3 minutes, shaking the pan frequently. Raise heat to high and add onion, garlic, and balsamic vinegar. Sauté until garlic is aromatic, about 1 minute more. Add apricots, raisins, and almonds. Sauté until almonds are toasted and the raisins are puffy, 2–3 minutes. Add kale and sauté until deep green, tender, and softened, 5–7 minutes more. Drain mixture if necessary. Taste, and adjust seasoning with salt and pepper. Serve immediately.

(SERVES 8–10)

3 tablespoons extra-virgin olive oil

4 ounces slab bacon, diced small

1 cup small-chopped Vidalia onions

1 tablespoon minced garlic

3 tablespoons white balsamic vinegar

½ cup dried apricots, quartered

½ cup golden raisins

¼ cup slivered almonds

2 pounds baby kale leaves

Pinch of kosher salt to taste

Dash of freshly cracked black pepper

Southern-Style Shelled Field Peas

A lot of things have changed over the years, and shucking peas by hand is one of them. This small but priceless tradition used to mean quality time for families, taking up large segments of the day. Many hours were spent deshelling and cooking peas and butter beans, exchanging old stories and events of the day.

White Acre peas (also called lady or creamer peas) are one of my favorite varieties. They are a delicious, small field pea particular to this neck of the woods. My friend Doug Bailey of Bailey's Produce and Nursery has the market cornered when it comes to gathering the region's freshest peas in their pods. Farmers far and wide bring their sacked-peas to Doug for personal shelling and for retail at the market. They supply the majority of the White Acres peas, pink-eye peas, black-eyed peas, zipper peas, and white and speckled butter beans to our community.

Yes, times have changed. Today, Bailey's Produce can process a sack of fresh pea pods in less than ten minutes using their garden-green-painted industrial pea shucking machines. It's fascinating to watch, and the process is incredibly efficient. I can buy fresh and frozen peas and butter beans year-round at Bailey's. Doug will gather and process them, put them in a ziplock bag (no blanching), and store them in his freezers for the offseason. I put them up in the same manner at the restaurant. Here is the simple way to make flavorful Southern peas.

(SERVES 6–8)

4 cups shelled White Acre peas (or fresh field peas)

1 tablespoon unsalted butter

1 cup small-chopped Vidalia onions

3 cups ham hock stock

Pinch of kosher salt

Dash of freshly ground black pepper

Carefully wash and pick over the shelled peas. Discard any discolored peas. I like a few pieces of pod shell, so I will only pick out the tough stems. Place deep saucepan over medium heat, add the butter and chopped onion, and sauté for 2 minutes. Stir in the peas and coat them well. Add hot ham hock stock and increase heat to medium-high to bring to a boil. Skim and remove any foam as they cook for the first 10 minutes, then lower the heat, cover, and gently simmer for 30 minutes, stirring occasionally. Taste and adjust seasoning. Use a slotted spoon and serve right away.

Red and White Creamer Potato Salad

Red-skinned new potatoes are a staple in the Florida Panhandle, and easy to grow. Often, they are boiled with some butter or roasted whole with a bit of extra-virgin olive oil, chopped fresh rosemary, and fresh-picked thyme leaves. At least that's how I like to do them. To keep them small, sweet, and tender, I suggest harvesting them before they mature. From Canada to the Deep South, these delicious, low-starch morsels come in other varieties such as Yukon gold, white, and purple.

It was only recently that I fully discovered the red-skinned variety. I was given a swift lesson on how to harvest them by urban gardener Robert Randal of Gulf Breeze Gardens, just a few miles south of Pensacola's Three-Mile Bridge. Robert walked me through his organic potato patch, stopping to kneel down, spread the potato plant leaves against the fertile soil, and then dig down about eight inches around the plant with his hands and pull up several one-inch-diameter potatoes.

If you can't find white-skinned potatoes, all red is fine. I often pick through them and size them accordingly, when I can find them. I love making this potato salad for gatherings; it makes for a wonderful side dish in the summer.

Rinse and place the potatoes in a large pot. Cover with water and add salt. Bring to a boil over high heat, then reduce heat and simmer for 8 minutes (cook 12–15 minutes if using regular-size new potatoes). Strain and let cool. Remove with a slotted spoon or dump the potatoes into a colander and cool under running water. Slice creamer potatoes in half (or in quarters if using regular-size potatoes) and place into a large mixing bowl.

In a skillet, render the bacon until crispy. Remove and chop small, reserving the drippings.

In a medium-size mixing bowl, use a small whisk and combine the mustard, mayonnaise, bacon drippings, sour cream, vinegar, red onions, pickles, green onions, and parsley. Then, using a wooden spoon, gently fold the wet mixture into the cooled and halved potatoes. Add in chopped bacon. Taste, and adjust seasoning with salt and pepper. Wrap bowl and let chill completely before serving.

(SERVES 6–8)

1 pound small red creamer potatoes

1 pound small white creamer potatoes

2 tablespoons kosher salt

10 strips smoky bacon

3 tablespoons Creole mustard

1½ cups mayonnaise (your favorite)

¾ cup sour cream (light or regular)

1 tablespoon apple cider vinegar

¼ cup minced red onion

½ cup chopped bread and butter pickles

3 stalks chopped green onions, white and green

2 tablespoons finely chopped flat-leaf parsley

Dash of freshly ground black pepper

Three-Cheese Macaroni

Sweet Home Farm is a family dairy located in Elberta, Alabama, approximately twenty-five miles west of Pensacola. It has the distinction of being the first farmstead cheese operation in the state. Owners Alyce Birchenough and Doug Wolbert have been making handcrafted cheeses since 1984. A handpainted Sweet Home Farm mailbox and dirt driveway lead to the retail store, which resembles a Norman Rockwell cover from the *Saturday Evening Post.* But you can only purchase their fine cheeses on Saturday.

Alyce explains, "Our mild Gulf Coast climate allows our herd of Guernsey cows to feed on pasture year-round. We use no herbicides, pesticides, or growth hormones on the farm. There are no preservatives or colorings in our cheese. We specialize in aged, unpasteurized cheeses aged ninety days or longer."

They make more than fifteen varieties based on seasonal agriculture and demand from what seems like some sort of cheese cult following. The cheese is hard to find because all of the cheese produced is sold on the farm. You have to go there to get it. No mail order, no Internet order. If you make the enjoyable drive in May or June, grab some strawberries from B J's Farm stand on the way home.

For this delicious and velvety macaroni and cheese dish, I include easy-to-find substitutions readily available at the grocery store in case you're not in Elberta on a Saturday. I suggest experimenting with similar semi-soft artisan cheeses found in your area.

Render bacon in a skillet and reserve the fat. Drain on a paper towel–lined plate and then chop fine. In a separate saucepot, pour in the bacon fat and butter, place over medium heat, and then whisk in flour. Stir over low heat for 3–4 minutes. Add milk and cream and stir until smooth. Increase heat to medium-high to thicken. Reduce heat and stir in cheeses to make sauce velvety smooth. Add cooked pasta, chopped bacon, green onions, parsley, and thyme. Season with salt and pepper. Serve.

(SERVES 4–6)

¼ pound bacon (optional)

6 tablespoons unsalted butter

6 tablespoons all-purpose flour

1 cup whole milk

½ cup heavy whipping cream

1 cup shredded Gouda (or Sweet Home Farm Perdido)

1 cup shredded Monterey Jack (or Sweet Home Farm Bama Jack)

1 cup shredded Fontina (or Sweet Home Farm Elberta)

6 ounces elbow macaroni, cooked

2 tablespoons chopped green onions

1 tablespoon chopped flat-leaf parsley

1 tablespoon fresh thyme, removed from stem

Pinch of kosher salt

Dash of freshly ground black pepper to taste

Hot Peppered Collards

Few chefs can say they learned how to properly prepare and cook collard greens alongside both Chef Edna Lewis and Chef Scott Peacock. I was fortunate enough to have experienced that joy, and it was a huge a-ha moment for me. Chef Edna was the supreme, gentle-spirited, iconic southern chef, and she was sweet and gracious enough to allow me to get the "flavor facts" from her and absorb her expert cooking technique, one-on-one. Edna's impact upon my culinary career is monumental.

The same goes for Chef Scott. Anything Chef Scott embarked upon, he prepared in the manner of Ms. Lewis. For example, when I cooked collards with him, he always cut away the thick center rib portions from the greens. He then cut the remains in half (lengthwise), stacked them, and then rolled them up like tobacco leaves. Handing them off to me, I then proceeded to slice the rolled-up greens into inch-wide strips. Once they were piled high, I plunged them into a five-quart pot that had been simmering for a couple of hours on the stove. The pot had upwards of half a pot of water and a flavorful pork bone in it, brewing a tasty stock. (You can use salt pork, ham hock, or, my favorite, smoked hog jowls.) Making sure they were submerged, I let those greens simmer for thirty to forty minutes, seasoning them with salt and freshly ground black pepper.

After living in the South for a few decades, I picked up on the habit of seasoning collard greens, turnip greens, mustard greens, and kale with hot pepper vinegar. Hot peppers (like Tabasco peppers) from the garden are steeped in vinegar, salt, and, often, a little sugar to balance out the spice, a sort of smoothing over. Many old-school Southerners who ask for hot sauce will generally want something like Tabasco to sprinkle on their greens. But if they want hot pepper vinegar, the general rule is that they'll ask for pepper sauce.

Place ham hocks in a 5-quart stockpot filled with 1 gallon of water. Add onions, celery, carrots, salt, bay leaves, and peppercorns. Bring to a boil, then turn heat down and simmer for 3 hours. Strain, reserving the liquid. Remove ham hocks from the broth, let cool, then remove meat, discarding bones and skin. Finely chop the meat and set aside.

Place the whole collard greens leaves on a flat work surface and, using a utility knife, remove ribs from leaves one leaf at a time. Cut collards into 1-inch wide strips, then into 1-inch cubes. Place strained ham hock broth in a 6-quart stockpot over medium-high heat. Bring to a boil, then reduce to a low simmer. Plunge the cut greens into the broth and use a wooden spoon to push them down into the broth as they begin to wilt and until they are totally submerged.

Simmer them for 40–50 minutes or until tender. Do not overcook or they will become mushy. If greens are slightly bitter, add a pinch of sugar. Season them in the pot with hot sauce and add in the ham hock meat, seasoning with salt and pepper if needed. Use a slotted spoon or tongs to remove cooked collards for serving. Reserve the cooking liquor or "potlikker" for dumplings, corn bread dunking, or soup.

(SERVES 4–6)

2 smoked ham hocks

2 yellow onions, cut into quarters

1 celery rib, cut into 2-inch lengths

2 carrots, peeled and coarsely chopped

2 tablespoons kosher salt

3 bay leaves

½ teaspoon whole black peppercorns

1 bunch collard greens (fresh or store bought)

Pinch of sugar (if needed)

Dash of hot sauce (such as Louisiana Hot Sauce brand)

Pinch of kosher salt

Dash of freshly ground black pepper

Spicy Fried Okra

One of the wonderful things to happen along our 100-mile, somewhat unimpeded stretch of Florida Panhandle is getting our weekly call from Covey Rise Farms. Located in Husser, Louisiana, the highly reputable fifty-acre farm supplies fresh-picked produce year-round right to my back door. I get a real-time text from the delivery driver, giving me a pretty good idea of when he will arrive at the restaurant. All I have to do is step up into their refrigerated truck to taste and handpick from their incredible harvest.

Covey Rise Farms handles multiple varieties of more than thirty types of vegetables throughout their year-round growing season, including cool- and warm-weather crops. In addition, they sell regional picks that aren't necessarily grown on their farm, but are piggybacked on the truck. Some of my favorite produce picks are Creole and Heirloom tomatoes, pink-eyed peas, speckled butter beans, English peas, fennel, tatsoi, Red Cardinal spinach, baby turnips, mizuna, squash blossoms, rainbow carrots, plus blood and candy-striped beets and okra. The centerpiece for this recipe is okra fried the spicy way.

(SERVES 2)

2 cups fresh okra, sliced in half lengthwise

½ cup buttermilk

3 tablespoons rice flour

3 tablespoons yellow cornmeal

¼ teaspoon kosher salt

¼ teaspoons cayenne pepper

¼ teaspoon sweet smoky paprika

¼ teaspoon granulated garlic

Oil for frying

Pinch of kosher salt

Dash of freshly ground black pepper

Pat okra dry with paper towels. Place buttermilk in a shallow bowl. In another shallow bowl, combine the flour, cornmeal, salt, cayenne pepper, paprika, and garlic.

Preheat fry oil to 365°F. Dip okra in buttermilk, and then roll in cornmeal mixture a few pieces at a time. Place into hot oil for 1–2 minutes on each side or until golden brown. Drain on paper towel–lined plate. Season to taste with salt and/or black pepper.

My Gumbo Greens

It may be somewhat confusing, but in this recipe, greens are prepared as a side dish and not used in gumbo at all. The preferred greens are varieties of freshly available, hearty greens, such as curled mustard greens, turnip greens, broccoli greens, collards, dino kale, Red Russian kale, red spinach, swiss chard, and okra. Whether alone or in combination, your batch needs to be cleaned and chopped, cooked in a flavored ham hock stock, and served piping hot with shredded or chopped sausage or ham hock meat, and topped off with hot sauce with an added splash of vinegar (which you would find in any typical green gumbo).

To add to the gumbo muddle, there is no dark roux, as would be used for fresh green gumbo. And finally, this recipe for My Gumbo Greens is not to be confused with the traditional, meatless Lenten dish in Louisiana's Gumbo Z' Herbs, which is made with various greens and fresh herbs. You'll see it clearer when you run through the ingredients and preparation.

I love okra, especially when quick panfried and not slimy, as in this recipe. As you may surmise, the recipe for My Gumbo Greens was spawned from a penchant for gumbo and a zeal for greens. For a meatless version, simply omit the sausage.

(SERVES 10–12)

4 tablespoons olive oil

2 cups cut okra (optional)

2 cups medium chopped yellow onions

1–2 cups medium-chopped andouille sausage

1½ cups medium-chopped celery

1 cup medium-chopped green bell pepper, cored and seeded

1 tablespoon minced garlic

6 cups ham hock broth or water

3 pounds fresh greens (any one of the greens mentioned on page 207), cleaned and chopped

Ham hock meat

2 tablespoons apple cider vinegar

2 teaspoons hot sauce (such as Tabasco brand or Ed's Red)

Pinch of kosher salt

Dash of freshly ground black pepper

Place a large heavy pot over medium heat, add the okra, and cook for 3–5 minutes or until edges turn brown. Remove from pan and set aside on a paper towel–lined plate. Add the onion and sausage to the hot pan, stirring frequently with a wooden spoon, until caramelized and light brown in color, 12–15 minutes. Add celery, bell peppers, and garlic and cook, stirring often, until soft, another 8–10 minutes. Add the broth and increase heat to medium high. Begin first with the heartier greens (chopped collard, turnip, and mustard greens) and stir until tender, about 25 minutes (depending on which ones you're using), reduce heat to medium, then add remaining greens and stir until wilted and leaves are tender, about 5 more minutes. Add the ham hock meat. Taste and adjust seasoning with vinegar, hot sauce, salt, and pepper. Sprinkle the browned okra over the greens. Serve right away.

Squash and Yukon Gold Potato Latkes

Raised Jewish, I have fond memories of family gatherings with my parents, brother, and cousins at the Passover supper table. Simple russet potato pancakes (latkes) were traditional for the holiday, served, of course, with applesauce and sour cream. After being a southerner for over three decades, I've felt an instinct to blend the two heritages, preserving Jewish traditional dishes while making effective use of Florida's regional ingredients.

As Jewish southerners, my own family down here grew up on bacon and pork as well as experiencing some traditional foods such as latkes, brisket, kugel, and fried matzo. Latkes became a year-round sensation, the norm if you will, and creating new versions of traditional latke dishes such as Squash and Yukon Gold Potato Latkes is this chef's attempt at enticing southerners to experience Jewish foods.

Rinse zucchini, pat dry, and split in half lengthwise. Scoop out seeds with a spoon to form a canoe. Discard seeds and feed zucchini into a food processor fitted with a grating attachment. Place grated zucchini onto a clean, dry kitchen towel and squeeze towel firmly to remove liquid.

Peel potatoes, then cut and shape them to fit into processor feed. Grate potatoes, place on another dry towel, and squeeze dry.

Transfer zucchini and potatoes to a large mixing bowl. Beat eggs in a small bowl with a fork and add to mixture. Add grated onion, chopped parsley, olive oil, and matzo meal. Season lightly with salt and pepper and blend well.

Preheat skillet and cook a small test latke for seasoning before frying the entire batch. Taste, and adjust seasoning with salt and pepper. Heat a heavy-bottomed skillet with frying oil to medium high. Spoon zucchini and potato mixture into the hot oil and shallow fry for 2 minutes, or until golden brown on each side. Pat dry and place on a paper towel–lined plate. If cooking several batches, place latkes on an uncovered plate in a warm oven. I suggest serving with sour cream, fresh chives, and applesauce.

(SERVES 6–8)

2 pounds skin-on zucchini or yellow squash

2 large Yukon Gold or russet potatoes

3 eggs

1 medium onion, grated

1 tablespoon chopped flat-leaf parsley

1 teaspoon olive oil

¾ cup matzo meal

Pinch of kosher salt

Dash of freshly ground black pepper

Vegetable oil for frying

Chapter 9

Paella, Pasta, Perloo, Risotto

Seafood Paella

Spain's extensive history and its variety of native ingredients have influenced cooking across the globe for hundreds of years. This is true for the United States, since, like many other western countries, we were occupied by the Spanish in years past. However, the quest for bold Spanish flavors in the States didn't really begin until about twenty-five years ago in South Florida, during the American Food Movement, and it would have a major impact on Florida cuisine for years to come.

In 2008, Visit Pensacola (a branch of the Pensacola Chamber of Commerce) called upon the area's longtime and well-known chefs—Gus Silivos, Jim Shirley, and me—to discuss the possibility of teaming up to promote our area's culinary tourism. Visit Pensacola organizers named us the "Pensacola Celebrity Chefs." Our first event was to celebrate our city's Five Flags (these are generally referred to as the flags that represent those who have occupied Pensacola at one time or another). But then we decided we needed two more local, talented, and established chefs to match the number of flags, so we nominated chefs Frank Taylor and Dan Dunn.

We have prepared dinner for events such as Capture the Fort at Fort Pickens; The Luncheon for King Juan Carlos and Queen Sophia of Spain, held at the Pensacola Naval Air Museum in 2009; the Pensacola Wine Festival, featuring a Taste of Spain with Jorge Ordonez; and four consecutive sold-out dinner events in New York benefitting the James Beard Foundation (including Pensacola Celebrates 450 Years, Pensacola Chefs Honor Gulf Cuisine, Viva Florida 500, and Pensacola Panache).

Certainly it is paella that is Spain's most popularized dish. This recipe was prepared for the 2009 Pensacola Wine Festival's Paella Cook-off, judged by Southern Food Alliance director and author John T. Edge. The King and Queen of Spain would be proud.

(SERVES 12–14)

For the shrimp stock

24 medium shrimp

3 tablespoons olive oil

2 cups white wine

3 cups coarse chopped yellow onions

1 cup coarse-chopped carrot

1 cup coarse-chopped celery

3 bay leaves

2 tablespoons kosher salt

20 whole black peppercorns

3 gallons water

To make the shrimp stock
Remove and reserve heads and shells from shrimp. Clean shrimp and set aside. Place a 4- or 5-gallon stockpot over medium-high heat and add the olive oil. When oil begins to shimmer, add the shrimp heads and shells and stir for 2–3 minutes. Add wine, onions, carrots, celery, bay leaves, salt, and peppercorns. Add water and bring to a boil. Let simmer for 45 minutes. Strain, reserve shrimp stock, and discard shells.

To make the ham hock stock
Combine all ingredients, place in a 4- or 5-gallon stockpot. Bring to a boil, let simmer for 2½–3 hours. Strain, reserving liquid and ham hock meat. Remove bones and fat from ham hocks and chop remaining meat small.

To make the paella

Preheat oven to 350°F. Have shrimp and ham hock stocks prepared and hot. Preheat paella pan and add the olive oil. Add the sausage and let brown for 2 minutes, remove, and place in drain pan. Add the onions, tomato, garlic, and bell pepper, stir, and cook 5–7 minutes or until onions become translucent and liquid from tomatoes has evaporated. Add the shrimp stock, saffron, paprika, rice, and peas. Stir rice to coat and blend ingredients well. Place browned sausage on top, being careful to not disturb the rice. Loosely cover with foil and let simmer over medium heat for 15 minutes.

After 15 minutes, add the mussels, clams, and shrimp. Arrange diced ham hock meat and bell peppers over top and re-cover with foil for another 10 minutes, for 25 minutes total cook time. When shellfish have opened, remove foil and turn up the heat for 2 minutes for a perfect saccorat (crispy bottom) just before serving. Sprinkle with fresh chopped flat-leaf parsley.

For the ham hock stock

4 ham hocks

3 cups coarse chopped yellow onions

1 cup coarse-chopped celery

1 cup coarse-chopped carrot

2 tablespoons kosher salt

3 bay leaves

20 whole black peppercorns

3½ gallons water

For the paella

¼ cup pure olive oil

3 cups ½–inch-thick-sliced chorizo sausage

2 cups medium-chopped yellow onion

2 cups coarse-chopped vine-ripe tomato, seeded

3 tablespoon minced garlic

1 cup small-chopped red bell pepper

7 cups shrimp stock (from heads and shells)

Generous pinch of saffron threads

1 teaspoon smoky paprika (La Chinata brand preferred)

4 cups bomba, calasparra, or traditional Spanish rice

2 cups southern peas (such as butter bean, white acre, or pink-eyed)

24 fresh blue-gold mussels, scrubbed, beards removed

24 middle neck clams, scrubbed and purged

3 tablespoons fine-chopped flat-leaf parsley

Chicken and Chorizo Paella

When it comes to rice dishes, seafood often takes center stage on the dinner tables of towns all along the Gulf Coast. However, this is not always the case for those who live in the interior, landlocked communities with less access to seafood. There, more attention is given to farm animal resources.

Raising hogs and chickens is a common practice throughout the countryside, and they are always readily available. A short drive up into the Florida Panhandle will take you to many functioning, sustainable farms. One great example of such a farm is Green Cedars Farm in Molino, Florida. Owners Roger and Pam Elliot raise and process hogs for ground meat and steaks, and sell their free-range chickens.

When it comes to paella, Spain and Florida share an equal cultural and historical inclination toward chorizo. Chorizo is primarily a Spanish sausage that delivers worlds of flavor by seasoning ground pork with spices such as smoky paprika, red pepper flakes, cayenne, cumin, coriander, and fennel seed, and is perfect for this Spanish-style rice-based dish.

Equally ideal for paella is chicken. I crave the flavorful, moist and tender, dark thigh-meat over white breast meat anytime. In particular, it's best for dishes such as barbeque, roasting, and rice dishes. This pork and chicken paella dish screams down home with the addition of pulled ham-hock meat and field peas.

(SERVES 10–12)

For the ham hock broth

1 gallon water

2–3 smoked ham hocks

2 yellow onions, coarsely chopped

1 celery rib, coarsely chopped

2 carrots, peeled and coarsely chopped

To make the ham hock broth
Place all ingredients in a 4-gallon stockpot over medium-high heat. Bring to a boil and simmer for 2 hours. Strain, reserving liquid and keeping it warm. Let cooked ham hocks cool and then remove meat, discarding bones and fat.

To make the paella
Preheat oven to 350°F. Place a large paella pan over medium-high heat and add olive oil, cubed chicken, and sausage. Let brown for 2 minutes, then remove and place in pan to hold.

Reduce heat to medium and add the onions and cook for 10–12 minutes or until onions have caramelized. Add the tomatoes, peppers, and garlic (this mixture is called sofrito), and continue cooking for another 5 minutes. Add the hot hamhock broth, saffron, paprika, rice, and peas and stir to blend well.

Place browned chicken, sausage, and pulled ham hock meat on top. Loosely cover with foil and cook over medium-low heat without stirring for 20–25 minutes. Do not disturb the rice, and be careful not to burn it. Taste and adjust seasoning with salt and pepper. Just before serving, turn up heat for 2 minutes for a perfect socarrat (crispy bottom). Add fresh-chopped parsley over top and serve.

2 tablespoons salt

3 bay leaves

½ teaspoon whole black peppercorns

For the paella

¼ cup pure olive oil

12 fresh boneless chicken thighs, diced into large cubes

3 pounds chorizo sausage, cut into 1-inch pieces

1 cup small-chopped yellow onions

2 vine-ripe tomatoes, peeled, seeded, and coarsely chopped

½ cup small-chopped red bell pepper

3 tablespoons minced garlic

Generous pinch of saffron threads

1 teaspoon smoky paprika (La Chinata brand preferred)

4 cups bomba rice (short-grain rice)

2 cups field peas (white acre or English)

Pinch of kosher salt

Freshly ground black pepper

4 tablespoons chopped parsley

Paul's Crawfish Fettuccine

When I was chef at Bud and Alley's Restaurant in Seaside in 1990, I was introduced to cooked and peeled crawfish sourced from crawfish farms in New Orleans and supplied by Harbor Dock's Seafood in Destin. My good friend and sous chef (right-hand man) Paul Crout came to us right from Louisiana and was new to the Florida Panhandle. Paul had gained extensive experience in New Orleans at Mr. B's Bistro in the French Quarter, where he had mentored under renowned Chef Gerard Maras, a long-time Brennan's restaurant executive chef.

Paul liked to use crawfish in étouffée, jambalaya, and pasta dishes when they were available. Boiled whole, these brackish water crustaceans deliver a tasty morsel with every bite. I have enjoyed them the most when doused with spicy Zatarain's Crawfish, Shrimp, and Crab Seasoning and boiled to perfection at local gatherings. They are especially a big deal at the annual Fiesta of Five Flags' Pensacola Crawfish Festival, which happens waterside, in downtown Pensacola at Bartram Park.

This recipe is dedicated to Paul, and this is how I remember his dish. It includes both peeled, boiled crawfish tails and quick buttermilk, crispy-fried, soft-shell crawfish. The dish is decadent and delicious, and it represents the best times to be had at special gatherings along the Gulf Coast. Tell your friends you're doing the crawfish and they'll bring the beer.

(SERVES 4–6)

For the fettuccine

1 pound fettuccine

Kosher salt

1 (16-ounce) can diced tomatoes

3 teaspoons olive oil

2 teaspoons minced shallots

To make the fettuccine

Bring a large pot filled with 6 quarts of water and a generous pinch of salt to a boil over high heat. Add the fettuccine noodles and boil for 6–8 minutes until al dente. Strain, reserving the pasta water.

In the meantime, place the tomatoes in a food processor fitted with an S blade and pulse to puree.

Place a large skillet over medium heat with olive oil, shallots, and garlic. Stir for 30–60 seconds to blend well. Add the white wine and increase the heat to medium high, letting most of the wine evaporate.

Reduce the heat for 3–4 minutes, then pour in the tomatoes and bring sauce to a boil. Reduce heat to low and simmer for 5–7 minutes. Add cream and bring to a boil again, then reduce heat to low and simmer for another 10–12 minutes, letting it reduce until slightly thick. Adjust consistency with reserved pasta water if desired.

Stir in the crawfish tails, add the cooked fettuccini, and stir to coat well. Season with Creole seasoning. Taste, and adjust seasoning with salt and pepper.

To make the soft-shell crawfish
Preheat a deep-fryer to 350°F. Pour buttermilk into a medium-size bowl. In another medium bowl, combine flour, Creole seasoning, cayenne, and salt and stir to combine. Place the soft-shell crawfish first in the buttermilk, then coat lightly with seasoned flour. Use a slotted spoon to carefully drop the breaded crawfish into the fryer and cook until golden brown, 2–3 minutes. Remove and place onto a paper towel–lined plate.

To assemble
Place fettuccine into pasta bowls or into a deep presentation platter, and top with the golden-fried, soft-shell crawfish.

1 tablespoon minced garlic

1 cup white wine

1 cup heavy cream

2 cups boiled and peeled crawfish tails

Pinch Creole Seasoning (your favorite brand)

Pinch of kosher salt (optional)

Freshly ground black pepper

For the soft-shell crawfish

1 cup buttermilk

1 cup all-purpose flour

2 tablespoons favorite Creole seasoning

½ teaspoon ground cayenne pepper

1 teaspoon kosher salt

1–2 soft-shell crawfish per person

Garlicky Gulf Coast Linguine

When temperatures drop to a cool chill along the Gulf Coast, I like to eat more pasta and stick-to-your-ribs, comfort-style food. And it's got to have lots of garlic in it! I also enjoy cream reduction sauces, butter sauces, and cheesy Mornay sauces. I love the flavor of rich-tasting pasta sauces. One of my go-to techniques when making a cream sauce of any kind is to make sure the sauce does not sit, is spooned onto the pasta, tossed to coat, and served right away!

In the warmer weather months, I prefer pasta cooked with broth, extra-virgin olive oil, and fresh herbs. (Dried pasta is my go-to, year-round; I always keep a good supply in the pantry.) Remember, after it's done cooking, reserve some of that cooked pasta water for thinning the sauce. A good rule of thumb is to use a tomato-based sauce with pocketed or cup-shaped noodles (such as shells or orecchiette). They will hold and absorb more of the sauce. I suggest you finish your tomato sauce dishes and light cream sauces by cooking the noodle right into the sauce. Long noodles such as spaghetti, linguine, and fettuccine are a perfect choice for cream sauces and clear-broth-based sauces. Here's my interpretation of Pescatori-style, or garlic butter, sauce, for shellfish and linguine.

(SERVES 4–6)

For the garlic butter

2 sticks (8-ounces) sweet cream butter

3 tablespoons extra-virgin olive oil

2 tablespoons fine-chopped parsley

2 tablespoons minced garlic

1 tablespoon lemon juice

Pinch of sea salt

Dash of freshly ground black pepper

For the pasta

2 tablespoons sea salt

1 pound dried linguine pasta

28 wild middle-neck clams, scrubbed and rinsed

To make the garlic butter

Place unwrapped butter in a mixing bowl. Let it sit at room temperature for 1 hour to soften. After 1 hour, stir in olive oil, parsley, garlic, lemon, salt, and pepper. Use a rubber spatula to mix and scrape down the sides of the bowl to make sure all ingredients are blended. Taste and adjust seasoning with salt and pepper. Cover bowl tightly with plastic.

To make the pasta

Fill a 6-quart soup pot halfway with water and place over medium-high heat. Add salt and bring to a boil. Add the pasta and cook, stirring to keep from sticking, for 5–7 minutes.

While pasta is cooking, place a large skillet over medium-high heat. Add clams, wine, and shallots. Cover and cook for 3 minutes. Add the broth, then cover and return to a boil until clams open, 6–8 minutes. Transfer the opened clams to a bowl and cover.

Meanwhile, simmer the pan juices over medium heat, add the shrimp, and cook for 3–4 minutes. Transfer the cooked linguine directly to the skillet. Whisk in 4–6 ounces of whipped garlic butter mixture and let simmer until sauce becomes slightly thick, 3–5 minutes. Add the tomatoes and stir well to incorporate the garlic butter. Add the open clams and all their juices and toss well.

To assemble
Portion the pasta into individual bowls and arrange seafood on top of pasta. Just before serving, pour the sauce and tomatoes over the seafood. Serve immediately, sprinkling with Parmesan if desired.

1 cup chardonnay

2 tablespoons minced shallots

2 cups seafood broth (store-bought is fine)

1 pound medium Gulf shrimp, peeled and deveined

12 red heirloom cherry tomatoes, cut in half

12 yellow pear tomatoes, cut in half

Parmesan cheese (optional)

Three-Cheese Ravioli

I love pasta. I believe most of us do. When I was the chef at Bud and Alley's restaurant in Seaside, Florida, I served pasta more than any other dish on the menu. I challenged myself and my cooks to think outside the box for a new pasta dish every day. Let's face it, pasta makes money!

No matter if it was fresh or dried, pasta was all the rage and graced restaurant tables for many years before the onset of the no-carbohydrate diet in the mid-1990s. Pasta dishes can merit good menu pricing with the addition of our glorious and diverse Gulf seafood options. My job in Seaside was to see the creation of a sellout pasta dish every day for over five-and-a-half years. One of my favorite pasta dishes to make was ravioli, and it still is.

Making ravioli should be fun. If you don't have a pasta machine and don't want to make the dough, I recommend buying freshly made sheets or noodles from a nearby pasta artisan. We have one just across the street from Jackson's Steakhouse called The Bodacious Olive. I can call-in an order and they will make spinach, wheat, or plain semolina pasta sheets and have them ready for me in a couple of hours.

I am delighted to share this easy-to-replicate recipe. Of course, feel free to swap out similar styled cheese varieties to your liking. For this one though, I use a perfect combination of mild soft cheese and lightly salted hard cheeses.

(SERVES 4–5)

1 cup ricotta cheese

1 cup grated mozzarella cheese

¼ cup finely grated fresh Parmesan cheese

2 eggs, beaten

1 teaspoon fresh thyme leaves

Pinch of kosher or sea salt, plus more for cooking

1 pound dough, rolled into thin sheets

Bring a small stockpot filled halfway with water to a boil over high heat. In a mixing bowl, combine ricotta, mozzarella, Parmesan, eggs, thyme leaves, and a pinch of salt. Blend well and set aside. Lay a sheet of dough lengthwise on a floured work surface. Place teaspoon-size dollop of the filling about 2 inches apart in the center of the bottom half of the dough. Use your finger dipped in water to moisten the area around each dollop of filling, and then fold the top half of the dough over the filling to meet the other edge. Press down around each dollop of filling, making sure to press out any air bubbles.

Use a pasta cutter or sharp knife and cut ravioli apart by making a cut halfway between each portion of filling, and trim the bottom edge of the pasta. Place filled raviolis on a parchment-lined sheet pan and repeat with the remaining pasta dough and filling. (At this point, the pasta could be covered with plastic wrap, and refrigerated for up to a day.)

Add about 1 tablespoon salt to the boiling water. Drop ravioli into boiling water for 3–4 minutes (pasta will float to the surface when done). Serve with the sauce or topping of your choice, such as brown butter or porcini mushroom bolognese sauce.

Mom's Kugel

During my youth, my mom cooked intuitively on every Jewish holiday. She used recipes her parents used to follow, and others that were shared between family and friends within the small Jewish community of York, Pennsylvania.

Nowadays, American Jewish fare has become popular for Jews and non-Jews alike. The common link in the desire to discover Jewish foods is their historically centered recipes and stories that provide information from the past. With a wealth of delicious recipes, preparing Jewish foods is no longer just for the Jewish calendar holidays.

The Sabbath is the basis for holiday cuisine in general. In Jewish cooking, recipes can easily transfer from one holiday to another. During the nineteenth century, German Jews were the leaders in most Jewish communities in the Unites States. The earlier Sephardic families had already integrated into American life, which to this day has

influenced American Jewish cooks. Kugel and matzo ball soup are two of my favorite Jewish foods. Some of my fondest childhood memories are of Mom and Dad battling over whose matzo ball recipe reigned supreme: Dad's hard matzo balls or Mom's soft matzo balls. The kugel crown always went to Mom, of course, and I'm thrilled to be able to share it with you. Don't wait for a Jewish holiday to try this recipe. It's perfect for any occasion.

1 (16-ounce) bag wide egg noodles

6 eggs

1 cup sugar

½ teaspoon kosher salt

1 pint low-fat, small-curd cottage cheese

1 pint low-fat sour cream

½ (15-ounce) box golden raisins

¼ cup melted butter

2 teaspoons vanilla

Pinch of cinnamon

Bring a 2-gallon stockpot filled halfway with water to a boil over medium-high heat. Add noodles and stir. Once the water returns to a boil, reduce heat to medium, and let noodles simmer for 6–8 minutes or until they become tender and al dente. Do not overcook. Empty stockpot into a large colander and run cold water over noodles, stirring well to cool and stop the cooking process. Drain off water completely and transfer the cooked noodles into a large mixing bowl.

Preheat oven to 350°F. Coat a casserole dish with butter pan spray. In a large mixing bowl add eggs, sugar, salt, cottage cheese, sour cream, raisins, butter, and vanilla. Use a whisk to blend well. Pour the wet mixture over the noodles and stir with your hands to distribute the mixture evenly. Transfer mixture to the coated casserole dish. Sprinkle several pinches of cinnamon over top of the kugel.

Cover with foil and bake on the middle rack in the oven for 30 minutes. For additional crispy noodle edges, remove the foil and cook uncovered for an additional 15–20 minutes. Total baking time is approximately 50 minutes. Let sit for 30 minutes before portioning into squares.

CHEF'S TIP: Eggs noodles vary in thickness and cooking time. Thin egg noodles may cook in 3–4 minutes while thick egg noodles may take 6–8 minutes.

CHEF'S TIP: Make the kugel one day ahead and store in the refrigerator. The next day, cut it into squares and reheat it, loosely covered, in the casserole dish for 20 minutes at 350°F just before serving.

Panhandle Perloo

Perloo (pronounced Per-low) is a dish that is as popular as jambalaya in the kitchens of the Florida Panhandle and throughout many regions in the heart of the South. It's not a fashionable dish, but if you're fond of rice dishes, then you know rice and a little meat can go a long way at the supper table. Although there are over a dozen different spellings (Perloo, Pilau, Pilaw, Purlo, Purloo, just to name some) and history books full of stories for the dish, they all stew up a similar rice-based dish filled with vegetables and spices.

The inland-based perloo is typically made with chicken, pork, or game. The coastal versions often include shrimp or shellfish, and sausage. For centuries, the dish has recurred as jambalaya in New Orleans, paella in South Florida, and has laid its claim to American fame in Charleston, South Carolina, as perloo in the sixteenth century. Whatever its true history, the dish has roots reaching back to Poland, Minorca, Greece, Iraq, Iran, India, and the Orient.

I love one-pot rice dishes in all their variations, and have never eaten two that were exactly alike. For this Northwest Florida recipe, I showcase locally harvested, farm-raised or wild shrimp, and clams, and use locally sourced food products.

Preheat oven to 400°F. Place the sliced sausage in a dutch oven over medium heat. Cook until the edges are turned up but not crispy, about 10 minutes. Stir in the onions, bell pepper, celery, and garlic and cook another 10–12 minutes or until the onions begin to take on a light color. Add the rice, tomatoes, spices, hot sauce and stock. Stir well, increase heat to medium high, and bring mixture to a boil. Stir one more time, cover loosely with foil, and cook over medium-low heat without stirring for 20–25 minutes. Do not disturb the rice.

Add the clams, shrimp, and oyster meat. Cover again until seafood is cooked, 12–15 minutes. Taste, and adjust seasoning with salt and pepper. Remove from oven and let rest for 10 minutes partially uncovered. Just before serving add fresh-chopped parsley over top.

(SERVES 8–10)

- 3 cups (2-links) thick-sliced andouille sausage
- 2 cups chopped yellow onions
- 1 cup chopped green bell pepper
- 1 cup chopped celery
- 2 teaspoons minced garlic
- 4 cups Plantation Gold rice or aromatic white rice
- 2 cups peeled tomatoes, seeded and coarsely chopped
- 1 teaspoon smoky paprika (La Chinata brand preferred)
- 1 teaspoon granulated garlic
- 1 teaspoon granulated onion
- 1 teaspoon ground cumin
- 1 teaspoon freshly ground black pepper
- 1 teaspoon kosher salt
- 1 teaspoon crushed red peppers
- 3 tablespoons hot sauce (Ed's Red brand preferred)
- 4 cups store-bought or homemade shrimp stock
- 24 middle-neck clams, scrubbed
- 1 pound medium shrimp, peeled and deveined
- 24 Gulf Coast oysters, shucked
- Fresh chopped parsley for garnish

Shrimp and Andouille Jambalaya

Whether the dish is Creole or Cajun, a gumbo, any type of jambalaya, or boiled crawfish, all are immensely popular along the Gulf Coast from Florida to Louisiana. The same can be said for the methods of cooking: cast-iron skillets, pots, and kettles. When it comes to jambalaya, cast-iron is the way to go. This ideal pot is perfect for even heat distribution, browning meats, and moist cooking.

As far as jambalaya's origin is concerned, the Spanish paella is largely seen as the source for its creation. But even the French had a dish called *jambalaia*. It also contained the same basic elements of meat, vegetables, rice, and stock. John T. Edge notes in his book *Foodways* that African-descendant New Orleanians were contributing such one-pot dishes as jambalaya (paella-like concoctions of shellfish, meat, rice, and tomatoes that might have had a Spanish ancestry as well). These heavy-duty cast-iron pots made it possible for Louisiana Cajuns to cook their jambalaya in their regional manner.

Today, when we think of jambalaya, we typically think of New Orleans. And to set the record straight, we still prefer a dutch oven to cook it (just don't say that to the Spanish and French). Here is my recipe that I have prepared with fresh Gulf shrimp and authentic-styled andouille sausage, and I'm keeping the tomatoes in it just to bridge the gap!

(SERVES 4–6)

3 tablespoons olive oil

1 cup medium-chopped andouille sausage

1 cup medium-chopped yellow onions

1 cup medium-chopped green bell peppers

½ cup medium-chopped celery

1 teaspoon finely minced garlic

1¼ cups medium-grain white rice

1 (16-ounce) can diced tomatoes

2 cups chicken or vegetable broth

2 tablespoons hot sauce (Louisiana brand preferred)

1 teaspoon dried basil leaves

½ teaspoon dried leaf thyme

1 bay leaf

Pinch of kosher salt

Dash of freshly ground black pepper

20 medium Gulf shrimp, peeled and deveined

Preheat the oven to 350°F. Place oil in a 4-quart dutch oven over medium heat for 5 minutes. Add andouille and stir for 3–4 minutes. Add the onions, bell peppers, and celery, and stir for another 3–4 minutes. Add garlic and rice, and stir to blend. Pour in the tomatoes, broth, hot sauce, herbs, and bay leaf, and then season lightly with salt and pepper. Add the shrimp and stir to blend well. Cover tightly with lid and bake for 50 minutes. The liquid should be absorbed and the rice thoroughly cooked. Remove lid and let sit 10 minutes before serving.

Creamy Crab over Saffron Risotto with Slab Bacon

The prized dish "risotto" hails from the Milan region of Italy. Authentic risotto begins with the finest short grain rice, in this case it's arborio. The art of cooking the rice begins by evenly coating the rice grains with butter and onions in a heavy-bottomed skillet, and then directly deglazing with white wine. After that, stir in the hot simmering broth in stages. By low simmering and frequent stirring, the liquid is absorbed and the rice begins to cook and tenderize.

Make no mistake, cooking risotto is time consuming, requiring about 25 minutes (from start to finish) of constant attention to simmering and broth absorption in order to cook the rice properly. All of this depends upon the quantity; the more you make, the longer it takes. It's important to remember that you want the outcome of this "regional rice dish" to be tender and creamy.

I recommend adding the simmering broth as needed. Add one or two ladles at a time, just enough for it to rise to the surface of the rice. Leave the skillet uncovered throughout the process! Simmer over low heat and stir mixture frequently until most of the liquid is absorbed. Repeat this 3–4 times until the rice grains are tender and cooked. Classic risotto is always finished with chunks of cold butter, and grated Parmesan or Romano cheese is added just before serving. Cheeses can be salty, so I recommend saving the salt and pepper for last.

A risotto main course can include chicken, shellfish, sausage, roasted vegetables, and much, much more. Once you are comfortable making risotto, the sky is the limit. It's the ultimate "comfort food."

Cut the bacon into ¼-inch-thick slices and place in a heavy skillet over medium heat to render crispy, 12–15 minutes, stirring occasionally. Pour off excess fat and reserve for risotto. Place bacon on a paper towel–lined plate and set aside.

In a small bowl, dissolve saffron in ½ cup broth and set aside. Set a heavy, non-reactive saucepan over medium-high heat. Add 2 tablespoons of bacon fat and sauté onions until tender, about 3 minutes. Add rice, stir well to coat the grains, then continue stirring as you deglaze with the white wine. Add saffron broth, and then add the hot broth in stages as you stir. As you stir and broth is absorbed, add more to cover. When rice is tender and broth is absorbed (about 25 minutes), finish risotto with grated cheese.

In a separate sauté pan, heat whipping cream over medium high and whisk frequently until slightly thickened, about 10 minutes. Add crab to the warm cream and reheat until hot (about 2 minutes). Season the mixture lightly with salt and pepper.

Pour crabmeat mixture over top of the risotto and top with remaining fresh-grated cheese, chopped bacon, and scallions.

(SERVES 4–6)

½ pound slab bacon

½ teaspoon crushed saffron threads

3–4 cups hot chicken broth, divided

1 cup small-chopped onions

1 cup arborio rice

½ cup dry white wine

1 cup Pecorino Romano cheese, freshly grated (plus additional for serving)

1 cup heavy whipping cream

2 cups backfin crabmeat

Pinch of kosher salt

Dash of freshly ground black pepper

¼ cup small chopped scallions

Chapter 10

Simple Breads and Such

Bourbon Banana-Pecan Bread

Banana bread is one of America's favorite, sweet, quick breads (and the best way to use over-ripened bananas). I've been baking it since the days I first began cooking at The Kitty Hawk Saloon in Ocean City, Maryland. Back in that day, when men ate quiche, I served sweet breads such as poppy-seed and zucchini at lunchtime. Usually I would prepare it with our restaurant's quiche lorraine.

While there's nothing particularly southern about banana bread, I still wind up baking it because it brings back fond memories of those early days at the beach on the East Coast. It's great warm or freshly sliced at room temperature, and can hold its own just fine when served with an ice-cold glass of milk.

Now that I'm living in the South, the recipe I developed for making banana bread naturally brought together some of this region's finest ingredients. The process includes bourbon (a favorite spirit of the South), pecans (need no introduction), and sorghum (an important crop worldwide). Banana-pecan bread is an excellent supper table accompaniment during the holidays, so make sure there is plenty of soft butter on the table for slathering. In a pinch, it can be transformed into a simple dessert—warmed and topped with vanilla ice cream.

(MAKES 1 9¼ × 5¼ × 2½-INCH LOAF PAN)

4 tablespoons (½ stick) unsalted butter, plus more for pan

½ cup sugar

2 eggs

4 cups mashed ripe banana

¼ cup sorghum or cane syrup

3 tablespoons bourbon

1 teaspoon lemon juice

½ cup chopped pecans

1½ cups all-purpose flour

1 teaspoon baking powder

1 teaspoon baking soda

1 teaspoon salt

Preheat the oven to 350°F. Lightly butter a loaf pan. Using a mixer on high speed, cream the butter and sugar together until light and blended well. Add the eggs one at a time, waiting until each egg disappears into the mixture before adding the next. The mixture will becomes light and fluffy. Add the mashed bananas, sorghum, bourbon, lemon juice, and chopped pecans and mix thoroughly (about 1 minute).

In another bowl, sift the flour, baking powder, baking soda, and salt. Adjust mixer speed to low and add the sifted dry ingredients to the creamed mixture and blend well (about 2 minutes). Do not overmix.

Pour batter into the prepared loaf pan and bake until a toothpick or wooden skewer comes out clean when inserted into the center of the loaf, about 1 hour. Remove from the oven and let sit 10 minutes before turning out onto a wire rack to cool. Serve warm or at room temperature.

Roasted Pumpkin and Zucchini Bread

To many of the locals, late fall and the "shoulder season" along the Florida Panhandle is the most peaceful time of the year. The Gulf of Mexico's water stays at a swimmable temperature, but the beaches start to empty out. At this time of year, we begin to experience some funky weather changes from week to week. It's not unusual to experience dramatic temperature changes. Arctic blasts push their way down to the Gulf Coast with temperatures occasionally dropping to the freezing point, but a few days later the thermometer will break seventy degrees. Talk about flip-flops.

During these shoulder months, "snowbirds" (U.S. northerners and Canadians) come to our coast to escape their harsh northern climate and enjoy the much more moderate weather, reasonable prices, and empty beaches. To some degree, Destin still depends on them to survive throughout its winter shoulder seasons. Downtown Pensacola experiences its busiest business days during those months. Thanksgiving, Christmas, and New Year's Eve inspire festive holiday table foods, and the smell of sweet quick breads permeates the kitchen throughout the holiday season.

There are a few extra steps involved when using fresh pumpkin for this holiday-inspired quick bread, but I think you will find it rewarding when you taste it.

To make the pumpkin
Preheat the oven to 400°F. Using a serrated knife, cut the pumpkin in half from stem to bottom. Use a heavy-duty vegetable peeler to remove the outer skin, and a large heavy-duty spoon to scoop out the seeds and the pulp string that coats the inside surface. (Save the seeds for drying or roasting if you desire.) Chop the pumpkin into ½-inch cubes, and place them in a small bowl. Toss them with the butter, sugar, and cinnamon. Spread them out on a baking pan and roast for 12–15 minutes, or until fork tender. Set aside.

To make the bread
Preheat the oven to 350°F. Lightly butter a loaf pan. Using the mixer on high speed, cream the butter and sugar together until light and blended well. Add the eggs one at a time, waiting until each egg disappears into the mixture before adding the next. The mixture should become light and fluffy.

In another bowl, sift the flour, baking powder, baking soda, salt, cinnamon, and allspice.

(MAKES 1 9¼ × 5 ¼ × 2½-INCH LOAF PAN)

For the pumpkin

1 small pie pumpkin

3 tablespoons unsalted butter, melted

2 teaspoons sugar

¼ teaspoon cinnamon

For the bread

4 tablespoon (½ stick) unsalted butter

½ cup sugar

3 eggs

2 cups all-purpose flour

2 teaspoons baking powder

1 teaspoons baking soda

¼ teaspoon salt

¼ teaspoon cinnamon

¼ teaspoon allspice

½ cup vegetable oil

1 teaspoon vanilla extract

1½ cups grated zucchini, squeezed

Adjust mixer speed to low and add the sifted dry ingredients to the creamed mixture and blend well, about 1 minute. Add the oil, vanilla, and zucchini and blend well. Fold in the roasted pumpkin with a rubber spatula.

Pour into the prepared loaf pan and bake. Bake until a tester toothpick or wooden skewer comes out clean when inserted into the center of the loaf, about 1 hour. Remove from the oven and let sit 10 minutes before turning out onto a wire rack to cool. Serve warm or at room temperature.

Yellow Cornmeal Soda Bread

Soda bread is a farmhouse staple and a specialty from Ireland. When immigrants traveled to America from Ireland in the nineteenth century, they brought this simple craft with them. Over there, Irish soda bread has traditionally been the bread of a poor population, just as corn bread has been to the American South—a rudimentary mixture made only with the farmhouse pantry ingredients available at the time. Far from ever being fashionable bread, baking soda bread was an integral part of daily life in almost every home, feeding many hungry farmers and their families for years.

I love to prepare soda bread and quick bread (breads with no yeast) because they are easy to personalize and very forgiving. I discovered soda bread's simplicity when tasked with creating a St. Patrick's Day meal for Jackson's, so I have modified it by enriching it with eggs. Most early recipes for Irish soda bread don't include eggs or baking powder. The sour milk, or buttermilk, does the job of activating the baking soda, creating a leavener.

Try this Panhandle version of cornmeal soda bread using locally ground cornmeal, one egg, and buttermilk. It's quick and easy to prepare and tastes great warm, but even better after sitting for a couple hours.

Preheat the oven to 450°F. Sift the cornmeal, flour, salt, and baking soda into a large bowl. Make a well in the center. Stir in egg and cane syrup (if using) with 1¼ cup buttermilk. Mix from the sides, adding more buttermilk if necessary. The dough should be soft and pliable, not too wet or sticky.

Turn out onto a floured board and knead 20 times. Pat and shape the dough into a round, about 2 inches high. With the blade of a sharp knife, make cross cuts about ½-inch deep over the top surface of the dough. Bake for 15 minutes, then brush top surface with the remaining buttermilk. Turn the oven down to 400°F and bake for 35 minutes or until cooked. Test for doneness by tapping the bottom of the bread; it should have a hollow sound. Place on wire rack to cool. Serve at room temperature.

(MAKES 1 LARGE BREAD ROUND)

1½ cups yellow cornmeal

2½ cups bread flour

1 teaspoon salt

1 teaspoon baking soda

1 egg, beaten

1–2 teaspoons cane syrup or sugar (optional)

1½ cups buttermilk, divided

Creamed-Corn Corn Bread

My favorite bread, corn bread, is savored throughout the country, particularly in the South. There are seemingly as many versions of corn bread in the Florida Panhandle as there are cooks. Simply stated, it is easy to prepare. However, there's a delicate balance between the savory, the sometimes sweet, and the often spicy versions representative of its region—Jalapeño in Texas and Mexico, sugar above the Mason-Dixon Line, and savory in the Deep South.

Cake and corn breads are great right out of the oven. But the true test of whether it's a good bread or not is whether or not it holds its moisture after it has cooled down (grab a corner piece). If I break it apart, sop something up with it and if it falls apart, it's too dry for me.

For one of my cooking classes at Jackson's Steakhouse, I wanted to make a moist corn bread. I developed this creamed-corn-infused corn bread recipe using the rich and delicious, homemade creamed corn recipe found within this book. It was a hit! I had a feeling that this could not have been a totally original thought, and I was right—I wasn't the first to come up with the idea.

About a year later, while enjoying a world-class cooking demonstration at the annual Taste of Pensacola on Pensacola Beach, I watched Andrew Zimmern share his very own creamed-corn corn bread with the audience. Andrew became a household name as co-creator and host of the Travel Channel series *Bizarre Foods*. At the gig, I smiled and thought to myself, Hmmm, apparently culinary geniuses think alike!

(MAKES 1 10-INCH LOAF)

10 tablespoons bacon fat, divided

½ cup finely chopped yellow onion

1¼ cup unbleached all-purpose flour

1½ cups yellow cornmeal

1 tablespoon baking powder

½ teaspoon kosher salt

1 teaspoon sugar

2 eggs, whisked

⅓ cup buttermilk

2 cups homemade creamed corn (see recipe in Chapter 8) or 1 (14-ounce) can creamed corn

Preheat oven to 425°F. Heat 3 tablespoons of bacon fat in a skillet. Add onions and sauté for several minutes. Remove pan from heat and set aside.

In a large mixing bowl, sift flour, cornmeal, baking powder, salt, and sugar and set aside.

In a separate large mixing bowl add the sautéed onions, whisked eggs, buttermilk, 5 tablespoons of bacon fat, and creamed corn. Add the dry ingredients to the wet ingredients and stir briefly to combine.

Place a skillet in the oven for 5 minutes to warm. Remove from oven and pour in the remaining 2 tablespoons of bacon fat. Use a paper towel to coat bottom and sides of pan. Pour in the batter.

Reduce heat to 375°F and bake bread for approximately 40 minutes, or until a toothpick inserted into middle comes out clean and top is golden brown. Remove corn bread and let cool for 30 minutes in the pan on a rack before cutting into wedges or squares and serving.

CHEF'S TIP: If a cast-iron skillet is not available, use an 8 × 8 × 2-inch casserole dish.

Edna Lewis–Inspired Biscuits

Few cooking memories evoke more happiness for me than those of making biscuits alongside seventy-six-year-old Chef Edna Lewis and Chef Scott Peacock, two of America's most respected southern chefs. They were heading up the Revival of Southern Foods tour throughout the country in 1992 and invited me to work alongside them. By some good fortune and chance, they trusted my hands at making their trademark biscuits for important events such as American Chefs Celebrate American Farmers; a tribute to the late James Beard; the theme for CityMeals-on-Wheels, held at New York's Rockefeller Center; Ms. Lewis's seventy-seventh birthday celebration, a dinner honoring her and inaugurating the James Beard Foundation's Living Legend Series; a Symposium for Revival of Southern Food at the Middleton Place in Charleston, South Carolina; and a Seaside Symposium on Southern Food, here in the Panhandle. The memories are still vivid.

There are two things in particular that made Edna Lewis's biscuits unique. One is that her homemade recipe calls for single-acting baking powder. Ms. Lewis explained, "Single-acting baking powder is less bitter than double-acting baking powder." The second is that the lard was always rendered fresh and on site from leaf lard (a sheet of fat—easy to melt, pulled from the vent area of the pig). I have adapted this recipe so it's a little easier to replicate, but will provide comparable results.

June 26 1993

Dear Irv and Coworkers,

Thank you all for coming to share with us the Work & Fun. I wish it could have been more so I am enclosing a letter from the People at city-meals on-wheels. We were afraid that they would not let us have such a staff but Scott convinced them that it would work and it did.

Thanks Irv to you and your Coworkers

Love
Edna Lewis

3 cups all-purpose flour, sifted,
plus more for dusting

½ teaspoon kosher salt

2½ teaspoons baking powder

½ teaspoon baking soda

⅔ cup good lard

1 cup buttermilk

Lightly salted butter, room
temperature for brushing

Preheat the oven to 450°F. Mix together sifted flour, salt, baking powder, and baking soda in a large mixing bowl. Add lard and blend with your fingertips until mixture has become the texture of cornmeal. Add milk all at once, scattering it all over the dough. Stir vigorously with a heavy-duty wooden spoon. The dough will be very soft in the beginning, but will stiffen in 2–3 minutes. Continue to stir a few minutes longer.

After dough has stiffened, scrape from the sides of the bowl and create a ball. Lightly dust a work surface with flour and turn out biscuit dough. Coat hands with flour and flatten dough by hand. Form a round cake and knead for a minute by folding the outer edges of the dough into the center of the circle. As you fold, overlap the dough ends. Turn the folded-in side face down. Lightly dust with more flour and use a rolling pin to roll dough to ¾-inch thick.

Dust a 2½-inch-diameter biscuit cutter with flour. Make cuts straight down—do not wriggle the cutter. Cut as close together as possible to utilize all the dough. Place the biscuits next to each other but not touching each other, on a heavy-duty cookie sheet or baking pan. Bake for 13–15 minutes. Remove from oven and let rest for 3–4 minutes. Don't re-roll dough trimmings. Bake them along with the perfect biscuits.

CHEF'S TIP: Select good-quality butter or lard, and use fresh baking powder or make your own. Be careful not to overwork the dough. Don't twist the biscuit cutter as you cut. Make these biscuits with love, bake them, and finally, brush 'em with soft butter as you pull them from the oven.

Bacon Hush Puppies

When I first arrived in the Florida Panhandle in 1982, hush puppies, fries, slaw, and lemon wedges were served with all seafood. I ate hush puppies every chance I got, especially at those mom-and-pop fried fish spots, shrimp and oyster barns, and dockside seafood shacks. There weren't many other restaurants to choose from back then, and believe me, not all the hush puppy and slaw recipes were good ones.

Some southern folklore legend claims that hush puppies got their name from the fishermen who would toss them to the barking dogs so they'd "hush up" and not scare away the fish. And it came as no surprise to me that North Florida has its own local lore. Posey's Oyster Bar in St. Marks, which was destroyed in 2005 by hurricane Dennis, was once known as "the home of the hush puppy." Residents there support this claim and have reported that one former owner of Posey's is credited with inventing the "hush puppy."

No matter which story holds true, we still hold this cornmeal concoction in high esteem with it's golden-brown exterior and moist and flavorful interior. As simple as it may seem, a good hush puppy recipe can be hard to find. Here is my recipe for bacon hush puppies. Bacon makes most everything taste better, particularly for the hush puppy. Feel free to double or triple the recipe for large gatherings. For the perfect batch, I suggest not cooking more than ten at a time, unless you have a battery of fryers.

Preheat frying oil to 365°F. In a large bowl, whisk together cornmeal, sugar, baking powder, baking soda, salt, black pepper, and cayenne. Make a 3-inch well in the center of the dry ingredients.

In a second bowl, combine chopped onions, pepper, jalapeño, egg, and buttermilk. Add to center of dry ingredients and whisk from the sides to make a smooth batter. Batter should be stiff and easily fall from the scoop.

To fry the hush puppies, use a 1-ounce scoop to portion batter and carefully release each hush puppy into the hot oil, one at a time. Fry for 3½ minutes or until they are deep golden brown and float. Place on paper towel–lined plate to drain.

(SERVES 6)

2 cups yellow or white cornmeal

1 teaspoon granulated sugar

2 teaspoons baking powder

1 teaspoon baking soda

¼ teaspoon salt

Dash of freshly ground black pepper

Pinch of cayenne pepper

½ cup finely minced yellow onion

¼ cup finely diced red sweet pepper

1 teaspoon finely diced jalapeño, seeds removed

1 large egg

1 cup buttermilk

Oil for frying

Sweet Corn Pudding with Fresh Herbs

One of the greatest things ever that makes the Deep South so special is sweet corn. Florida, in particular, is sweet on corn. The Sunshine State ranks corn as one of the state's most valuable vegetable crops. A handful of Florida varieties that come to mind are Silver Queen, Gold Cup, Guardian, Bonanza, and Florida Staysweet. In the Panhandle region, Silver Queen and its hybrid, Silver King, are most prevalent.

I'm a huge fan of fresh, sweet corn right from the cob. I'm not picky about whether it's white or yellow as long as it's sweet and not too starchy or waxy. When the corncobs are roasted or grilled in their husks, sweet corn has a remarkable earthy flavor profile, making it perfect for shaving (for relish or salsa) or eating it right off the cob.

For my sweet corn pudding, shaved raw corn is first sautéed and then simmered in cream to maximize flavor extraction. This recipe was originally designed for biscuit or muffin-size cast-iron molds, and was best served under fresh Gulf Coast fish such as grouper, snapper, or triggerfish. However, I have changed the recipe slightly to make it more of a casserole-style dish for scooping and serving just out of the oven.

(SERVES 6–8)

4 tablespoons (½ stick) unsalted butter

1 cup finely diced Vidalia onions

1 jalapeño pepper, seeded and chopped fine

3 cups fresh sweet corn kernels

½ teaspoon fresh thyme leaves

½ teaspoon fine-chopped fresh rosemary needles

1 cup heavy cream

3 eggs, beaten

1 cup whole milk

½ cup stone-ground yellow cornmeal (C&D Mill brand preferred)

⅓ cup granulated sugar

1 cup ricotta cheese

½ teaspoon kosher salt

Dash of fresh ground black pepper

Freshly grated nutmeg

Add butter to medium skillet over medium heat and sweat onions for 3 minutes. Stir in jalapeño, corn kernels, and herbs and cook for another 2 minutes. Add the whipping cream to skillet, increase heat, stir, and bring to a boil, then reduce heat to medium-low, stir, and simmer for 5–7 minutes, or until slightly thick to make creamed corn. Remove from heat to cool slightly.

In a medium-size mixing bowl, combine eggs and milk. Slowly whisk in cornmeal, sugar, then ricotta. Stir the cooked creamed corn into the egg mixture, then season with salt and pepper.

Coat a 10–12-cup cast-iron skillet or casserole dish with pan spray, then pour in the pudding mixture. Add freshly grated nutmeg over top.

Preheat the oven to 350°F. Bake 35–40 minutes, until top begins to brown and a toothpick in the center comes out clean. Let rest 5 minutes. Serve warm.

HERBS

Chapter 11
Grab a Plate and a Beer

Country-Style Fried Chicken

Unbeknownst to me, I was captured on film working alongside Chef Edna Lewis (the late doyenne of southern cooking) and Scott Peacock during a Seaside feast in 1991. The film segment became forever known in the award-winning documentary, *Fried Chicken and Sweet Potato Pie*. During the film, Chef Lewis narrates her life story. It's extraordinary and can be found on YouTube.

When you watch, look closely in the background and you'll see a young bearded chef chopping in the kitchen. That's me! The three of us were cooking historic southern foods for notable southern cookbook authors John Egerton, Eugene Walter, Marie Rudisill, and of course, Edna Lewis. History was made and it was a very special time indeed!

As for fried chicken, it's practically a religion in the Deep South and the Florida Panhandle. It's one of the many meals I was privileged to cook with them, and still love to cook for my friends. As for my fried chicken recipe, I borrow the techniques I learned from Scott Peacock, Edna Lewis, and Art Smith. What they shared with me was their penchant for cooking with the best and freshest ingredients, and preparing food with love and extra care.

Combine chicken broth (or water), lemon juice, 1 tablespoon salt, garlic, and bay leaf in a large mixing bowl. Add cut-up chicken and marinate for 2 hours.

Place flour, remaining 4 tablespoons of salt, and pepper into the paper bag, close top, and shake to blend well.

Pour buttermilk into a separate large mixing bowl.

Pour shortening and lard into a cast-iron dutch oven and preheat to 365°F.

Remove chicken from brine and wipe off any garlic pieces. Dip brined chicken into the buttermilk and then transfer directly into flour mixture in the paper bag. Shake well to coat lightly all over. Remove from bag and place on the wire rack to let excess flour drop. Let coated chicken rest for 20 minutes before frying.

Place coated chicken in hot oil mixture, skin side down, leaving 1 inch between the pieces. Add the chunk of bacon. Cook for 10 minutes, use the tongs to turn the chicken, and fry for an additional 12–15 minutes. Chicken will be crispy and mahogany in color. Place fried chicken on a wire rack with a baking pan underneath to catch any drippings. Add remaining cuts of chicken and repeat. Let rest 30 minutes and serve.

CHEF'S TIP: If possible use farm-raised and young chickens for making this recipe. I recommend avoiding chickens over 3½ pounds—they take too long to cook and the outside often becomes too dark before the meat is done.

(SERVES 4)

For the chicken

2 cups chicken broth or water

4 tablespoons lemon juice

5 tablespoons kosher salt, divided

1 teaspoon coarse-chopped garlic

1 bay leaf, broken

2½–3 pounds fresh chicken, cut into 8 pieces

5 cups all-purpose flour

4 tablespoons freshly ground black pepper

2 cups buttermilk

All-vegetable shortening (Crisco brand preferred)

1 pound lard

1 (2-inch) chunk of smoky bacon

Chicken and Drop Dumplings

Chicken and dumplings is a Southern favorite, and in my opinion one of the top comfort foods of North America. During my early days at Bud and Alley's, my prep team consisted of an elderly husband and wife team, Ms. Louise and her husband, Leo. Every day they drove to the restaurant from their remote family home in Point Washington. There's dedication for you.

From time-to-time, Louise would bring in her yard bird eggs in exchange for kitchen scraps to feed their chickens. I loved these people. They worked until they were physically exhausted, and then went home to tend their farm. Louise would occasionally cook her chicken and dumplings, and bring them in for break-time and share with me. And that was when I became a believer.

The first time I made chicken and dumplings was in 1994, when I was tasked to outline daily specials as Food Development Chef for Destin Development Co. They owned the Destin Diner at that time, along with six other restaurants. However, it wasn't until last year that I perfected my own dumpling style. Here is my recipe for chicken and puffy cornmeal dumplings.

(SERVES 8–10)

For the chicken stock

1 (2½–3 pound) chicken

Olive oil

Pinch of kosher salt

Dash of freshly ground black pepper

1 small onion, coarsely chopped

3–4 stalks celery, coarsely chopped, leaves reserved for garnish

3 bay leaves

For the chicken and dumpling sauce

¾ cup chicken fat (reserved from roasting)

1 cup medium chopped yellow onion

1 teaspoon minced garlic

1 cup all-purpose flour

To make the chicken stock

Preheat oven to 350° F. Rub the chicken with oil, salt, and pepper. Roast for 1½ hours or until juices run clear when chicken is poked with a skewer in the thickest part of the thigh. Remove from oven and allow to cool. Pour pan juices and fat into a small bowl and reserve. After about 1 hour, pull the meat from the bones and set aside. Place all the bones in a 5-quart stockpot and cover with water. Add onion, celery, and bay leaves, bring to a rolling boil, and lower to a simmer. Simmer for 1½–2 hours. Strain and reserve liquid and lightly season with salt and pepper.

To make the chicken and dumpling sauce

In same stock pot add chicken fat, onions, and garlic and sauté for 2–3 minutes or until onions become soft and opaque. Add the flour and stir for another 3–5 minutes. Add the remaining pan juices, stock, cream, and mushrooms and bring to a low boil, then reduce to a simmer. Taste, and adjust seasoning with salt and pepper. Simmer for 20 minutes. Add green onions.

To make the dumplings

Sift the cornmeal, flour, baking powder, and sugar into a large bowl. In a small bowl combine the egg and milk to a smooth mixture. Make a well in the center of the dry ingredients, add the milk mixture, and stir in. Fold in the parsley. Cover with plastic wrap and place in refrigerator for 1 hour.

To assemble
Coarsely chop the pulled chicken meat and add to the chicken and dumpling sauce. Bring sauce to a low simmer and drop 8–10 tablespoons of the dumpling mixture into the simmering sauce. Cover and simmer for 10 minutes. Stir and check seasoning. Serve in a soup tureen, deep platter, or individual soup bowls. Garnish with reserved celery leaves.

1 cup heavy cream

2 cups sliced button mushrooms

Pinch of kosher salt

Dash of freshly ground black pepper

3 green onions, coarsely chopped whites and some green

For the dumplings

1 cup yellow cornmeal

¼ cup all-purpose flour

1 teaspoon baking powder

1 teaspoon granulated sugar

1 egg, beaten

¾ cup milk

2 tablespoons finely chopped flat-leaf parsley

Braised Beef Short Ribs

I grew up on braised beef. And to this day, the simplest way I know how to cook beef short ribs is the way my mom prepared her Sabbath brisket way back when. The technique I took over from her is boiling the meat in broth with onions, carrots, and celery, along with other seasonings, until the meat is very tender, and the broth is rich. Thick-cut beef short ribs are perfect for large gatherings, but must be prepared far in advance because they require several hours of cook time. This slow-braising cooking method is foolproof.

It's not difficult to find beef short ribs nowadays. You just have to look for them. Beef ribs tend to play second fiddle to pork ribs, so that's the hard part. In Asia, however, they have a different mindset. Beef short ribs are a national dish (*Kalbi-kui*) in Korea, and the thin butterfly short ribs are perfect for smoking and quick-grilling on the barbecue.

In this neck of the woods, more often than not, beef short ribs are prepared like a southern *pot-au-feu* of beef and vegetables, wine broth, and herbs. The meat is slow braised until it is succulent and ready to fall off the bone. Often the braising liquid flavor profile can be altered by interchanging fresh herbs or vegetables such as fresh fennel, or by spices such as star anise for that distinct licorice flavor.

(SERVES 4–6)

½ cup vegetable oil

6 portions (about 2–3 pounds) beef short ribs

1–2 cups red wine

1 cup small-chopped carrots

2 cups small-chopped onions

1 cup small-chopped celery

1 cup small-chopped tomato, peeled and seeded

1 quart chicken broth

1 quart beef broth

4 tablespoons minced garlic

1 sprig fresh rosemary

1 sprig fresh thyme

1 orange skin, zest into wide strips

Pinch of kosher salt

Freshly ground black pepper

Preheat oven to 325°F. Place a large dutch oven over medium-high heat and add oil. Heat oil to shimmer, about 3 minutes, and then add the ribs one by one, leaving 1 inch between them. Brown the short ribs for 3 minutes on each side. Remove from oil and pat dry with paper towels. Pour off excess oil, then add wine and all vegetables. Place the seared short ribs over vegetables, cover with broths, and bring to a boil. Add garlic, rosemary, thyme, and orange zest, lightly season with salt and pepper, and cover. Place in preheated oven for 3–3½ hours. Check to see if connective fat is tender, meat should be easy to pull away from the bone.

When beef is tender, use a slotted spoon to remove the ribs from the braising liquid and transfer onto a plate, cover, and set aside. Pour the braising liquid into a small saucepan and skim surface to remove any fat. Cook until the liquid is reduced by half or slightly thickened. Place the braised short ribs over cooked rice or pasta and pour sauce with vegetables over the short ribs. Serve right away.

Panhandle Shrimp Boil

A fresh harvest of Florida hoppers is a great excuse for an impromptu Panhandle-style shrimp boil. Hoppers are a delicacy of the Florida Panhandle. They are to Apalachicola Bay what lobster is to Maine. These pink shrimp migrate off the grass flats of the bay and can always be identified by the spots in the middle of their backs. I believe these succulent shrimp to be the sweetest shrimp I have ever eaten and a prized iconic Panhandle crustacean.

Fresh head-on wild shrimp from any coast will work for this recipe. If you're landlocked, it's easy to find frozen head-off shrimp at a reputable seafood market. Shrimp processors often individually quick-freeze them for shipping and retail; this is your second-best option. I recommend wild shrimp for boiling, as they will be more tender than supple farm-raised. Should you decide on headless shrimp for your shrimp boil, cut the purchase weight by approximately one-third.

Here is my recipe for a shrimp boil made with our regional shrimp. Don't be intimidated by preparing a shrimp boil. Borrow or purchase a boiling pot at an outdoor/sports store and a gumbo burner works perfect. Remember you will also need an oar-like paddle for stirring.

(SERVES 8–10)

¼ cup salt

1 bag Zatarain's boil bag

4 cups Zatarain's spice powder

3 large onions, quartered

4 whole garlic heads, halved

6 bay leaves

4 lemons, halved

8 sweet corn ears, shucked and cut into 2-inch lengths

2–3 pounds red creamer potatoes

10 pounds head-on shrimp (fresh Florida hoppers preferred)

Fill a 30-gallon boiling pot and basket ¾ full with water or a 40-gallon boiling pot and basket ½ full with water. Bring the water to a boil and add the salt, boil bag, boiling spices, onions, garlic, and bay leaves. Squeeze the lemons into the water and then drop them in. Let simmer for 20 minutes.

I like to use a hacksaw to cut the fresh corn into 2-inch lengths or simply break them in half by hand. Add the corn and potatoes and let simmer for 15 minutes. Next, increase heat to a rapid boil and add the shrimp. Let boil for 5–7 minutes, stirring frequently. Turn off the heat and carefully remove the basket. Pour the shrimp, corn, and potatoes onto a long table lined with newspaper. Grab a plate and let the feast begin!

Amber Beer–Battered Fish

One of the Panhandle's favorite ways to prepare freshly caught fish such as grouper, scamp, mahi-mahi, or lionfish is to lightly fry it. My personal favorite frying method is dipping and coating using a thin beer batter made with a craft amber beer. Trust me when I tell you there is nothing better for building a flavorful beer batter than our own distinguished craft beers brewed right here in Pensacola.

The new craft beer movement is sweeping the Florida and Alabama coast, and Pensacola brewmaster Mark Robertson is one of the regional pioneers brewing flavorful, authentic beer. Pensacola Bay Brewery is housed in the historic Pensacola district, and leads the microbreweries for the Panhandle. Mark selects the highest quality ingredients, turning hops and malts into signature, flavorful brew. He prides himself on both classic styles and creative fine beer recipes, making for unique creations–all without preservatives and chemicals.

The humble brewery located across from historic Pensacola Old Christ Church is often the hub for folks to gather and celebrate life, and is a favorite local watering hole. Area service women and men, food and beverage industry residents, and chefs and artists gather at the brewery to celebrate good people, good beer, good food, and good times. Among the fifteen unique handcrafted beers, my favorite for a memorable beer battered fish fry is their Rip Tide Amber.

Preheat frying oil to 375°F. Cut the fish fillets into ¾ × 1–2-inch chunks. Thoroughly rinse all the fish and drain off excess water. Pat dry with paper towels and season with salt.

Combine then sift the all-purpose and rice flours into a mixing bowl. Make a well in the center and pour in 2 tablespoons olive oil and eggs. Gradually beat in beer using a heavy-duty whisk to make a smooth, thick batter. Cover and refrigerate for 1 hour.

Dip the seasoned fish chunks in the prepared batter and place directly into hot oil, frying for 3–5 minutes until crisp and golden. Lift out and drain onto a platter lined with paper towels. Taste a crispy fish nugget, and adjust seasoning with salt. Divide onto serving plates. Garnish with lemon wedges and serve immediately with your favorite tartar sauce or spicy aioli.

(SERVES 6–8)

Vegetable oil for frying

3 pounds skinless fish fillets

1 teaspoon kosher salt

2 cups all-purpose flour

1½ cup rice flour

2 tablespoons pure olive oil

2 eggs, beaten

2 (12-ounce) bottles amber beer (Rip Tide Amber label preferred)

3 lemons, cut into wedges

Oven-Roasted Suckling Pig

The University of West Florida Division of Anthropology and Archaeology reported that "Pigs were initially introduced into Florida by Spanish explorer Hernando de Soto in 1539. Pork was an important and favorite meat in the Iberian diet. Cured hams, bacon, and pork preserved in brine were indispensable meats for sea voyages and for overland expeditions through unfamiliar territories."

My good friends Dorothy and Brandy Bruton celebrate life with a pig roast every spring. Here's a direct quote from their invitation: "Let's get together for no special reason. Just to celebrate good food, good friends, and the grillin' season. Winter is finally over, no more chillin'! The Brutons are hosting a pig roast and it's time to do some grillin'."

Along the Florida Panhandle, a pig roast typically takes place after winter, and before it gets too hot. A large, heavy-duty barbecue works nicely. Just build a cinder block pit or a dug-in hole and fill it with a stockpile of charcoal and wood. Seasoned pecan or hickory wood adds a good smoke flavor. The seasoned pig is placed on a metal grill rack (often homemade) and slow-cooked over the open fire. It's a true social event, often taking eight hours (depending on the size of the pig) or an entire day, from start to finish.

Often times an outdoor event of this caliber is not feasible, so I adapted this recipe for an indoor oven. This way it can happen at any time of the year, for a few close family and friends, or a small gathering. I recommend having friends bring their favorite side dishes for the feast.

(SERVES 10)

For the brine

3½ gallons water

5 cups kosher salt

4 cups granulated sugar

1 (5-pound) bag of ice

1 (15–20 pound) dressed suckling pig

For the basting sauce

½ cup olive oil

1 cup apple cider vinegar

½ cup water

1 cup brown sugar

To make the brine
Use a deep plastic tub or box or heavy-duty plastic food storage box. Add the water, salt, and sugar and stir to dissolve, about 5 minutes. Add the ice and stir to blend well. Submerge the pig in the water mixture. Place in a cool dark area of the house, turning once, for 6–12 hours. It's important to be sure the water temperature stays below 40 degrees at all times. Add additional ice if needed.

To make the basting sauce
Combine all ingredients in a small saucepan and stir over low heat to dissolve brown sugar. Turn off heat and set aside.

To roast the pig
Preheat oven to 275°F. Remove all but the lowest oven rack. Remove the pig from the brine and place in the kitchen sink to drain. Discard the brine. Transfer the pig to a baking or roasting pan fitted with a rack to keep the pig raised off the bottom. Fill the cavity with lightly crumpled aluminum foil to fill it out. It will take about twenty

12-inch-long sheets of foil. Sit pig upright, position legs snugly to the sides, and prop up head on a pie pan or with more crumpled foil to align nicely with the spine. Cover snugly with foil and place in the oven.

Rotate the pan after each hour. After 3 hours, remove pan from the oven and carefully lay pig on its side to remove the foil. Reposition the pig to sit upright, increase oven temperature to 425°F, and begin the basting process.

Continue roasting uncovered, applying the basting sauce with a basting mop or brush every 10 minutes for the next hour. Adjust to lower temperature setting if needed. Apply foil to cover any head parts that may start to become too brown. The pig is done when a thermometer inserted in the thickest part of the meat reads 160°F. Remove from the oven and let rest for 30 minutes before carving.

CHEF'S TIP: Suckling pigs range in size depending on the provider and age of the pig when slaughtered. Use a reputable butcher or local farmer who can have the pig processed and dressed. For a general rule of thumb to calculate how much pig will be needed for your gathering, simply figure 2 pounds of raw weight per person. Pigs larger than 22–24 pounds most likely will not fit in a standard oven and will require a commercial oven or outdoor cooking.

Here is a general guideline of cooking times for unstuffed suckling pigs:

18–20 pounds 4¼–4½ hours

20–24 pounds 4½–5 hours

Pit-Roasted Oysters

From my current hometown of Pensacola to the oyster town that is Apalachicola, one of my favorite Florida Panhandle occasions is an oyster roast. The main requirements for an oyster roast are cleaned oysters, a hot bed of amber wood coals, heavy-duty gloves, garlic butter, and plenty of cold beer! A pit-fire is my favorite method. However, it requires a bit of planning and making sure that all the materials are in place before you get started.

Pit-fires are best during the chilly weather months. After all the oysters have been roasted and eaten, the ambers can be restoked with more wood and transformed into a campfire for toasting marshmallows on a stick or making s'mores. This is great when you're near the water as the sun sets on the beach, bay, or sound. I guarantee that this occasion will be fondly remembered by your friends, family, and loved ones.

It's a tradition to keep it simple, which means once the oysters are popped open and the top shell is removed, you can spear these little roasted jewels with a cocktail fork and then dip them into a side dish of garlic butter mixed with hot sauce or crushed red peppers and perhaps a squeeze of lemon.

To make the fire pit

A pit-style fire can be done in your backyard or on a stretch of beach over a dug-in campfire. This method requires selecting a remote area away from trees and buildings, and building a fire pit 2 cinder blocks high and 2 cinder blocks wide. Leave one side open for stoking the fire. Use the kindling and a starter stick, and stack 5 or 6 split hickory logs inside the pit. Add a bit of lighter fluid, and ignite the fire. Let burn down for 20 minutes, then add a few more logs. In about an hour, the wood ambers should be hot enough to spread over the bottom of the pit. Place the grill grate over top.

To make the oysters

Place the butter, minced garlic, and crushed red pepper in a saucepan on the grill rack and stir to blend well. Set aside. Line the front of the grill with tightly sealed oysters and cover them with soaked untreated burlap. As the oyster begin to pop open, in 7–10 minutes, transfer them to a pan and use a shucking knife to pop off the top shell. Place oysters on individual plates or a large platter. Pour the garlic butter mixture into individual ramekins for dipping. Serve and eat them using a cocktail fork, accompanied by lemon wedges, hot sauce, and garlic butter.

(SERVES APPROXIMATELY 10)

For the fire pit

12–16 cinder blocks

Plenty of kindling (sticks and tree branches, broken into manageable lengths)

Fire starter stick or lighter fluid

10–20 pieces split hickory or pecan logs

Matches

3 × 3-foot grill grate or metal rack

For the oysters

1 pound unsalted butter

¼ cup minced garlic

Pinch crushed red pepper (optional)

1 sack Gulf Coast oysters, rinsed with a hose

Large burlap sack from the oysters (soaked in sea water)

Lemon wedges (optional)

Hot sauce (Ed's Red brand preferred)

Chapter 12

A Gulf Coast Thanksgiving

Boudin-Stuffed Quail with Madeira Sauce

Florida farm-raised quail can be ordered fresh via the Internet from Agrilicious.org. They can also be found in most grocery stores throughout the country in the counter-freezer section along with duck, goose, Cornish hen, and turkey. They are usually semi-boneless, which means the rib cage and cavity bones have been removed.

On the other hand, if you're adventurous and looking for the ultimate quail hunting experience, try Blackwater Farms, a privately owned farm and hunting preserve located west of Pensacola near Loxley, Alabama. The native grasses and fields of northwest Florida and lower Alabama are plush with Panhandle Bobwhites, so load up the rifles and hop in an old-timey army jeep to find these game birds in the wild.

One of my favorite and most delectable ways to prepare quail is to stuff it. Simplifying the stuffed quail preparation is as simple as chasing down a good quality, succulent boudin (pork and rice sausage with Cajun spices). A couple hundred miles to the west of here is Cajun country, the heart of Louisiana, where boudin-sausage making is as much about tradition as it is about taste. And for this neck of the woods, a good quality boudin made by generations-old recipes can be found at Cajun Specialty Meats in Pensacola, or on the Internet at cajungrocer.com.

(SERVES 4)

1 pound medium or hot (spicy) boudin sausage

8 whole bone-in or semi-boneless quail

1 cup Madeira wine

1 cup chicken broth

1 sprig fresh thyme

1 sprig fresh savory

1 teaspoon Cajun seasoning

1 tablespoon all-purpose flour

2 teaspoons unsalted butter

Pinch of kosher salt

Pinch of sugar

Preheat oven to 350°F. Remove the sausage and rice mixture from its casing. Stuff each quail with the boudin, then place the birds, breast side up, on a wire rack over a baking pan with the wine, ¾ cup of broth, herbs, and Cajun seasoning. Bake for 30–40 minutes, or until a meat thermometer reads 165°F when inserted into the center of the stuffing.

Remove rack and the stuffed quail from the pan and set aside. Place the roasting pan directly over medium-high burner. Scrape pan with a wooden spoon to release any tiny caramelized bits. In a small bowl whisk together the flour and remaining ¼ cup of chicken broth until smooth. Pour flour mixture (white wash) into the roasting pan, reduce heat, and simmer for 5 minutes or until slightly thickened. Whisk in butter until it disappears. Taste and adjust seasoning with salt or sugar. Pour through a strainer and spoon over the top of the stuffed quail.

Porcini-Dusted Sweetbreads

In the early 1980s, I began my love affair with sweet breads working the kitchens of French restaurants, and today they make a reappearance on my menus for special occasions. It is a special dish. The unusual name for and texture of the veal thymus gland meat has provided a love/hate relationship with Gulf Coast tasters. I find that seasoned travelers and foodies, who are more than likely to be familiar with how they taste, have already formulated an opinion.

The best way to introduce sweetbreads to new tasters is to break them up into smaller pieces, make them crispy, and serve them as an appetizer with a dipping sauce on the side. Another way to make sweetbreads more approachable is to combine them with other proteins such as chicken or country ham. It's all about semi-concealment.

The following preparation for sweet breads made its way to the appetizer platters during my second visit to the James Beard Foundation in 2001 for a Gulf Coast Thanksgiving.

(SERVES 2–4)

½ **pound veal sweet breads**

¼ **cup all-purpose flour**

2 **tablespoons dried porcini mushroom powder**

¾ **teaspoon salt**

4 **tablespoons (½ stick) chilled unsalted butter, divided**

1 **tablespoon fine-chopped shallots**

¼ **cup dry sherry**

1 **sprig fresh thyme**

1 **tablespoon fine-chopped flat-leaf parsley**

Freshly ground black pepper

Rinse the sweet breads and soak them in water for 2 hours. Prepare an ice bath with equal parts water and ice in a medium bowl. Place a saucepan over medium-high heat, and add the sweet breads and tepid water to cover. Bring to a boil, reduce heat, and simmer the sweet breads for 6–7 minutes. Using a slotted spoon, transfer them to the ice bath. When cooled completely (about 10 minutes) remove the membrane and connective tissue and then separate them by seam into small nuggets. Nugget sizes will vary so do not worry.

In a medium bowl combine the flour, mushroom powder, and salt. Coast the sweet bread nuggets with the seasoned flour. Place a sauté pan over medium heat and melt 3 tablespoons of the butter. When bubbling, fill the pan with the sweetbreads, leaving ½ inch between them in order to fry them crispy. It will take 3–4 minutes for the small nuggets and 5–6 minutes for the larger ones. Remove them from the pan and place them on a plate lined with a paper towels. Pour off excess butter from pan.

In the same pan, add the shallots and sherry and scrape the bottom of the pan. Adjust heat to a low simmer, add the thyme, and reduce by half. Just before serving, finish pan sauce by swirling in remaining chilled butter. Add the chopped parsley, taste, and adjust seasoning with salt and pepper. Add the sweetbread nuggets back to the pan and then swirl to coat them. Divide onto individual plates and serve right away with the sauce on the side for dipping.

Slow-Roasted Turkey

When we were growing up, we were taught that the celebration that came to be officially known as Thanksgiving first happened in Plymouth Colony in 1621 between the Pilgrims and the Wampanoag Indians. And of course, as young schoolchildren, we were taught that the centerpiece of their feast was turkey. Given the abundance of wild turkeys and other native game at the time, it is certainly believable; but we'll never know for sure.

According to Florida historian Michael Gannon, "When on September 8, 1565, Pedro Menéndez de Avilés and his 800 Spanish settlers founded the settlement of St. Augustine in La Florida, the landing party celebrated a Mass of Thanksgiving, and, afterward, Menéndez laid out a meal to which he invited as guests the native Seloy tribe who occupied the site. . . . What was the meal that followed? Again we do not know. But, from our knowledge of what the Spaniards had on board their five ships, we can surmise that it was cocido, a stew made from salted pork and garbanzo beans, laced with garlic seasoning, and accompanied by hard sea biscuits and red wine. If it happened that the Seloy contributed to the meal from their own food stores, fresh or smoked, then the menu could have included as well: turkey, venison, and gopher tortoise; seafood such as mullet, rum, and sea catfish; maize (corn), beans, and squash." That was quite a few years before the Mayflower hit Plymouth Rock, but some stories just stick.

As with dressing or stuffing, most people prefer their turkey prepared the way it was when they were growing up, and for me that preparation is slow-roasted. I also like to brine my turkey when possible, and, before roasting, lift up the breast skin and stuff it with a fresh herb rub. I offer my thanks with a recipe for both brining and roasting the perfect turkey to enjoy at Thanksgiving, or any time of year.

To make the brine

Unwrap turkey and set aside giblets and livers. Rinse the turkey thoroughly. Place salt, sugar, 2–3 pounds ice, and 2 gallons of cold water in a 5-gallon bucket and stir until salt and sugar are dissolved. Add the turkey and submerge. There are no hard-and-fast rules for brining, but I suggest 10–12 hours brine time in a cool spot. Check ice after several hours of brining, and add more ice if needed to keep 38°F or colder.

To make the turkey

Have the Saucepot Gravy ready and set aside on stove burner.

Preheat oven to 400°F. In a shallow roasting pan, add the giblets and livers (optional), onions, carrots, celery, thyme leaves, chopped rosemary, and water. Set a V-rack to its widest setting in the pan.

(SERVES 10–12)

For the brine

1 (14- to 16-pound) turkey

2 cups kosher salt

1 cup sugar

1 (5-pound) bag ice

2 gallons water

For the turkey

Saucepot Gravy (page 263)

3 cups medium-chopped onion

1 cup medium-chopped carrots

1 cup medium-chopped celery

1 teaspoon fresh thyme leaves

1 teaspoon finely chopped fresh rosemary

3 cups water

1 stick butter for basting, softened

1 teaspoon fresh savory leaves

2 sprigs fresh thyme

2 sprigs fresh rosemary

2 teaspoons olive oil

Brush the backside of the turkey with butter before setting the bird in the rack. Place savory, thyme sprigs, rosemary, and olive oil in a small bowl and blend well. Lift breast skin and rub herb mixture onto the meat. Place, breast side up, in rack and brush entire breast side of the turkey with 2 tablespoons of butter.

Roast for 1 hour. Remove pan from oven and baste turkey leg, thigh, and breast with 2 tablespoons of butter. Rotate the oven pan and add more water if evaporated. Return turkey to the oven and roast for another 30 minutes. Remove from oven and baste turkey leg, thigh, and breast with 2 more tablespoons of butter. Rotate the pan and return turkey to oven and roast another 20 minutes. Remove turkey for the final time and repeat basting with remaining butter. Roast until a meat thermometer inserted into the thigh registers 170°F–175°F, about 30 additional minutes. When done, transfer to a platter and let rest 25 minutes before carving.

Skim fat from roasting pan, then place the pan over 2 open burners set on medium. Use a wooden spoon to stir and loosen the brown bits. Stir in 3 cups of water and increase heat to medium high to boil and then reduce heat to low and simmer for 3–5 minutes. Strain contents of roasting pan into the prepared Saucepot Gravy. Simmer over medium-low heat to thicken or add more beurre manier (kneaded butter and flour; see Saucepot Gravy recipe). Taste, and adjust seasoning with salt and pepper. Reserve and chop up giblets and livers (optional) and add to the saucepan gravy. Carve turkey and serve gravy separately.

Standing Rib Roast with Vegetables

A slow-roasted beef rib or prime rib is one of my favorite ways to cook a basic rib roast. For the holidays, there's nothing more impressive than presenting a bone-in standing rib roast on a platter with roasted vegetables. I love a crispy and charred hunk of meat that's juicy and cooked to perfection, and, for me, the quintessential cut of beef is the standing rib roast.

It's not likely that you will find a standing rib roast on the meat counter at your grocery store, so ask the butcher to cut a 4-bone-in rib roast from a beef rib and have him tie it for roasting, too. Ask for USDA Choice grade. There is no need to go to the expense for Prime grade, since there is plenty of fat and the roast will be cooked at a fairly low temperature. I guarantee the roast will be flavorful and juicy, and will melt in your mouth.

If your butcher didn't do it, tie cotton string or butcher's twine between each bone to secure the beef for roasting. In a mixing bowl combine salt, pepper, garlic, onion, paprika, thyme, and rosemary and blend well. Rub and massage the entire roast with the spices. Place in refrigerator to marinate overnight. Before cooking, let the roast sit at room temperature for 45 minutes. Place a large, heavy-duty skillet or roasting pan over medium-high heat and add the oil. When oil shimmers, sear the roast on all sides and brown the ends (about 5 minutes each side) to seal in the juices.

In a medium-size mixing bowl, combine the cut vegetables and garlic cloves. Place rib roast on middle rack in roasting pan, loosely covered with foil, in a 325°F oven for 1 hour. Remove roast and rack, and add cut vegetables to the hot drippings and stir to coat well. Return roast and rack over vegetables and cook an additional 45 minutes loosely covered with foil, or until internal temperature reaches 130°F.

Let roast rest 20 minutes before carving. Present standing with bones up on a platter, surrounded with the roasted vegetables. To make au jus, place the roasting pan over a stovetop burner on medium-high heat, add the broth, and scrape the pan bottom with a wooden spoon to lift the caramelized bits and pieces. Reduce heat, taste, and adjust seasoning. Strain the au jus before serving along with the roast. Once the standing rib roast has been presented, transfer the meat to a carving board and lay flat. Slice between the bones, against the grain, and cut them in half for smaller portions. Serve immediately along with vegetables and au jus.

(SERVES 5–6)

- 4-bone prime rib roast
- 1 tablespoon kosher salt
- 1 teaspoon fresh-ground black pepper
- 1 teaspoon granulated garlic
- 1 teaspoon granulated onion
- 1 teaspoon smoky paprika (La Chinata brand preferred)
- 1 teaspoon dried thyme leaves
- 1 teaspoon minced fresh rosemary
- 1 cup olive oil
- 2 cups thick-sliced Vidalia onions
- 2 cups ½-inch-wide-wedge-cut sweet potatoes, peeled
- 2 cups ½-inch-wide-wedge-cut turnip roots, peeled
- 2 ears corn, cut into 1-inch pieces
- 2 cups beef broth
- 20 peeled garlic cloves

Andouille Corn Bread Dressing

Did you know that dressing is prepared separately and only becomes stuffing once you put it in the bird? Regardless of whether you're from the North or South, at Thanksgiving time, dressing is a traditional side to accompany your bird of choice: turkey, goose, duck, or what have you. I'm sure you can agree that north of the Mason-Dixon Line, most of the bread used for dressing will be the white bread sort. On the south side, cooked and crumbled corn bread is the bread of choice. In the past, I have also used a rich French-style brioche (egg bread).

In the north, sweet apples and nuts are often included in dressing, while in the south a good spicy pork sausage and beer frequent recipes, as well as pecans. I'm one who believes that if it isn't broke, then one shouldn't try to fix it, which leads me to my sausage and corn bread dressing. I make this recipe every year for the restaurant and it's proved to be a local favorite year after year.

Eggs are often used in recipes to help bind cubed-bread dressings. I include eggs in my corn bread dressing recipe for richness and body. However, the fine corn bread will remain together as long as the dressing remains moist. If you decide to leave out the eggs, keep plenty of hot broth available to moisten the cooked dressing as it sits.

(SERVES 8–10)

8 cups fine-broken corn bread

2 cups small-chopped andouille sausage

1 cup (2 sticks) unsalted butter

2 cups small-chopped Vidalia onions

1 cup small-chopped celery

2 tablespoons minced garlic

⅛ cup fine-chopped fresh sage

3 eggs, whisked (optional for firm texture)

½ (12-ounce) bottle beer

About 4 cups hot broth (chicken, turkey, or duck)

2 teaspoons celery salt

Pinch of kosher salt

Freshly ground black pepper

Preheat oven to 350°F. Coat a 9 × 13 × 2-inch casserole dish with pan spray. Place the broken corn bread into a large mixing bowl and set aside. Place a large skillet over medium-high heat, add sausage, and cook for 5–7 minutes until juices are released. Add butter and, when it foams, add onions, celery, and garlic. Stir to coat vegetables and cook until vegetables become tender, 8–10 minutes. Add the sage and stir in to blend. Pour entire mixture over the broken corn bread. Stir together to blend well; I like to put on my food handler's gloves and use my hands from this point on. Whisk together the eggs, beer, broth, and celery salt, and season lightly salt and pepper. Turn out dressing into the casserole dish and form to fit. Cover with foil and bake 30 minutes.

Saucepot Gravy

Most folks agree it's practically sacrilegious to work on Thanksgiving Day. Chances are, every year you're home enjoying the holiday with family and friends, like most of America. Unless, of course, you work in the restaurant industry. For me, that means suiting up for our Thanksgiving brunch and making a difference in the lives of people in the Florida Panhandle area the best way I know how. I get to make them happy by being open all afternoon, producing turkey and all the fixings at a reasonable price. It's been a tradition at Jackson's since 2000. And it's a good thing, because many people prefer to dine out on that day.

One key ingredient to my Thanksgiving plate is the Saucepot Gravy. It was inspired decades ago by my longtime neighbors and great friends, Debra and Mike Desouza, while I was living in Destin. They knew firsthand that I worked every holiday and weekend, and for Thanksgiving they would invite me to their house for an early supper. Often exhausted and empty-handed, I would offer to make the gravy as a contribution to the feast. I would grab a small saucepot and start chopping onions, celery, and carrots as the foundation. This was my famous "Saucepot Gravy," which I still make every year, only now I make it in a five-gallon pot!

Place the oil in a large heavy-duty saucepot over medium-high heat for 3 minutes or until oil shimmers, and then brown turkey neck all over (about 5 minutes).

Place softened butter in a small mixing bowl. Use a fork to blend in the flour until all the flour has been absorbed, creating a *buerre manié*.

Add the cut vegetables and thyme and stir for 2–3 minutes. Add garlic and seasoning and stir to blend well. Add broth, stir, and bring to a boil. Reduce to a low simmer and use a whisk to blend in the *beurre manié* to thicken the gravy to your liking. Add bay leaves, taste, and adjust seasoning with salt and pepper or poultry and herb seasoning, and gently simmer for 30 minutes.

Remove saucepot from heat and set aside. When turkey is ready to serve, pour any pan drippings into a bowl and skim to remove the fat. Do not use burnt drippings. Add up to a cup of drippings to the prepared gravy and stir to blend well. Discard neck and bay leaves before serving. If using a smoked jowl, remove any meat from the bone, chop small, and add to the gravy. I like my gravy with all the vegetables and meat included. Straining is optional.

CHEF'S TIP: *Beurre manié* can be used soft by adding dollops with a spoon, or made in advance and stored in a tightly sealed container in the refrigerator for 2–3 weeks. Break into small nugget-size pieces before using.

(MAKES ABOUT 1 QUART)

For the gravy

3 tablespoons olive oil

1 (8-ounce) smoked turkey neck or smoked hog jowl

½ cup (2 sticks) softened butter

¾ cup all-purpose flour

1 cup small-chopped onions

½ cup small-chopped celery

½ cup small-chopped carrots

1 teaspoon fresh thyme leaves

1 teaspoon minced garlic

1–2 teaspoons poultry and herb seasoning

5 cups chicken broth

2 bay leaves

Pinch of kosher salt

Freshly ground black pepper

Turkey pan drippings (optional)

Country Ham with Cane-Mustard Seed Glaze

In the Jewish household where I was born and raised, pork was taboo. My first experience preparing a true salt-cured (uncooked) ham was with one sourced from Smithfield in Virginia. Chefs Scott Peacock and Edna Lewis used them frequently. It wasn't till 1992 that I watched them soak them and change out the water several times and learned how to cook them.

Well, a lot of things have changed since those days, including America's fascination, and mine, with country ham. I am a huge fan of thinly sliced, aged country ham, especially when it is cut into paper-thin, almost translucent slices. In fact, I am serving country ham on my current fall menu at Jackson's along with my crab cakes with corn and snap bean salad. The ham sliced in this manner provides a subtle and salty flavor and creates "umami" with every bite.

Domestic-aged country ham and imported prosciutto have become the darling of pork aficionados. These wonderful hams are being served on charcutiere boards in restaurants all around the country. While working alongside the chef duo of Peacock and Lewis, I also learned how to cook and apply a sweet glaze to cooked whole ham to counter the intense salt flavor. This recipe is one of my creations using local cane syrup, and is perfect for a last minute, applied glaze on a fully cooked ham.

(MAKES ABOUT 1½ CUPS GLAZE)

1 country ham, uncooked (Benton's, Edwards, Smithfield, or your favorite brand)

½ cup pure cane syrup

½ cup water

6 tablespoons apple cider vinegar

2 tablespoons brown mustard seeds

¼ cup Dijon mustard

2–3 cups water (for roasting pan)

Follow instructions for soaking, trimming, and cooking on whatever particular country ham you have purchased.

Place cane syrup, water, vinegar, mustard seeds, and Dijon mustard in a saucepan over medium heat and stir to blend well. Reduce heat and simmer for 15 minutes or until mustard seeds become soft. Set aside.

Preheat oven to 350°F. Put the fully cooked and ready-to-be-served trimmed ham in a roasting pan and score the surface of the trimmed fat with a sharp knife. Add the water to the roasting pan. Apply glaze with a brush or spoon and spread evenly all over the scored ham. Bake for 10 minutes, then repeat the process 2 more times. Remove from pan and place on a serving platter for carving. Serve with remaining glaze.

Cooked Pear and Cranberry Relish

Every country has some sort of relish that it relishes, though the kind that I like to make is a not-so-traditional American chutney, which is sweet and tart. I take cranberry sauce, as we know it, and transform it into a cooked relish, but not exactly the chilled version traditionally found on a hot dog or burger. The mix is not too wild, loose, and loud, but this combination of short-cooked fresh and dried fruits is a refreshing alternative to old-style cranberry sauce.

It's not like gelled cranberry sauce from a can, nor is it a solid red mass of cooked cranberry sauce and sugar as some of us remember from our childhood. It's not southern or classic, but after years of serving this relish, I think you'll find this recipe has the necessary pedigree and flavor characteristics to grace the Thanksgiving supper table. The flavors are fresh and bold, and a little relish goes a long way. I like to think of this cooked relish as a condiment more than a side dish.

I recommend this recipe be prepared a day in advance and chilled in the refrigerator. To serve, reheat in a saucepot and serve warm, or bring down to room temperature (my favorite). You might just simply cook it and set it aside until needed and then serve it right on the turkey plate. After Turkey Day, I love to puree the leftover relish down and use it instead of jarred applesauce with pork or alongside latkes.

Place a heavy-duty saucepan over medium heat, add the butter, onions, and vinegar, and cook for 3 minutes or until onions become translucent. Add the pears and cornstarch and stir in to blend well or until cornstarch disappears. Add cranberries, apricots, raisins, ginger, honey, and mint. Increase heat to medium-high. Once the mixture reaches a boil, reduce heat, stir well, and let simmer 15–20 minutes or until pears are fork tender. Serve or set aside until needed.

(SERVES 8–10)

3 tablespoons unsalted butter

1 cup small-chopped Vidalia onions

3 tablespoons raspberry vinegar

6 Anjou or bosc pears, peeled, seeded, and medium-chopped

2 tablespoons cornstarch

¾ cup dried cranberries

1 cup small-chopped dried apricots

½ cup golden raisins

1 tablespoon grated fresh ginger

1 tablespoon artisan honey

3 tablespoons fine threads fresh mint

Red Wine Poached Pears with Blue Cheese Brule

There's nothing quite like the combination of a sweet pear and blue-veined cheese. For this dessert, I use Bayside blue cheese, an aged farmstead cow's milk cheese from Sweet Home Farm in Elberta, Alabama. However, most any artisan blue cheese will work. For poaching pears, I like to use an affordable red wine that complements food, such as Pinot Noir, Cabernet Sauvignon, or even a Ruby Port. These varietals have lush flavors, ample fruit, and great balance—something I would pair with fruit and cheese. Avoid standalone, full-bodied, high-tannin Bordeaux-style wines for poaching dessert. They are excellent with steaks, but for dessert they tend to overpower the fruitiness of the pear.

You can customize the poaching liquid to suit your taste by adding various spices, fresh ginger, vanilla beans, or a particular wine to the mix. Once the poaching liquid has been reduced, this makes for a perfect sauce. Also, I frequently change sweeteners, swapping out honey or cane syrup for sugar. The butane-torched sugar provides a crunchy texture to the soft blue cheese.

(SERVES 8)

1 (750-milliliter) bottle Pinot Noir or choice red wine

1 cup water

¼ cup cane syrup

1 cinnamon stick

1 vanilla bean, split

4 medium Anjou or Bosc pears, peeled

1 cup artisan blue cheese, broken into chunks

6 tablespoons turbinado sugar

In a saucepan bring wine, water, cane syrup, cinnamon, and split vanilla bean to a boil over medium-high heat. Add pears snugly into the simmering wine. Cover and simmer for 25 minutes, stirring occasionally to rotate the pears. Pears are done when they pierce easily with the tip of a knife. Remove the pears from the poaching liquid using a slotted spoon and set aside.

Remove cinnamon stick and return poaching liquid to a boil. Reduce by a third or until it coats the back of a spoon, about 20 minutes. Turn off heat and set aside. Slice the pears lengthwise in half. Use a Parisian scoop to remove a perfect sphere from the center of each pear half.

Fill each pear cavity with 1 tablespoon of blue cheese. Repeat for each pear half. Just before serving, dust the entire surface of each pear with the sugar. Tap to remove any excess sugar. Turn on flame and torch each cheese-filled pear for only 8–10 seconds. Spoon a pool of sauce onto each plate and serve with one pear half.

Sweet Potato Pecan Pie

As with many of my recipes, I use instinct to pair classic southern ingredients. For this recipe, I combined sweet potato pie and pecan pie. This seemed like an original idea to me, and a delicious one at that. However, on a recent visit to K-Paul's Louisiana Kitchen in New Orleans, I discovered that one of their signature in-house desserts is Chef Paul Prudhomme's sweet potato pecan pie.

That trip to the Crescent City inspired me to thumb through my dog-eared and wine-stained copy of Chef Paul Prudhomme's Louisiana Kitchen, which has graced my cookbook collection since its publication in 1984. I indexed the book to confirm what I already knew: this pie combination had been done before. But that's okay.

Chef Paul's recipe requires making the two pie fillings separately and then carefully layering them before baking, resulting in a few extra steps but a pie that is eye-catching. My version is basically a pecan pie filling with a couple of baked sweet potatoes that are mashed and incorporated into the filling. It's simple, luscious, and easy as pie! Make sure you use a graham cracker crust, though, and I highly recommend melting homemade marshmallow over the top before serving.

For the piecrust

1¾ cups fine graham cracker crumbs (about 15 crackers)

¼ cup dark brown sugar

8 tablespoons (1 stick) unsalted butter, melted

For the sweet potato and pecan filling

2 sweet potatoes, about 10 ounces each

1 cup dark corn syrup

1 cup granulated sugar

1 teaspoon salt

½ teaspoon cinnamon

⅔ cup unsalted butter

1 teaspoon vanilla extract

1 cup coarsely chopped pecans

3 eggs, beaten

Freshly grated nutmeg

To make the piecrust

Stir graham cracker crumbs and dark brown sugar in a bowl until well combined. Add melted butter and mix until crumbs are evenly moistened. Press firmly and evenly on the bottom and sides of a 9-inch pie plate to create a crust, making sure there are no cracks. Bake in the oven for 10 minutes or until golden. Remove from oven.

To make the sweet potato and pecan filling

Preheat oven to 350°F. Wrap the sweet potatoes tightly in aluminum foil and bake them until they are very soft, about 1 hour. Remove from oven and allow them to cool in the foil. Unwrap the potatoes and remove the skin. Put the flesh into a bowl and mash well with a fork, transfer to a 2-quart saucepot, and add the corn syrup, sugar, salt, cinnamon, and butter. Bring to a boil, using a wooden spoon to blend until the sugar has dissolved. Remove saucepot from heat for 20 minutes to allow the mixture to cool down. Whisk in vanilla, nuts, and eggs and blend well. Skim to remove any foam from the top of the filling. Add freshly grated nutmeg on top.

To assemble

Pour the mixture into the partially cooked piecrust and use a rubber spatula to scrape all of the filling out of the saucepot. Place pie in the oven on the middle rack and bake for 40–50 minutes or until center is firm and no longer jiggles. Remove and let cool on a wire rack for 1 hour. Chill in refrigerator for 2 hours before slicing.

CHEF'S TIP: Add a slab of homemade marshmallow to melt and toast over the top of the pie before serving. Homemade marshmallow can be made days in advance, dusted with confectioners' sugar, and stored until needed.

Pumpkin Bread Pudding with Gingersnap Streusel

Bread pudding, no matter what country it's from, is not a complicated dessert. From a chef and restaurateur standpoint, it's perfect for utilizing leftover French or brioche bread. The sweet custard-based dessert first appeared on New Orleans menus long before it made its way here. It became a signature menu dessert throughout the Florida Panhandle in the 1980s.

There is no fixed recipe, and yes, you can omit the raisins. I believe bread pudding was not really intended to be a fashionable dish, but it turned out differently, as countless things do.

To make the streusel
Place the gingersnap cookies in a food processor, pulse, and crush the cookies fine. Continue to pulse. Drop in cold butter pieces and alternate with sugar, and continue to pulse to blend well. Place mixture in the refrigerator in a bowl and cover with plastic until needed.

To make the whiskey sauce
Place the sugar, corn syrup, whiskey, cream, salt, and vanilla in a medium saucepan over medium heat. Whisk over heat until sugar is dissolved and sauce is slightly thickened, about 15 minutes. Remove from heat.

To make the bread pudding
Preheat the oven to 350°F. Place the raisins in a small saucepan over medium-high heat and cover with water. Boil for 5 minutes, turn off the heat, and continue to steep raisins in the water for another 5 minutes. Strain off the water and reserve raisins.

In a large mixing bowl, whisk together the eggs and sugar, then add the milk, half and half, pumpkin meat, cinnamon, vanilla, and clove. Add several grindings of freshly grated nutmeg. Stir in the bread cubes and soak them for 30 minutes, stirring occasionally.

Coat the baking dish to avoid sticking. Pour the mixture into the baking dish and add the raisins, pushing them into the bread pudding. Cover with foil and bake for 45 minutes. Remove foil and spread the streusel topping evenly over the bread pudding. Press down gently on the streusel, and then bake for 15 more minutes, uncovered. Let the bread rest for 30 minutes before serving. Scoop pudding into individual bowls and serve with whiskey sauce.

(MAKES 1 9 × 13-INCH BAKING DISH)

For the streusel

5 cups gingersnap cookies

4 sticks (16 ounces) cold unsalted butter, cut into small pieces

1 cup granulated sugar

For the whiskey sauce

1 cup granulated sugar

½ cup corn syrup

¾ cup bourbon or whiskey

1 cup heavy cream

Pinch of kosher salt

1 teaspoon vanilla extract

For the bread pudding

1 cup raisins

7 whole eggs

1½ cups granulated sugar

3 cups milk

2 cups half and half

2 cups pure pumpkin meat

2 teaspoons ground cinnamon

1 teaspoon vanilla extract

½ teaspoon ground clove

Freshly ground nutmeg

12 cups (¾-inch) cubed bread

Chapter 13
Confectionaries

Bourbon Pecan Pie

There's more to pecan pie than meets the eye. Homemade golden, flakey pie dough filled with a sweet pecan mixture symbolizes comfort and pleasure, and is a tradition here in the Deep South. The French-inspired custard for pecan pie with Native American pecans is bound together with eggs. The sweeteners for the recipe can vary from clear or dark corn syrups, white or brown sugar, black strap molasses, or raw honey to maple or cane syrup.

Bourbon pecan pie is the South's favorite version, and I prefer mine with brown sugar and clear corn and dark corn syrup. First, cook it in a saucepan before you add the eggs, or whisk it all together and pour it into piecrust and bake it. Both ways work just fine. Most serious cooks will whip up their favorite pecan pie recipe during the holidays, and baking them along the Florida Panhandle is no exception. I like to serve up my version of this classic pie during Thanksgiving and Christmas.

Here is my flakey pie dough recipe that was passed along to me from Chef Lucy when I attended the Culinary Institute of America in New York. It's soft, elastic, and easy to work with a rolling pin. Best of all, it works perfectly when paired with my pecan pie filling inspired by the legendary Grand Dame of southern cooking herself, Chef Edna Lewis.

(MAKES 1 9-INCH STANDARD PIE)

Flakey pie dough

¼ cup chilled milk

½ teaspoon salt

1½ cups all-purpose flour

½ cup vegetable shortening, cut into pea-size cubes and frozen

To make the pie dough

Pour milk into a mixing bowl and stir in salt until it dissolves.

Sift the flour into a medium-size mixing bowl. Add cubes of shortening and coat them in the flour by rubbing with both hands until the cubes are broken down to pea size (about 2 minutes). Do not make too small or crust will become mealy.

Dust work surface with flour. Make a well in the center of the flour and add the milk mixture. Blend flour into the milk mixture with hands until dough ball is formed. When dough gathers, turn out onto the floured surface. Knead the dough 30 times; do not overknead. Gather dough into a ball, press it into a disk, and cover with plastic wrap. Refrigerate it for 1 hour.

Remove dough from the refrigerator and let sit for 10 minutes. Unwrap and place dough on a work surface lightly dusted with flour. Dust the rolling pin with flour and roll out the dough to ⅛-inch thickness in all directions from the center.

Invert a pie pan and place it over rolled-out dough, leaving a 1-inch overlap for forming the crust. Use the point of a knife and cut a complete circle around the overlap. Dust hands with flour and fold the circle in half to place inside of the pie pan. Unfold and center the dough in the pie pan. Press down evenly to conform into the pan. Fold dough under and flute the edges. Place in refrigerator for 1 hour before filling.

To make the pecan pie filling

Preheat oven to 350°F. In a saucepan, combine the syrups, sugar, butter, and salt. Whisk over medium heat until sugar is dissolved. Remove from heat and let cool down (about 20 minutes). When cool, whisk in eggs, bourbon, and vanilla. Blend well. Skim to remove any foam on the surface from whisking, then add the pecans. Pour filling into pie shell on a cookie sheet and place on the middle oven rack. Bake for 40–45 minutes until filling soufflés and the center is set and firm. Remove and let cool completely on a wire rack. Chill one hour before slicing.

CHEF'S TIP: This recipe is designed for an 8- or 9-inch-deep-dish pan. Some of the newer pie dishes range from 9½ inches to 10 inches; these also produce beautiful deep pies. I simply double both the piecrust and the filling. You may need to place foil over the crust to ensure it does not overcook before the center sets. Add an extra 12–15 minutes to the baking time for a deep-dish pie.

For the pecan pie filling

¾ cup light corn syrup

½ cup dark corn syrup

1 cup sugar

4 tablespoons (½ stick) unsalted butter

¼ teaspoon salt

3 eggs, room temperature, beaten

3 tablespoons bourbon

1 teaspoon vanilla extract

1¼ cups pecans halves

Bushwacker Tres Leches Cake

A tres leches cake is one of the desserts that intrigued me while preparing a class on Latin American cooking. This cake is popular in Central and South America, North America, including South Florida, and many parts of the Caribbean, but typically it's not as prominent along the Florida Panhandle. The traditional soaked-cake dessert consists of 3 milks: evaporated, sweet condensed, and heavy cream.

I admit that rich coffee with cream and sugar is one of my favorite beverages. Maybe that's why I'm in love with White Russian–style cocktails. As a Pensacola local, the "Bushwacker" has turned out to be one of my favorite summer time, piña colada–type concoctions and is recorded as being first served at the Sandshaker on Pensacola Beach in the mid-1970s.

In honor of that Pensacola tradition, we served Bushwacker Tres Leches cake for the Pensacola Celebrity Chef's dinner at the James Beard Foundation in New York in 2014. Chefs Dan Dunn, Gus Silivos, Frank Taylor, Jim Shirley, and I all agreed that the Bushwacker would be representative of Pensacola, and particularly of Pensacola Beach.

At the event, a shot glass was filled with an icy-smooth Bushwacker, crafted by photographer Bill Strength, one of Pensacola Beach's longtime bartenders, and was served alongside the Bushwacker-soaked cake.

(MAKES 1 13 × 9-INCH CAKE PAN)

For the Bushwhacker tres leches sauce

3 pints old-fashioned vanilla ice cream

1 cup heavy cream

3 tablespoons sweet condensed milk

6 ounces light rum (such as Bacardi Silver)

To make the Bushwhacker tres leches sauce
Place the vanilla ice cream into a medium stainless steel saucepot over low heat and stir until melted. Remove from heat and stir in heavy cream, sweet condensed milk, light rum, Bacardi 151, coffee liqueur, and Crème de Cocoa. Place in refrigerator until needed.

To make the cake
Preheat oven to 350°F. Sift flour, baking powder, and salt onto a piece of parchment paper and set aside. In a mixing bowl, beat the eggs and sugar with an electric hand mixer on high speed for 2 minutes. While beating, pour in the milk and vanilla all at once. Continue beating for an additional 10 minutes. Turn mixer off. Crease

the paper holding the sifted dry ingredients and then add them to the batter. Use a rubber spatula to incorporate dry ingredients. Add oil to the cake batter and continue to fold in until it disappears.

Pour mixture into a lightly buttered cake pan. Tap the pan on the table to remove any air pockets, and then bake for 20–25 minutes, or until an inserted toothpick comes out clean. Set baked cake aside and let cool for 30 minutes. Run a sharp knife along the edges of the cake and poke holes over the entire top of the cake's surface with a toothpick. Pour entire Bushwacker mixture over the cake and let it sit for 1 hour in the refrigerator before serving.

2 ounces Bacardi 151

3 ounces coffee liqueur (such as Kahlua)

3 ounces dark Crème de Cocoa

For the cake

2 cups all-purpose flour

2 teaspoons baking powder

1 teaspoon salt

8 eggs

2 cups sugar

⅓ cup milk

2 teaspoons vanilla

⅓ cup vegetable oil

Warm Fig Squares with Hard Sauce

I love sweet and succulent fresh figs simply prepared. In almost every place I have lived in the Florida Panhandle, I've had a fig tree in my yard. It's usually the little sweet mission fig variety. They ripen in late June and July, and then it's a race against the blue jays and mockingbirds to gather them intact. If you can find them without tiny beak holes, they are best just picked, lightly rinsed, air-dried, then wrapped with a paper-thin slice of cured country ham as an appetizer, or served with a little sweet cream for dessert.

In this neck of the woods and throughout the south, preserving figs is a family practice if you are privy to a lot of fig trees. Freshly gathered figs are fragile and highly perishable if not consumed within a few days. Because the season is short and supply abundant, we put up figs for year-round use.

I created this recipe centered on put-up figs, which I frequently purchase from J.W. Renfroe Pecan Company in Pensacola, who keeps a steady supply of whole figs in syrup on their retail shelves.

(SERVES 8)

For the pudding

1 (16-ounce) jar whole figs in syrup (J.W. Renfroe Pecan Co. brand preferred) or 16 whole figs and ½ cup sugar syrup

2 tablespoons backstrap molasses

4 tablespoons Madeira wine

⅓ cup yellow cornmeal

¼ cup sugar

¼ teaspoon salt

¼ teaspoon cinnamon

2 eggs, beaten

2 cups heavy cream

For the hard sauce

½ cup (1 stick) unsalted butter, softened

1 cup confectioners' sugar

1 tablespoon Madeira wine

1 tablespoon unsalted butter, melted for coating the pan

To make the pudding

Preheat the oven to 300°F. Place the figs and syrup in a food processor and puree. Pour the puree into a saucepot and add the molasses and Madeira. Sift together cornmeal, sugar, salt, and cinnamon, then whisk that mixture into the fig mixture, and stir over medium heat until sugar has dissolved, 5–7 minutes.

In a separate mixing bowl, add the eggs and whisk in cream until blended well. Ladle the hot fig mixture into the cream mixture one ladle at a time. Pour the entire pudding mixture into the saucepot and whisk to blend well. Turn off heat.

To make the hard sauce

While the pudding is setting, prepare the hard sauce. In a mixing bowl, cream the butter and sugar together with an electric hand mixer. Beat in the Madeira. Place in refrigerator for 1 hour. Spoon into a bowl and serve, or keep in the fridge (it will last for days covered in plastic wrap) until you need it. Serve with the warm pudding.

To assemble

Coat a 6- or 8-cup casserole dish or an 8 × 8 × 2-inch baking dish with the melted butter. Pour in pudding mixture. Set the casserole into a pan of hot water and bake for 1 hour and 15 minutes, or until mixture is firm in the center and set. Test for doneness by inserting the tip of a knife into the center of the casserole. As soon as it comes out clean, the pudding is done. Serve warm and top with hard sauce.

CHEF'S TIP: The hard sauce will harden (probably how it got its name) in the fridge, so be sure to remove it at least a couple of hours before you want to serve it. Hard sauce should be smooth and easily spooned onto desserts.

Semolina Fritters with Blackberry–Maple Filling

In Italy, the king of pasta cultures, pasta dough is usually made with durum wheat (semolina). In countries such as Morocco, Algeria, and Tunisia, couscous acts as the pasta and semolina is used instead of more traditional grains such as bulgur, millet, and corn flour.

I discovered this semolina-style dessert fritter when researching Mardi Gras–like pastry for one of my Italian cooking classes. Beignets (French for fritter) include the once-classic New Orleans street food known as *calas* (crispy rice fritters). Café du Monde in New Orleans made beignets famous, and these flour-and-yeast–based fritters are still a tradition today. My variation on fritters features semolina, which means there is no yeast in these incredibly moist and tasty fritters!

(MAKES 24 2-OUNCE FRITTERS)

To make the blackberry-maple filling

Combine berries and cornstarch in a small mixing bowl and toss to coat the berries evenly. Place a small saucepot over medium-high heat and add the coated berries, water, lemon juice, sugar, and maple syrup. Reduce heat to a low simmer and simmer for 5 minutes or until sugar is dissolved and mixture is thick. Remove from heat and let cool for 20 minutes. Spoon the cooked blackberry mixture into a pastry bag with doughnut-filling tip. Twist top of pastry bag to seal and set the filled bag aside until it's time to fill the fritters.

To make the fritters

Place a medium-size soup pot over medium-high heat. Add the semolina, milk, water, sugar, and lemon zest. Bring to a boil and use a wooden spoon to stir until thick, about 5 minutes.

Transfer mixture to a baking pan and smooth over to spread mixture evenly. Place in refrigerator to cool down completely.

Use the whip attachment of a tabletop mixer on high speed to whip the egg whites to stiff peaks. Set aside.

Sift flour and baking powder together and set aside.

Place the chilled mixture into a clean mixing bowl. Using a mixer fitted with a paddle attachment on low speed, pulse to blend in the egg yolks and flour mixture. Scrape down the sides and remove bowl from mixer. Use a spatula to fold in the whipped egg whites.

To assemble

Preheat frying oil to 350°F. Using a 2-ounce scoop, place level scoops of batter into the oil and deep-fry each fritter until golden brown, 3–4 minutes. Remove from fryer, drain onto paper towels, and roll directly in granulated sugar. Poke a hole with the tip of the pastry bag and fill the center of each fritter with the blackberry filling and serve.

CHEF'S NOTE: If you want, you can omit filling the semolina fritters altogether and serve them as is.

For the blackberry-maple filling

1 cup fresh blackberries

3 teaspoons cornstarch

⅛ cup water

1 teaspoon lemon juice

¼ cup granulated sugar

2 tablespoons pure maple syrup

For the fritters

2 cups semolina

2 cups milk

2 cups water

2 tablespoons granulated sugar

Zest of 1 lemon

2 eggs, separated

2 tablespoons, plus 1 teaspoon all-purpose flour

1 teaspoon baking powder

Vegetable oil for skillet or deep-frying

Extra granulated sugar for rolling

Pecan Cake with Sweet Cream and Praline Sauce

This recipe is modeled after the classic Southern Pecan Cake with Caramel. Who could deny the pleasure of combining praline sauce with homemade pecan cake? I have seen a number of interpretations for the dessert over the years, but this one I adapted to my palate with fundamental specifications. While the recipe looks complex, much of the work can be done several hours in advance. Good things come with time.

(MAKES 1 3-LAYER CAKE)

For the praline sauce

2 sticks (1 cup) unsalted butter

1½ cups packed light-brown sugar

¾ cup light corn syrup

1 (14-ounce) can sweet condensed milk

½ teaspoon fresh lemon juice

1 teaspoon vanilla extract

Pinch of ground cinnamon

Pinch of kosher salt

For the icing

1½ cups heavy whipping cream

¼ cup confectioners' sugar

1 teaspoon vanilla extract

For the pecan cake

1½ cups granulated sugar

2 sticks (1 cup) unsalted butter, softened

4 large eggs

3 cups cake flour

2 teaspoons baking powder

1 teaspoon baking soda

½ teaspoon salt

1 cup pecan meal

1 cup milk

1 teaspoon vanilla extract

1 cup vegetable oil

1 cup sour cream

To make the praline sauce
Place butter, brown sugar, corn syrup, and condensed milk in a medium-size saucepan and heat over medium heat, stirring to dissolve sugar, about 5 minutes. Stir in lemon juice, vanilla, cinnamon, and salt. Remove from heat. Chill down by stirring over an ice and water bath.

To make the icing
Place cream in a chilled mixing bowl and beat until almost thick, about 3 minutes on high speed. Add sugar and vanilla and continue to beat until it reaches a firm peak. Set aside.

To make the pecan cake
Preheat oven to 350°F. Place the sugar and butter in a mixer bowl using a paddle (or a hand mixer) and cream together until light and fluffy, about 4 minutes. Add eggs, one at a time, beating well after each addition.

Sift together the flour, baking powder, baking soda, and salt. Combine the sifted flour mixture and pecan meal. Add the flour mixture and milk alternately to the creamed mixture and beat just until incorporated, beginning and ending with the flour mixture. Reduce speed to low and beat in the vanilla, oil, and sour cream. Mix until sour cream disappears. Do not over mix.

Coat three 9-inch nonstick cake pans with baking spray and divide batter evenly between them, about 1-inch thick. Bake for 20 minutes or until a wooden pick inserted in center comes out with moist crumbs clinging. Place a wire cooling rack over a sheet pan and let cakes cool in their pans for 10 minutes. Turn out to remove from pans and cool completely on the wire rack.

To assemble
After cakes have cooled, use a slicing knife and remove the tops from 2 of the 3 cakes, so the cakes are about 1-inch thick, reserving the best-looking one for the top. Divide the icing over the cut tops and use a spatula to spread evenly onto the 2 layers. Stack them neatly atop each other and finish with the uncut cake on top. Place entire cake onto a wire rack over a drip pan. Pour praline sauce over the cakes and arrange the toasted pecans on top. Place in refrigerator for 2 hours. Slice to serve.

Blueberry Volcano Cheesecake

I don't think I have ever met anyone who doesn't like cheesecake, especially a thick slice of the tall, classic, New York–style cheesecake. I admit that baking is not my strong point, and I make silly mistakes in baking simply because I prefer not to measure—a baking no-no for the unaccustomed! Mistakes are often made at home, but at restaurants, too. And some of the coolest things in the world happen by mistake. Like in the case of this recipe.

My baker accidentally undercooked a whole cheesecake. Just prior to service, it was brought to my attention that the freshly baked cheesecake was indeed not cooked enough or firm enough to slice. I had to think quickly! "I must have cheesecake," I explained. "It's on the dessert menu." At the time, I didn't think it was a good idea to recook the entire cheesecake, so I offered an idea to my baker, who still argues that it was her idea! "Miko," I said, "let's try to remix the entire half-cooked cake, and then use an ice cream scoop to scoop it into individual small baking dishes." I then suggested that we bake it the rest of the way and see if it firmed up. Well, it did! And, as it turned out, it was essentially a genius of a method in utilizing under-cooked cheesecake.

Honest to goodness, this dessert has been on my menu ever since that day. Each individual baking dish is lined with a typical graham cracker crust and prebaked. The chilled half-cooked cheesecake is scooped into each dish and a hole is formed in the center and filled with fresh blueberry sauce. It is then baked until the center is like molten blueberry lava.

(SERVES 10)

For the crust

15 whole graham crackers

½ cup lightly packed brown sugar

8 tablespoons (1 stick) unsalted butter, melted

For the blueberry filling

1½ cups blueberries

½ cup water

2 tablespoons sugar

1 teaspoon cornstarch

½ teaspoon zest of lemon

For the cheesecake

1½ pounds cream cheese

1 cup granulated sugar

4 eggs

5 tablespoons all-purpose flour

1 teaspoon vanilla extract

For garnish

½ cup blueberries

Confectioners' sugar

To make the crust

Preheat oven to 350°F. Place crackers in a food processor and pulse to a fine meal. Combine graham cracker crumbs and brown sugar in a bowl and blend well. Add melted butter and blend until the crumbs are evenly moistened.

Divide the graham cracker crumb mixture evenly among ten 5-ounce ovenproof gratin dishes. Press firmly and evenly on the bottom and sides of the dishes to create a crust, making sure there are no cracks. Place them on a baking pan and bake for 10 minutes or until golden. Remove from the oven.

To make the blueberry filling

Place ingredients into a small saucepot and bring to a boil. Turn off and remove from stove, stir well to blend, and set aside until assembling.

To make the cheesecake

Preheat oven to 350°F. Place cream cheese and sugar in a mixing bowl and blend with a hand mixer until smooth. Beat in eggs one at a time, letting each egg disappear into the batter before adding another. Add the flour and vanilla and beat to blend. Place a 10-inch springform pan onto a baking pan and pour batter into the springform pan. Place both pans into oven on center rack. Once the pan is level, carefully pour 1–2 cups water into the baking pan. Bake uncovered on center rack for 30 minutes. Remove and let cool completely in refrigerator. The cheesecake is about half cooked at this point.

To assemble

Using a 4-ounce ice cream scoop, fill each gratin dish with chilled, half-cooked cheesecake. Once each dish has been filled, dip your index finger in oil, then into the cheesecake to create a hole in the center, about 1 inch wide, down to the crust. Fill each hole to the top with the blueberry filling. Bake for 10–12 minutes. Remove from oven and, before serving, top individually filled cheesecakes with a few fresh blueberries, dust with confectioners' sugar, and serve.

Triple Chocolate Cake

According to the University of West Florida Division of Anthropology and Archaeology, "Chocolate was often requested by the Spanish in Pensacola from supplies in New Spain (Mexico). It was used both as a high-status drink and for medicinal purposes."

Rum and coffee were once brought by ships to the New World and is the perfect match for this confection masterpiece. I created this recipe for the Jackson's dessert menu in 2008 and it remains on the menu today.

To make the chocolate mousse

Place chocolate and butter in a large bowl set over a saucepot or in a double boiler at a low simmer. Stir chocolate and butter until melted. Turn off the heat and let stand.

Beat the cream in a stainless-steel bowl set over ice until it forms soft peaks, add the sugar, coffee, and rum, and continue to whip until firm. Do not overwhip.

Transfer melted chocolate to a large bowl. Using a runner spatula, fold in the whipped cream one large spoon at a time, scraping from the sides and turning the bowl each time. Repeat three times until cream disappears, then add all the remaining whipped cream at once and fold in until cream disappears. Do not whip any further. Cover the mousse and refrigerate for approximately 1 hour before filling the cake.

To make the cake

Preheat the oven to 350°F. Grease three 9-inch cake pans with the butter. Sift together the cocoa powder, flour, sugar, baking soda, baking powder, and salt and place in the bowl of a heavy-duty mixer.

In a separate mixing bowl, combine the eggs, milk, buttermilk, oil, rum, and vanilla. Slowly pour the egg mixture into the flour mixture, beating in on low speed using a paddle attachment until cake batter is smooth. Do not overmix. Divide the batter among the three prepared pans. Bake for 40–50 minutes or until toothpick inserted into the center comes out clean. Remove from oven and let cool for 10 minutes before inverting pan and removing the cakes. Place right side up on wire racks to cool completely, about 1 hour.

(MAKES 3 9-INCH CAKES)

For the chocolate mousse

8 ounces bittersweet chocolate

2 tablespoons (¼ stick) sweet cream butter

2 cups heavy cream

6 tablespoons sugar

4 tablespoons dark roast coffee, room temperature

4 tablespoons dark rum

For the cake

1 tablespoon unsalted butter, softened

1 cup cocoa powder

3½ cups all-purpose flour

3 cups sugar

1 tablespoon baking soda

2 teaspoons baking powder

¾ teaspoon kosher salt

3 eggs, beaten

1 cup milk

1½ cups buttermilk

1 cup vegetable oil

4 tablespoons dark rum

1 teaspoon pure vanilla extract

Chocolate ganache

16 ounces semisweet chocolate, finely chopped

12 ounces bittersweet chocolate, finely chopped

3 cups heavy cream

1 teaspoon pure vanilla extract

Pinch of kosher salt

Once cakes have cooled, use a long, serrated knife to trim off the top cake layer to make a flat surface. Set the layer aside. Repeat for the second layer. Use a small offset spatula or a palette knife, and evenly coat the top of the first layer with about 1 cup of the chocolate mousse filling. Spread so the mousse extends beyond the edges of the layer. Place the second layer on top of mousse and press to make level. Cover with about 1 cup of chocolate mousse filling. Top with the uncut remaining cake layer. Smooth the sides and fill any gaps with the chocolate mousse. Refrigerate for 2 hours to set the mousse. Meanwhile begin assembling the ganache.

To make the chocolate ganache

Place the chocolates in a large stainless-steel bowl. Pour the cream in a saucepan over medium heat to warm, about 10 minutes. Add the vanilla and salt. Stir mixture to blend well, and then pour over the chocolate. Cover with a towel and let sit for 5 minutes. Remove towel and use a rubber spatula to stir until smooth and blended well. Cool down the ganache by stirring until mixture has thickened slightly. Reheat ganache if necessary.

To assemble

When the mousse has set, place cake on wire rack over a baking pan. Pour the ganache over the entire top of the cake as evenly as possible, starting at the center and moving outward. Let it drip down the sides. Store in an airtight container in the refrigerator and serve anytime.

Homemade Marshmallows

In January of 2015, I was tasked as guest chef to prepare an outdoor feast for 120 folks at 13 Mile Seafood. Outstanding in the Field was a farm-to-table event in Apalachicola, Florida. For dessert, I decided to make bourbon pecan squares incorporating local raw honey. I wanted the end result to be a s'mores-like dessert with toasted marshmallow over the pie, so I added chocolate ganache and graham cracker. It was the perfect combination that still has folks talking!

I adapted this marshmallow recipe to be handled well in the field and at home. These homemade marshmallows are both firm enough to slice easily and yet melt perfectly over pie using a food torch. Try making this recipe a day in advance and storing marshmallows cut and heavily dusted with confectioners' sugar. I recommend melting them over my recipe for Sweet Potato-Pecan Pie or Bourbon Pecan pie.

**3 (¼-ounce) envelopes
unflavored gelatin**

1 cup cold water, divided

2 cups granulated sugar

**1 cup light corn syrup (Karo
Syrup brand preferred)**

¼ teaspoon salt

2 teaspoons pure vanilla extract

**Confectioners' sugar, to sift
over top**

Place the gelatin and ½ cup of water in the bowl of an electric mixer
fitted with the whisk attachment, and let it bloom for about 10
minutes. Meanwhile, in a small saucepan combine the sugar, corn
syrup, salt, and remaining water. Cook the mixture over medium-high
heat, stirring, until the sugar dissolves and the syrup reaches 240°F
on a candy thermometer. Remove from the heat.

Turn the mixer on low speed and slowly pour the sugar syrup into
the softened gelatin. Increase the speed to high, and whip until the
mixture is very thick and fluffy, about 12 minutes. Add the vanilla in
the last minute of whipping. The mixture will become lukewarm and
should be cool enough that you can spread it into the pan.

Spray one 13 × 9-inch baking pan with butter pan spray.

Dip a runner spatula into water and spread the marshmallow mixture
into the buttered dish. Dip your hands in water and then smooth and
flatten the marshmallows. Sift confectioners' sugar liberally over the
top and let sit for several hours (or overnight) before cutting. Use a
butter-sprayed knife to cut any sized squares.

CHEF'S TIP: To create a brûlée, use a utility knife dipped in water to
slice the marshmallows into ½–inch slabs. Lay the slabs over pie (or
other dessert) and melt and toast the marshmallows with a small food
torch for 10 seconds before serving.

Upside-Down Peach Skillet Cake

I love anything cooked in a cast-iron skillet, especially upside-down cake. This dessert encompasses the best of both worlds. Peaches are found locally beginning in late June in the outer Florida and Alabama regions and throughout the summer months. One of my favorite and juiciest peaches is from Chilton County, Alabama, located just a few hours north of the Florida Panhandle.

Peaches are grown and available on a smaller scale throughout the Florida and Alabama Panhandle. However, the 100-acre orchard at Durbin Farms Market is in the heart of Alabama peach country. They begin unloading crates of peaches picked from their orchards early in the morning. The peaches are then trucked and made available at Bailey's Produce and Nursery, Flora Bama Farms, and other local produce companies. At Durbin Farms, peaches from Chilton County are handpicked for baskets or individually stacked onto a mound for selecting.

Any ripe variety of peaches will work for this upside-down cake, but my favorite is still the white-fleshed peach. These are lower in acidity and taste sweet, whether firm or soft.

Preheat oven to 350°F. Place a 12-inch cast-iron skillet over medium-low heat and add the butter and brown sugar. Cook until sugar is melted. Remove from heat. Arrange peach halves, cut side down, over the sugar mixture and cover the bottom of the skillet. Place pitted cherries in between all the peach halves.

In a large mixing bowl, beat egg yolks with a whisk until thick and lemon colored. Add nectar and vanilla and blend well. In separate mixing bowl sift salt, flour, and baking powder together. Whisk the flour mixture into the egg mixture and blend well.

Beat the egg whites and the sugar together. The egg whites will become light and a meringue will form stiff peaks. Make sure all the sugar has been used. Fold the meringue into the batter until smooth. Do not over mix.

Pour the batter over the peaches and place on middle oven rack. Bake for 25–30 minutes. Remove from oven and let sit for 5 minutes. Cover the skillet with a plate and invert the skillet to remove the cake. Serve warm with whipped cream.

(SERVES 8–10)

3 tablespoons butter

1 cup light brown sugar

6 medium ripe peaches, halved, stones removed

¼ pound fresh Rainier or Bing cherries, pitted

4 eggs, separated, room temperature

½ cup peach or pear nectar

1 teaspoon vanilla

¼ teaspoon salt

1½ cups all-purpose flour

1½ teaspoons baking powder

1 cup sugar

Whipped cream

Resources

Bad Byron's Specialty
Food Products
PO Box 1262
Santa Rosa Beach, FL
32459
buttrub.com

Bailey's Produce and
Nursery
4301 N. Davis Hwy.
Pensacola, FL 32503
facebook.com/
BaileysProduce

Benton's Smoky Mountain
Country Hams
2603 Hwy. 411 N.
Madisonville, TN 37354-
6356
bentonscountryhams2
.com

Blackwater Farms (Quail)
CR 65
Loxley, AL
Blackwaterfarms.info

The Bodacious Olive
407-D South Palafox St.
Pensacola, FL 32502
bodaciousolive.com

Bud and Alleys
Waterfront Restaurant
2236 East County Road
30-A

Santa Rosa Beach, Florida
32549
budandalleys.com

C & D Mill
700 Benjulyn Rd.
Cantonment, FL 32533-
6976

Clear Creek Farm
6065 Clear Creek Rd.
Milton, FL 32570
Clearcreekfarm.net

Cold Water Gardens
7009 Creek Stone Rd.
Milton, FL 32570
Coldwatergardens.com

Craine Creek Farm, LLC
17353 County Road 64
Loxley, AL 36551
crainecreekfarm.com

Dragonfly Fields
1600 County Hwy. 192
Defuniak Springs, FL
32433

Durbin Farms Market
2130 7th St. S
Clanton, AL 35045
durbinfarms.com

East Hill Honey
Company
PO Box 30093
Pensacola, FL 32503
Easthillhoney.com

Ed's Red
5911 Garrison Ave.
Port St. Joe, FL 32456
edsred.com

Fish House
Barracks St.
P.O. Box 710
Pensacola, FL 32591
Fishhousepensacola.com

Flora Bama Farms
6404 Mobile Hwy.
Pensacola, FL 32526
facebook.com/
florabamafarms
ofpensacola

Flora-Bama Lounge
17401 Perdido Key Dr.
Perdido Key Beach, FL
32507
florabama.com

Green Cedars Farm
9280 Gibson Rd.
Molino, FL 32577
greencedarsfarm.com
facebook.com/
greencedarsfarm

Gulf Breeze Gardens
3042 Rosa Del Villa
Gulf Breeze, FL 32563

Harbor Docks Wholesale
  Seafood Market
538 Hwy. 98 E.
Destin, FL 32541
harbordocks.com

Indian Pass Trading Post
  and Raw Bar
8391 CR 30A
Port St Joe, FL 32456
indianpassrawbar.com

Jackson's Steakhouse
400 S. Palafox St.
Pensacola, FL 32503
jacksonsrestaurant.com

Joe Patti's Seafood
524 S. B St.
Pensacola, FL 32502
joepattis.com

J.W. Renfroe Pecan Co.
2400 West Fairfield Dr.
Pensacola, FL 32505
renfroepecan.com

Marias Fresh Seafood
  Market
621 E. Cervantes St.
Pensacola, FL 32501
mariasfreshseafood
  market.com

McCreery's Heirloom
  Liberty Garden
Liberty Gardens,
  Innerarity Island
Pensacola, FL 32507

Modica Market
109 Seaside Central
  Square
Santa Rosa Beach, FL
  32459
modicamarket.com

Palafox Market
19 N. Palafox St.
Pensacola, FL 32502
http://palafoxmarket.com

Pensacola Bay Brewery
255 E. Zaragoza St.
Pensacola, FL 32502
http://pbbrew.com/

Red Bar
70 Hotz Avenue
Santa Rosa Beach, Florida
  32459
http://theredbar.com/

Sand Shaker Lounge
731 Pensacola Beach
  Blvd, Gulf Breeze, FL
  32561
sandshaker.com

SoGourmet
407 S. Palafox St.
Pensacola, FL 32502
sogourmetpensacola.com

Sweet Home Farm,
  Specialty Grocery Store
27107 Schoen Rd.
Elberta, AL
southerncheese.org

13 Mile Seafood Market
227 Water St.
Apalachicola, FL 32320
13milebrand.com

US Wellness Meats
204 E Lafayette St.
Monticello, MO 63457
uswellnessmeats.com
facebook.com/
  USWellnessMeats

Viet Hoa Oriental Food
  Market
3707 Mobile Hwy.
Pensacola, FL 32505

Welding Shop BBQ
  (smoked mullet)
501 Gulf Beach Hwy.
Pensacola, FL 32507

Woods Fisheries
464 Angelfish Rd.
Port St. Joe, FL 32456
Woodsfisheries.com

Acknowledgments

To my daughter: Sienna, you are my greatest accomplishment in life. Thanks for understanding who I am and for being such a support in everything I do. I am so proud of you and the fine person you have become. I love you.

To my parents: Thank you for letting me discover the color of my parachute in my own time and providing me with faith and support through the years. Thanks for raising me and Steve to be independent, hard-working men and loving husbands and fathers. Thanks for showing up for all my life accomplishments. I miss you, Pop. I love you, Mom. I know you're beaming with joy. Who would have thought I would write a book?

To Jerry Gill, my friend and copy editor for many of my articles, newsletters, stories, cooking class recipes, and newspaper columns. You were one of the first people I took my idea to about writing a regional Florida Panhandle cookbook. Thank you for believing I could do it and helping me shape and outline my initial ideas. Thank you for the countless hours assisting me in formatting my first commercial cookbook proposal. Most of all, thank you for teaching me to be proud to be called a Redneck!

To Lisa Ekus, my friend and trusted advisor. You are and have always been my biggest advocate. Thanks for taking immediate interest in my cookbook concept, requesting to see my proposal long before it was completed, and for pitching the concept prior to its final title. Though we may have sold more cookbooks, from the bottom of my heart thanks for trusting that we should not call my cookbook *The Redneck Riviera Cookbook,* no matter what anyone in New York had to say.

Thanks for having me rewrite my first cookbook proposal numerous times before we collectively agreed it was time to pass the pieces along to Ken Bookman to organize the puzzle. Thank you for taking me by the hand and walking me through my first cookbook project. You and your brilliant team are responsible for the final book title, *Panhandle to Pan: Recipes and Stories from Florida's New Redneck Riviera,* and for finding the right publishing company, Globe Pequot. Thanks for having faith in my Florida Panhandle project and for sharing your belief in me with your longtime literary friend Norman Van Aken.

Huge thanks go to a fellow Miller, Scotty Miller. No relation here, but a real friend. Scotty has a passion for writing, a keen eye for grammar, and a one-of-a-kind sense of humor. Scotty willingly accepted the task of being a third set of eyes for all of my stories because he simply enjoys it. Many of them he rearranged to make better sense. I had many good chuckles when I spotted his side-splitting comments hidden within my stories, knowing he wanted to see if I was indeed reading over his work. Many of them I deleted, thank goodness!

Many thanks to Norman Van Aken for decades of inspiration, sharing of culinary visions, and contributions to Florida cuisine. Thanks for taking the time to reconnect with a Florida Panhandle chef from the early days of your guest chef appearances. You're one of my biggest Florida culinary influences, and you never cease to amaze me with your remarkable writing skills and cooking. You're a living legend, and I'm certain I will be seeing you again in the near future. What an incredible joyride you continue to have! Your words of encouragement were essential for me in taking on this solo project. Thanks, Chef!

Thanks to Chef Jason Perry, General Manager Steve Ooms, and the entire staff and team at Jackson's for keeping the restaurant on course, and for all your support and assistance with "Cookbook Saturday" writing time. Thank you Chefs Jason Perry, Mikosha Franklin, and Jonathan Gardner for assisting with ingredient preparation and recipe-making for food images.

Thank you Maria Goldberg for your support in marketing and your long-time friendship, and to Collier Merrill and brothers Burney and Will, for changing my life and believing in all my culinary efforts, particularly in the significance of Jackson's for downtown Pensacola and my ability to write this book.

Special thanks for images provided in this book, go to photographer Bill Strength and an array friends from near and far—Margo S. Stringfield, Tony Riesinger, Jamie Hall, Deborah Dunlap/*Historic Pensacola Photographs*, Sandy Cessaretti and WSRE TV Foundation, Inc., Phillip Makselan and *Pensacola Home & Garden Magazine,* Nathan Holler, Lisa and Gerald Burwell and *VIE Magazine,* Linda Jordan and Lynn Jordan Photography, Scott Harrell, Rishy Studer, Susan Ozburn, SoGourmet and The Bodacious Olive, Tommy Van Horn, Craine Creek Farm, Flora Bama Farms, Jason Perry, and Laurel Woodfin.

Special thanks to my friend and chef Johnny Earles, formerly of Criolla's in Grayton Beach, along County Road 30-A, for his significant culinary contributions in shaping the foods of the new Redneck Riviera during the American food movement.

I would like to extend a heartfelt thanks to influential chefs, authors, and friends: Norman Van Aken, Edna Lewis, Scott Peacock, Art Smith, Chris

Hastings, Frank Stitt, Virginia Willis, Joe Truex, David Burke, John Folse, John Besh, Susan Spicer, Emeril Lagasse, Duane Nutter, Kevin Gillespie, John Folse, Jacques Pepin, Justin Timinerie, Byron Chism, Paul Crout, John Jacob, Tim Dutrow, Jeff Dutrow, Carolyn O'Neil, Jo Manning, Margo Stringfield, Leon Galatoire, John Egerton, John T. Edge, John de Mers, Clay Triplet, Dan Dunn, Gus Silivos, Frank Taylor, Jim Shirley, Curtis Flower, David Penniman, Mark Robertson, Chris Robertson, Erin Street Shaw, Susan Benton, Bill Campbell, Robert Tolf, Chris Sherman, *Fish Fry Magazine*, Ken Bookman, and my sweetest, Simone Boswell.

Farmers and artisans I'd like to acknowledge are Alyce Birchenough and Doug Wolbert, Robert Randel, Ed Creamer, Tommy Van Horn, Roger and Pam Elliot, Natalie and Michael Ritter, Ray Davis, Wanda Davis, Will Davis, Tommy Ward, Sarah Ward and T.J. Ward, Ed Wood, Mark Godwin, Don Bailey, John Wood, Jake Renfroe, Cloyed and Dorothy Bruton, Mark and Chris Robertson, Cat McCreery, Barbara Williams, Sandy Veillieux, Covey Rise Farm, Shueh-Mei Pong and Charles Bush, Frank Patti, Alice Guy, Todd James, Ray Boyer, Charlie Knodt, Micah Craine, and Charles Modica.

Additional Photo Credits

Craine Creek Farm p. 61; East Hill Honey Co. p. 37; Flora-Bama Farms p. 62; Irv Miller pp. 40, 55, 59, 125, 156, 198, 204, 221, 233; Jamie Hall/Emerald Grande pp. 10, 4, 230; Jason Perry p. 57; Jeff Dutrow p. 129; John Wood/Grassland Beef, LLC p. 171; Laurel Woodfin p. 270; Lisa and Gerald Burwell and *VIE Magazine* pp. 16, 17 (top), 78, 199, 214, 254; Lynn Jordan Photography pp. 9, 10, 28, 185; Deborah Dunlap's Historic Pensacola Photographs pp. 86, 90, 92, 94, 97, 100; Tony Reisinger/Cabeza del Huachinango Fine Gyotaku Art/Huachinango en Azul p. 88; Nathan Holler p. 17 (bottom); Phillip Makselan/*Penasacola Home and Garden Magazine* pp. 91, 108; Scott Harrell p. 110; University of West Florida Archeology Institute pp. viii-ix; WSRE TV Foundation pp. 144, 163.

Index

About the Author

Irv Miller settled in the Panhandle in 1982, helping to pioneer fine dining in Destin, introducing country French cuisine to the Emerald Coast and then along Santa Rosa County's 30A, focusing on bold flavors of the Mediterranean and locally sourced ingredients. Since 1999, he's been in Pensacola, emphatically preserving and cooking the iconic foods of the region. As a culinary ambassador for seafood and agriculture, Miller has been promoting the Florida Panhandle and the Redneck Riviera as a culinary destination for more than three decades.

One of the region's most personable and notable chefs, Miller has garnered more country-wide recognition for the Florida Panhandle than any other chef. Most of his cooking experience is from hands-on restaurant experience and supporting community efforts. He is proud of the fact that he put himself through culinary school. He did not train under renowned chefs, but has worked beside a few. He has a library of cookbooks that he uses frequently for inspiration, research, and guidance. He worked in restaurants for six years before choosing his culinary career path (which many of his friends questioned).

He graduated from the Culinary Institute of America in 1982, and believes in working hard to attain his goals. He maintains that he became a chef because he enjoys it and is good at it. He has little patience for misguided dreams of chef stardom, entitlement, and, most of all, lack of enthusiasm for the love of cooking, which flows naturally through his veins and is his life's blood.